PHNOM PENH

Books are to be returned on or before
the last date below.

LIBREX-

Cities of the Imagination

Cities OF THE IMAGINATION

PHNOM PENH

A cultural and literary history

Milton Osborne

Signal Books
Oxford

First published in 2008 by
Signal Books Limited
36 Minster Road
Oxford OX4 1LY
www.signalbooks.co.uk

A catalogue record for this book is available from the British Library

ISBN 978-1-904955-40-5 Paper

Drawings by Wendy Skinner Smith
Image p.36 courtesy Museu Nacional de Arte Antiga, Lisbon
Cover Design: Baseline Arts
Production: Devdan Sen
Cover Images: Per-Andre Hoffmann/Alamy; Richard Connors/istockphoto
Printed in India

Contents

For Leslie Fielding
A friend indeed in Phnom Penh in 1966, and ever since

Foreword

Milton Osborne has loved Phnom Penh, Cambodia and the Cambodians since he first arrived in the country as a young Australian Foreign Service Officer in April 1959. In all the decades that have followed he has followed the city's painful transformations and the agony of the Cambodian people through civil war, communist mass murder, foreign occupation and a return to something that approaches normality today, albeit a corrupt and brutal dispensation.

As soon as he arrived in 1959, he fell in love with Phnom Penh. It's a sickness which is quite common amongst westerners and it is very hard to cure. Osborne never shook it off. If truth be told, he probably never wanted to do so, because love of Phnom Penh, Cambodia and the Cambodian people brings great joy as well as pain and exasperation.

This, his latest book, is just wonderful, a fruit of a lifetime of diligent and critical love. He tells extraordinary stories of conspiracy and romance and conquest, including the arrival of Portuguese and Spanish missionaries and adventurers in the sixteenth century, the perpetual struggles by Siam and Vietnam to dominate the land in between them, the arrival and departure of the Dutch and then the one hundred-year protectorate imposed by France, which had just ended when Osborne first stopped by.

He arrived in classic style—on a DC-3 (Dakota) in the Elysian days of Cambodia, at least in terms of modern memory. The little kingdom was virtually unknown in the western world, except in France which had colonized it for the best part of a century. It had kept its independence between its traditional enemies, Thailand to the west and Vietnam, to the east. Even more important, it was managing to remain neutral in the growing dispute within Vietnam between communist Hanoi and anti-communist Saigon.

Cambodia in these days was a truly charming backwater, where French culture and cuisine were important, where service was plentiful but merchandise was not. The country was presided over by the eclectic King Norodom Sihanouk who was, to his people, a God King. He had won its independence from France and his rule were inspired, irresponsible, quixotic, self-obsessed and ultimately a tragic failure.

Phnom Penh then numbered only about half a million people. The pace of life was slow. There were few cars in the wide streets laid out by the French, and very few planes came into the little airport on the edge of town. There was almost no telephone contact with the world. It was like a little French provincial town, with cafés and bistros along the river's edge, gentle monks and with luscious agriculture. American aid stimulated the economy and at least the richer classes of society. Enough of this money trickled down to help the poor.

Osborne was charmed by Cambodia and he has remained charmed, appalled and fascinated by it to this day. As a result of his youthful posting he became one of the most diligent historians of Cambodia's past, ancient and modern, and today the canon of his work on Cambodia is known and rightly celebrated around the world. Modern Cambodian scholarship can be tendentious and is riven with sectarian disputes—but in Osborne the Cambodians have one of the fairest champions imaginable.

He returned for the second time in the mid-1960s as a graduate student and found that the last five years had not been kind to Phnom Penh. Sihanouk had renounced American aid and broken relations with the United States; the economy suffered and Phnom Penh was no longer quite such a delightful place to live. The scars beneath the soft skin were more painful now. The growing war in Vietnam next door was having more and more impact on Cambodia, even as Prince Sihanouk struggled to keep the country outside of it—by declaring neutrality but in fact allying himself closer to the communists. The United States found him exasperating.

There was growing tension and discontent both within Phnom Penh itself and also amongst the peasantry, and finally in March 1970 Sihanouk was overthrown in a coup d'état whose leaders at once brought Cambodia into the war on the side of the United States. In 1971 when Osborne returned on what was to be his last visit for ten years, war was already stalking through and closing down much of the countryside, and Phnom Penh was swollen with refugees. The city became more and more crowded and putrid until the communist Khmer Rouge won victory and brutally expelled the entire population in the summer of 1975. For the next three years the city that Osborne chronicles had its weirdest period—emptiness.

The Khmer Rouge terror throughout Cambodia lasted until they were overthrown by their former Vietnamese comrades in early 1979. Osborne kept in touch with the country he loved by interviewing refugees along the Thai-Cambodian border who gave him "an indelible impression of the true horror" inside Cambodia. When he next returned to Phnom Penh in 1981, he was shocked: it was now "a shattered city, with large sections still empty of people, and much of it "had the air of a vast, insanitary transit camp, as poorly nourished survivors of the Pol Pot tyranny returned to the city and sought to scrape a living." He visited Tuol Sleng, the banal high school where the Khmer Rouge had tortured and murdered their suspected enemies, and mass graves outside Phnom Penh which still had the horrible sweet and sour stench of death about them. He suddenly realized with a shock that the Khmer Rouge had completely demolished the city's Catholic cathedral.

The horrors of the Khmer Rouge's brutal madness reverberate still. Osborne has gone back many times since and has recorded many of the changes that have happened to Cambodian society and to Phnom Penh since. The city has come back to "an apparent degree of normality". But, as Osborne points out, it has had a government which brooks no challenge. In 1993 the people of Cambodia enthusiastically took part in elections run very well by the United Nations. They voted to remove the corrupt communist government that the Vietnamese installed. The government refused to accept the vote and the UN left. Now autocracy and corruption discolours all.

There was corruption in 1959 when Milton Osborne first came to Phnom Penh, but nothing on the scale of that which prevails today. Today in Phnom Penh power is money and money is power and people in shanty towns fear the powerful men's bulldozers which can tear through their homes to construct a new shopping mall. There is a culture of impunity which continues the Cambodian trauma.

As Osborne says, "the tragedy of Cambodian history" has been played out decade after decade in the lifetime that he has known it and chronicled it so movingly and so well. He concludes that "only a supremely unperceptive optimist would suggest that tragedy is no longer part of the drama played out each day in Phnom Penh."

William Shawcross

Preface

There are probably as many ways to write about a city as there are cities, and this is surely so when writing about Phnom Penh, Cambodia's capital. In ways apparent even to a first-time visitor, it has its own, special character, notably different, for example, from the great cities of Europe. Phnom Penh has nothing to match their millennial histories and the variety of their great stores of art, though it has one of the most notable collections of sculpture from the Angkorian period of Cambodian history. Nor, shifting geographic perspective to Asia, does Phnom Penh possess the literary tradition of a Calcutta or the imperial history of a Beijing. In so many ways and by comparison with so many cities, Phnom Penh is different—newer, in terms of its significance as a capital, never a centre for the production of great art itself, and with an indigenous literary tradition which, while rich in itself, is barely accessible for outsiders. But to think any of these facts rob it of interest is to be badly mistaken.

Phnom Penh has only attained its fixed status as a capital city recently. This is true despite the fact that it was Cambodia's capital for about thirty years in the fifteenth century, and for short periods in succeeding centuries. It was, remarkably enough, briefly the site of imperial derring-do in the sixteenth and seventeenth centuries when Iberian adventurers played a brief role in Cambodian affairs. But its life as a city of consequence really did not begin until 1866, when Cambodia's French "protectors" persuaded the Cambodian king to move his capital to Phnom Penh from Udong, a site a little to the north. So in its modern form it is a little younger than Singapore and a little older than Kuala Lumpur. But it is much younger, as a major Southeast Asian centre, than Jakarta, which was known as Batavia when the Dutch imposed their rule there in the seventeenth century.

With one notable exception, the visitor to Phnom Penh will not be rewarded by finding an abundance of great art, but that exception is the superb collection of pre-Angkorian, before 802 Common Era (CE), and Angkorian, 802-1431 CE, statuary in the National Museum. None of these wonderful items was produced in Phnom Penh. The Royal Palace is a relatively recent construction and much smaller in size and interest than the better known Grand Palace in Bangkok. Throughout Phnom Penh there is some interesting architecture. There is enough remaining from the colonial years to remind a visitor that this city was once part of France's colonial empire. And there are architecturally interesting buildings from the independent years but, like those of the colonial period, they are limited in number.

What really makes Phnom Penh a city of interest is the extraordinary human aspect of its short modern history. For although the city's name is forever linked in the mind of outsiders with the horrors of the Pol Pot regime in the 1970s, there is much more to its history from the middle of the nineteenth century than those blood-soaked years when rationality appeared to have vanished forever from Cambodia. Beyond the little-known Iberian interlude of the late sixteenth century, the history that grips the imagination involves the personalities and passions of the men and women whose lives determined the city's evolution. This is a story that encompasses the bitter battle between Norodom I, the first king to reign under French "protection", and the colonial officials who sought to diminish his power; the determination and apparent success of those same officials to transform a deeply traditional society; and the role of Norodom Sihanouk, Norodom I's flamboyant great grandson, in his various guises as king, prime minister, chief of state, and ally of the Khmer Rouge (Red Khmer or Cambodians, a term originally coined by Sihanouk himself to describe those who were then his communist opponents). It is a story that encompasses the bloodstained tyranny of the Pol Pot period; and now, finally, the emergence of a city under an authoritarian leader which is as sharply divided between rich and poor as any in the developing world.

Phnom Penh is also a city with a largely forgotten literary past, so far as western writers are concerned. Although for many it was only a way station for travel to the ruins at Angkor Pierre Loti and Somerset Maugham visited, as did noted travel writers such as Houghton Brodrick and Norman Lewis much later. André Malraux briefly spent time in Phnom Penh on his way to steal statuary from a temple at Angkor, and rather longer after he had been apprehended for doing so. Perhaps this latter experience was what coloured his short and disdainful reference to Phnom Penh in his famous novel, *La Voie royale* [The Royal Way, 1930], the book born of his attempted theft. Sadly, the amount of memorable writing about the city in the period since independence in 1953, outside the genre of political analysis, is limited indeed. What does exist mostly focuses on conflict.

There are local literary and other artistic worlds to be found in Phnom Penh, though access for a foreigner to the former is constrained by a lack of accessible translations. And this is a book written, without apology, by a foreigner, for foreigners.

It is sadly the case that much of Phnom Penh's tradition has vanished and is never likely to return, despite the sterling and dedicated efforts of Cambodians and foreigners alike to save as much of the cultural past as possible. Few would argue that there is a substantial body of contemporary visual art of note, though this may be changing. But traditional dance and theatre survive, with difficulty. Indeed, tradition of all kinds is under threat, not least because so many of the people who were the guardians of tradition died in the years when Pol Pot ruled the city. Charting tradition's survival in a sharply changed world, in which power and impunity are the prevailing values of contemporary Phnom Penh, forms the closing chapter of this book.

Milton Osborne
Sydney, 2007

Acknowledgements

My initial thanks are to Michael Dwyer and James Ferguson who asked me to write this book and who have patiently waited for its completion. In writing it I owe debts of gratitude that stretch back to my first arrival in Phnom Penh in 1959. To list all those who first helped me gain an understanding of the city would take an excessive amount of space. So while my thanks go to many whom I do not mention, I must make particular mention of my head of mission in Phnom Penh, the late Francis Hamilton Stuart, and the Cambodian friends whom I met during the first years I lived in Phnom Penh and after, when I returned as a student in 1966: Prince Sisowath Phandaravong and his parents, Prince and Princess Sisowath Entaravong; Colonel Kim Kosal; and Monsignor Paulus Tep Im Sotha. It is a telling comment on modern Cambodian history that both Kim Kosal and Tep Im Sotha were executed by the Khmer Rouge, while Prince and Princess Entaravong disappeared in the course of being driven out of Phnom Penh in April 1966. My time in Phnom Penh in 1966, when I witnessed the prelude to Sihanouk's political decline at the same time as I carried out research into the nineteenth century, was made greatly more pleasant by the kindness of the personnel of the Australian Embassy, and by the beginning of a particular friendship with the then British chargé d'affaires, Leslie Fielding, with whom I have continued to discuss developments in Cambodia over many years.

In more recent years, and in the course of regular visits to Phnom Penh, I have continued to benefit from the kindness of Australian diplomats and received assistance from a wide range of other residents. These include Michael Hayes, the courageous owner and publisher of the *Phnom Penh Post*; Frank Bochmann, the Food and Beverage Director of the Hôtel le Royal, and its honorary historian; Helen Grant Ross, who assisted me in understanding Phnom Penh's architectural history; Henri Locard, who expanded my knowledge of Khmer Rouge slogans and provincial prisons; and Gregor Muller, whose book on "bad Frenchmen" opened up a new picture of life in nineteenth-century Cambodia. Additionally, there are Cambodians who have been of great assistance but who would prefer that their names do not appear in a public document. My expression of thanks to them is no less sincere.

Away from Cambodia I have also incurred a large number of intellectual debts, reaching back to the years in the 1960s when I first started working in the French colonial archives, where I received every assistance. More recently I was grateful for the introduction Charley Todd gave me to his colleagues in the NGO Cambodian Living Arts. I am also grateful to Annette Hamilton for sharing her insights into Cambodian cinema with me. And over many years it has been a privilege to discuss developments in Cambodia with two outstanding journalists who have reported on the country for many years, Henry Kamm of the *New York Times* and Denis Gray of Associated Press. Both were among the first to recognize and write about the horrors of the Pol Pot regime.

My final and most particular expressions of gratitude go to two individuals who, from different perspectives, have once again been ready to read the whole of my manuscript in draft and to comment extensively on it, Dinah Goddard and David Chandler. Without their assistance the book would have been lacking what I hope is both its measure of accuracy and its insight.

As must always be the case, none of those to whom I owe my thanks and gratitude bears any responsibility for the facts as I present them in this book or for the judgments and conclusions that I offer. For these I alone am responsible.

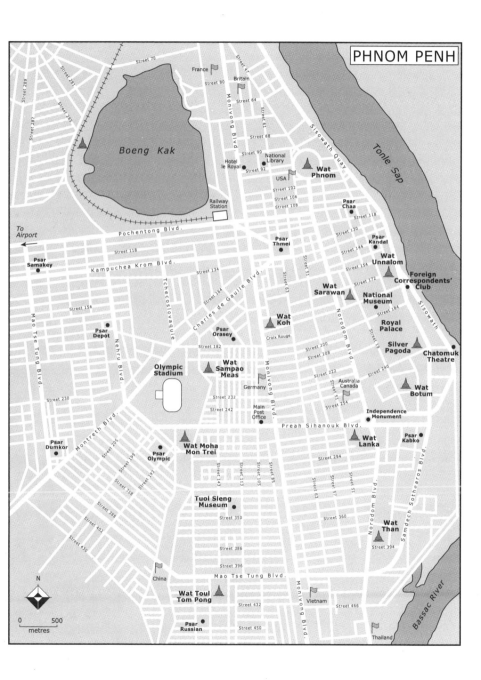

PHNOM PENH

Street 70
France
Britain
Street 80
Street 47
Street 84
Street 289
Street 281
Street 61
Street 88
Monivong Blvd.
Street 285
Street 287
Boeng Kak
Street 90
National Library
Hotel le Royal
Street 92
USA
Sisowath Quay
Tonle Sap
Wat Phnom
Street 102
Psar Chaa
Street 106
Street 108
Street 118
Railway Station
To Airport
Pochentong Blvd.
Psar Thmei
Street 130
Psar Kandal
Street 118
Street 144
Kampuchea Krom Blvd.
Psar Samakey
Street 134
Street 154
Wat Unnalom
Foreign Correspondents' Club
Wat Sarawan
Street 172
National Museum
Street 164
Charles de Gaulle Blvd.
Wat Koh
Croix Rouge
Street 184
Royal Palace
Tchecoslovaquie
Street 156
Psar Depot
Psar Orasey
Street 182
Street 200
Street 208
Silver Pagoda
Chatomuk Theatre
Mao Tse Tung Blvd.
Nehru Blvd.
Olympic Stadium
Wat Sampao Meas
Germany
Monivong Blvd.
Street 222
Street 240
Wat Botum
Australia
Canada
Street 232
Street 242
Main Post Office
Street 254
Independence Monument
Street 230
Preah Sihanouk Blvd.
Psar Dumkor
Montreth Blvd.
Street 205
Psar Olympic
Wat Moha Mon Trei
Wat Lanka
Psar Kabko
Street 294
Street 199
Street 193
Street 143
Street 113
Street 105
Street 85
Street 63
Street 57
Street 51
Samdech Sothearos Blvd.
Street 158
Tuol Sleng Museum
Street 350
Street 360
Norodom Blvd.
Wat Than
Street 388
Street 102
Street 386
Street 394
Street 430
Street 396
China
Mao Tse Tung Blvd.
Vietnam
Street 466
Wat Toul Tom Pong
Street 432
N
Psar Russian
Street 450
Thailand
Bassac River
0   500
metres

Chapter One

A PERSONAL INTRODUCTION TO A CHANGING CITY

Before 1958 I barely knew of Phnom Penh's existence and had not the slightest expectation that this city that would be a continuing part of my life for nearly fifty years, a cause of happiness and of deepest despair. When, in 1958, as a twenty-two-year-old trainee diplomat in Canberra, I learned I was being posted to the Australian mission in the Cambodian capital, my ignorance of Phnom Penh, and of the country in which it was located, was profound. Not only did I know little more than the city's name, I also knew nothing of Cambodia's archaeological riches, the great temples of Angkor, neither of their existence, nor their remarkable history. This sounds shameful now, but it is true.

I had difficulty imagining what I would find in Phnom Penh, even though the mission's "post report" summoned up a set of remarkably exotic images. I learned I would attend ceremonies at the Royal Palace, where the king was the father of the man who had been king before him. I found I should equip myself with a white sharkskin suit, the prescribed dress for the diplomatic corps at daytime ceremonies. When I later came to wear it with my colleagues in the corps I could never rid myself of the feeling that we looked like a rather seedy collection of Italian ice cream vendors. For my representational duties, the post report noted, I should be aware that offering a *coupe de champagne* at the end of the day was a favoured form of entertainment. This was only one testimony to a continuing link with France, the former colonial power, whose language was still widely used by the Cambodian government. This, I was told, was the reason for my being sent to Phnom Penh. With some capacity in the language, I was an appropriate, if very junior, choice for the slot falling vacant the following year. (Since in 1958 Phnom Penh was psychologically, about as far distant from Canberra as it as possible to be, I could not discount the thought that I was also chosen for this out-of-the-way posting by the "mandarin" who headed the foreign service as a consequence of my having dropped a catch off his bowling in a social cricket match.)

Daily life, the post report told me, would be both eased and complicated by Phnom Penh's setting. In a city where labour was cheap, there would be domestic help. But many everyday necessities would not be obtainable, or not at a price that was reasonable: no fresh milk, no butter other than what came in tins, a paucity or complete lack of standard pharmaceutical supplies. Reliable medical assistance was unavailable, so that serious illness would require evacuation to Bangkok—something I ultimately experienced when I contracted amoebic dysentery. And I should anticipate that the city's one so-called department store, the "Magasins Modernes", was distinguished more by what it did not have in stock than by the variety of its merchandise.

Then, as the time to leave Australia drew closer, an attempted rebellion in February 1959 against the authority of Prince Norodom Sihanouk, then Cambodia's undisputed leader, ended with the chief rebel being "shot while attempting to escape". It was clear that there was more to Cambodian politics than the comic opera picture conjured up by references to princes and palaces, royal elephants and exquisite dancing by the court ballet. Phnom Penh was indeed exotic, but part of that exoticism involved a political world that already had a deeply dark character and which within less than ten years would begin a descent into terrible bloodshed and, ultimately, a remorseless tyranny of an order that no one had foreseen or could imagine.

FIRST IMPRESSIONS

First impressions have a powerful place in memory, and so it is that I remember with startling clarity stepping out of a Royal Air Cambodge DC-3, at nine in the morning on 6 April 1959, on to the baking tarmac of Pochentong airport and into a stifling blanket of heat. I had spent the previous night in Saigon (today's Ho Chi Minh City), a brief stopover which had left me with a vivid impression of a big city that still had strong echoes of France in the Orient, even though Vietnam had gained its independence five years previously. Now, at Phnom Penh's airport, I stood in a setting surrounded by a rural landscape with few buildings in sight apart from the airport's terminal. The paddy fields stretching away from the airport's perimeter were dull khaki-grey in colour, for this was the height of the dry season, and the fields were empty except for the stubble of crops harvested months before. Tall sugar palms provided

The *Phnom* (Hill) from which the city takes its name

some sense of scale in the dust-filled air. And here and there in the distance I saw pillars of dust rising into the sky from the bone-dry tracks that wound through the countryside. They seemed like some Cambodian version of the biblical "pillars of smoke by day", as they marked the slow passage of ox carts traversing areas impassable for motor traffic.

Pochentong airport is only two and a half miles from the centre of Phnom Penh and in 1959 the first of these ran through largely open country before entering a city that, like Saigon, still preserved strong memories of its past as part of France's colonial empire. Strung out along the Tonle Sap river, the tributary of the Mekong that runs from the Great Lake until it reaches the river's main stream at Phnom Penh, Cambodia's capital seemed at first sight blessed by location and an apparent prosperity. As I was later to realize, the landmarks remarked on by nineteenth-century travellers and by literary visitors as diverse as Pierre-Loti and Somerset Maugham were there, unchanged. The *phnom* or "hill", from which the city takes part of its name, matched the image recorded by the French explorers who had travelled up the Mekong in the 1860s. And the Royal Palace, with the multicoloured tiles of its scattered buildings glistening in the sun, stood beside the river as both the symbolic and actual centre of Phnom Penh.

In 1959, the city's architectural and demographic character still reflected the tripartite division that had come into being after the French established their "protectorate" over Cambodia in 1863. (The supposed difference between a protectorate and a colony was no more than a legal fig leaf to cover the fact that from the 1860s until it gained independence in 1953, Cambodia was in every way that mattered a French colony.) There were still sections of the city that could be identified with the colonial "European Quarter", a "Chinese Quarter" and a "Cambodian Quarter". These were no longer as clearly defined as they had been in colonial times, but the names by which they were known still reflected their essential character. Added to these three main divisions were scattered groupings in which Vietnamese predominated. One was in central Phnom Penh to the west of the Cambodian Quarter. The other two locations where Vietnamese were numerous were in the area to the north of the European Quarter and in the peninsula formed by the Mekong and Tonle Sap rivers and reached, today, by the "Japanese Friendship Bridge". This area, a peninsula known as Chruoy Changvar, was once mostly occupied by members of Cambodia's Islamic community. Today they number half a million in the whole of the country, but they were barely half that number in 1959. By the 1950s the peninsula's large number of Vietnamese inhabitants also gave it a strongly Catholic religious identification. This fact did nothing to save it from being the site of a terrible, ethnically-motivated massacre in the turbulent first months of Cambodia's civil war in 1970. Today the main road running north past Chruoy Changvar has become home to a series of large, noisy bars and restaurants, many tawdry in character and more than a few combining their proclaimed services as massage parlours with undisguised identities as the capital's busiest brothels.

With the French element of Phnom Penh's population greatly reduced after Cambodia gained independence in 1953, the half million people who lived in the city in 1959 were divided, into three roughly equal groups: Cambodians, Chinese and Vietnamese. These were groups that largely lived apart socially as well as in their choice of residence, however much their working lives intersected. If not at the bottom of the social pyramid as coolies or cycle rickshaw (*cyclopousse* in local terminology) riders, Cambodians filled the ranks of the civil service, were teachers and only occasionally, notably if they were part Chinese in ancestry, engaged in commerce. And it was Cambodians who made up the ranks of the Buddhist monks, still referred to by the French term at this time as *bonzes*. In their saffron coloured robes, they were a ubiquitous presence at every state ceremony and they filled the streets near the palace with colour when they poured out of the Buddhist University in the late morning. To succeed in commerce was the aim of Phnom Penh's vigorous and noisy Chinese population, and some did so spectacularly well. Then there were the Vietnamese, many of them Catholic, and an object of dislike and distrust for most Cambodians who saw them as both traditional enemies and as the ethnic group the French had imported into the country to act in the lower ranks of the colonial administration. In 1959 the men of the Vietnamese community mostly filled roles as clerks and small-scale merchants, while their women folk frequently worked as domestics, particularly for western expatriates.

THE "GOOD YEARS"

For a western foreigner, Phnom Penh at the beginning of the 1960s was an attractive place to be. Fuelled by the presence of a large, free-spending American community, with its embassy and its aid and military missions, the economy was kind to Cambodia's elite, who reaped enormous profits by renting out their real estate holdings at inflated prices. To a surprising degree, some of the elite's prosperity did trickle down to the rest of Phnom Penh's community. There was poverty, of course, some of it dire. It was largely hidden by the fact that the poor lived in shanty settlements far from the centre of the city, where, in any event, the police moved swiftly to remove the occasional beggar from the streets. And if American money was a key to much of Phnom Penh's prosperity, there were still important French commercial interests in the country, notably in the huge rubber plantations on the red earth lands across the Mekong beyond the north-eastern provincial centre of Kompong Cham. The French had surrendered government control to Cambodians, but they were still a powerful, if discreet, force in relation to the country's external politics. They also had a clearly observable presence in cultural terms, from the Lycée Descartes staffed by French teachers, the preferred institution for the children of Phnom Penh's elite, to the pervasive

A billboard advertising "Alain Delon" cigarettes, a link with the city's French past

presence of French products, though not yet of Alain Delon cigarettes, named in honour of the French film star. Advertised widely, they are a relatively recent addition to the Phnom Penh scene. But bread in the characteristic French-style *baguette* was present everywhere, so much so that it had become as much a Cambodian as a French food staple. It remains so today.

In everyday terms the French presence was apparent in such quintessentially Gallic establishments as the Bar Jean and the Zigzag Bar, both drinking haunts which seemed to have been transplanted, together with their customers, from Marseille. I had a particular affection for a now-vanished, traditionally-run restaurant, La Taverne, with Monsieur Mignon as its *patron*, in the post office square. Categorizing Australians as *Anglo-Saxons* and so not truly appreciative of the joys of food and wine, he would upbraid me for asking whether the seafood he served had been kept on ice as it journeyed up from the coast during the hottest months of the year. The taste is what matters, he would insist over and again, not what happens in your stomach afterwards.

My concern for the freshness of Monsieur Mignon's seafood was only part of an awareness that I shared with all the city's residents of the difference between Phnom Penh's two main seasons. I quickly became aware of the monsoons that determined the city's climate, then and now. From November to late May or early June the north-east monsoon dominates Phnom Penh's climate. In November the skies are clear and the daytime temperatures seldom rise above 25 degrees Celsius. December is much the same, and on occasion a cold front moving down from China will temporarily lower the temperature to the mid-teens. When this happens the city's inhabitants suddenly reveal that they have a stock of "winter" clothing as they appear wrapped up against the "cold". But from December onwards the temperature continues to rise steadily and by March the increasing heat is accompanied by ever greater humidity. But except for the scattered showers of the "mango rains" which sometimes fall in March it is not until the end of May, or early June, that the arrival of the south-western monsoon begins to bring relief from the oppressive climate, which by then is reaching the high thirties day after day.

When the south-western monsoon becomes dominant its arrival is not marked by a sudden onset of continuous downpours. These come later, in September and October. At first, in the early weeks, whole days will pass without rain. But then, by August, the rainfall becomes more regular until, eventually, it pounds down throughout each day, leaving the city awash with water under grey skies that block out the sun from dawn to dusk.

The Chinese community, never missing an opportunity to gamble in the far-off days just described, placed bets on when the rain started falling. A "rain king" played a role akin to those who ran the numbers rackets in Harlem. It was up to the rain king to decide when the rainfall actually began and so whether to provide a "payoff" to the punters who had guessed the time correctly. The opportunities for corruption in this arrangement never seemed to dim the enthusiasm of those for whom this game was seen as an opportunity to make money.

The French, the Chinese and the Vietnamese communities each played a part in giving Phnom Penh its character, but for all that it was a Cambodian city, with its calendar of Cambodian festivals and a special world linked to the monarchy and the palace. Sihanouk may have abdicated in his father's favour in 1955, but from then until he was deposed in 1970 he was seen in almost every way as a king. While his father was alive, the palace was the supreme location for royal ceremonies and for performances by the dancers of the traditional court ballet. When heads of state visited Phnom Penh they were entertained by a performance of the ballet which drew for its repertoire from both

Dancers from the royal ballet troupe, 1959

indigenous legend and the Indian epics, the *Ramayana* and the *Mahabharata*. The dancers performed in costumes of the richest silks shot through with gold and silver thread, wearing golden tiered crowns or the masks of chimerical beasts, their every gesture full of meaning as their hands and feet struck poses that could only have been achieved by years of rigorous training.

There was other dancing, too. For the general population, watching folk dancers and participating in them at times of festivals was part of a continuing traditional way of life, less so in the city than in the countryside, but pervasive nonetheless. And for young, well-to-do men-about-town, both Cambodian and Chinese, there were the *dancings*, nightclubs of a sort where one could pay to dance with a female partner who more often than not was ready to supplement her income by offering other services later in the night. But perhaps most exotically of all there were the *soirées dansantes* offered by Prince Sihanouk, and held within the palace walls. Here senior Cambodians and members of the diplomatic corps danced to a band of princes led by Sihanouk as he played a saxophone or crooned French pop songs and his own compositions, such as *Phnom Penh* and *Brise de Novembre*.

The death of Sihanouk's father King Suramarit in April 1960 brought a sombre end both to entertainment of this kind staged in the shadow of kingly majesty and to the presence of a king on the Cambodian throne. Dancing evenings continued to be held in the palace, but they were never quite the same. And more than those of us living

Prince Norodom Sihanouk bearing an urn containing his father's ashes

in Phnom Penh initially realized at the time, it also signalled a crisis for Sihanouk in terms of who should take his father's place on the Cambodian throne. In the event, he chose to avoid making a choice by orchestrating his own elevation to the new position of chief of state. But much of the political manoeuvring of the time was overshadowed by the pomp of arrangements for the late king's cremation. In accordance with

King Suramarit's funeral pagoda at night in 1960

age-old tradition the king's body was placed in a golden urn filled with mercury to hasten decomposition while a great funeral pagoda was constructed on the *men* or royal cremation ground in front of the National Museum. There, five months later and after a great funeral procession that wound through the streets of the city, Suramarit's remains were cremated. Some of his ashes were, according to tradition, cast into the Mekong, while others were placed in a stupa in the grounds of the Silver Pagoda.

GATHERING CLOUDS

After nearly two and a half years, I left Phnom Penh in 1961 and did not return until April 1966, almost exactly seven years to the day since I had first stepped into the enveloping heat at Pochentong airport. I had returned as a Cornell University graduate student, lacking both the funds and the diplomatic privileges that had previously made living there so agreeable. The passage of years had not been kind to Phnom Penh. It had grown in size, it is true, so that most of the empty land along the road to the airport was now occupied. Following a burst of government-supported construction, major new public buildings had been completed. Many, such as the Faculty of Arts buildings along the Pochentong road, were the work of a talented Cambodian architect,

Vann Molyvann. But what had changed most importantly was the mood of the city, determined by its politics and its economy. In 1963 Prince Norodom Sihanouk, by then chief of state following his father's death in 1960 and the failure to appoint a new king, had renounced American aid. This was a bold political gesture made even bolder by his decision two years later to break diplomatic relations with the United States. Both these decisions were supported by the radical elements in Cambodia's political life, however much they were regretted by the powerful conservative interests who remained Sihanouk's most important supporters. With an end to American aid and Sihanouk's embrace of a new economic system of nationalized import and export, the funds that had made Phnom Penh such a pleasant place to live for the Cambodian elite and expatriates alike disappeared and the economy was faltering.

Certainly, the city retained some of its former panache. Fine meals could still be eaten at the Café de Paris, where Monsieur Spacesi, the corpulent Corsican owner, wore his Legion of Honour ribbon next to his trousers' flies as his derisory comment on the politics of metropolitan France. The Bar Jean continued to function by the river and La Taverne stayed agelessly the same. The Hôtel le Royal still had pretensions to being Phnom Penh's Raffles. (By great good fortune I found that I could live in one of its few non-air-conditioned rooms at a cost of less than three American dollars a day.) Sihanouk had not abandoned his plans for grand buildings, and construction was still taking place, but this was all superficial due to an overall decline in his readiness to address the hard issues of government. As the international environment deteriorated, with the increasing pace of the Vietnam War steadily drawing Cambodia into its orbit, Phnom Penh was more than ever a city of rumour and perceived conspiracies. Its citizens began, for the first time, to ask whether Sihanouk's luck was running out. For many in the elite there seemed no clearer reason to ask this question than the manner in which Sihanouk had suddenly immersed himself in a feverish programme of feature filmmaking while neglecting a growing list of policy dilemmas.

Much of my understanding of the changed character of Phnom Penh, and of Cambodia as a whole, came from an unlikely source, Father Paulus Tep Im Sotha, a Catholic priest who was the son of a Cambodian father and a Franco-Vietnamese mother. Educated at a seminary in Montpellier and then at the Angelicum University in Rome, Father Tep

Im had been ordained in Paris in 1959. His parish church was the Eglise Hoalong (sometimes rendered as Hoaland), a site whose name remembered the distant time when men from Holland had sited one of their trading factories in this location by the Tonle Sap river. I came to know Tep Im because we shared a common interest in history and, in contrast to so many of his compatriots, he thought of history in a western fashion rather than as a matter of events determined by mystical or superhuman forces. Moving freely throughout Phnom Penh society Tep Im knew of the doubts and uncertainties that plagued so many in the capital and of the unanswered questions that hung about the future.

By the end of 1967 such questions were being posed more urgently without clear and reassuring answers. There were few signs of unrest in Phnom Penh itself, but its population was increasingly unnerved by the reports filtering in from the north-west of the country, from a place named Samlaut, a distant location in Battambang province outside the knowledge of almost all who lived in Phnom Penh. A peasant rising against the authority of the state which had begun in Samlaut signalled the start of a rural insurgency that steadily gathered strength over the next three years. There were grisly tales told of bounties being offered to the army for the despatch of severed heads to the capital to verify the success of its efforts in putting down the increasing challenges to the state. And it was becoming clear, despite Sihanouk's repeated claims to the contrary, that sections of Cambodian territory along the country's eastern borders were being occupied as sanctuaries by the Vietnamese communist forces arrayed against the American-backed South Vietnamese regime.

SIHANOUK DEPOSED

As I returned to Cambodia each year between 1966 and 1971, I found Phnom Penh's mood increasingly morose as its citizens recognized that the good times had passed and puzzled over whether they might ever return. Then, in March 1970, while Sihanouk was in the Soviet Union, men on the right of Cambodian politics—almost all previously his trusted associates—staged a coup that threw him out of office. For some among them, the decision to act was taken on the basis of principle, since they genuinely believed that Sihanouk's policies had led the country into an impasse from which it had to be rescued. For others, ambition joined to greed was the driving force for their actions. None, surely, ever imagined that as a consequence of their actions they were opening the way to one of the most vicious civil wars in modern history that, within the space of five years, was to turn much of Phnom Penh into a largely empty wasteland.

That point was still some way away when, in 1971, I made my last visit before the terrible triumph of Pol Pot's force four years later. Yet with war growing in intensity in the countryside, Phnom Penh was already a city under partial siege. Travel by road to some provincial centres was still possible, but others, such as Battambang, could only be reached by air. Key government buildings in the capital were ringed by sandbags and barbed wire, and refugees fleeing the fighting in the countryside were flocking into the city and straining its resources.

There were many grim stories told of the way in which the war was being prosecuted, but grimmest of all was the account I heard of the massacre of over a thousand of Phnom Penh's Vietnamese community, mostly those living in the area of the Chruoy Changvar peninsula. Carried out by units from both the army and police, the slaughter began at the end of April 1970 and continued through the following month. Even today the reasons for this brutal business are not fully clear. In part it seems to have been an atavistic act of vengeance against traditional enemies as a "pay back" for the fact that Vietnamese communist forces were aiding Cambodia's own left-wing rebels fighting the Phnom Penh regime. In part, too, it appears to have been a channelling of anger against an easy target at a time when the loss of lives in the first pitched battles of the civil war, particularly among the students who had flocked to the government's colours after Sihanouk's overthrow, had been so grievous. Whatever the explanation, after the massacre large numbers from Phnom Penh's Vietnamese community fled the city.

After Pol Pot

I did not see Phnom Penh again for ten years, a period when it swelled to more than two million inhabitants as the war in the countryside grew ever more savage and refugees poured into the city. In the last year before the Cambodian communists' victory, the Khmer Rouge forces were close enough to Phnom Penh to lay down random rocket and artillery attacks that tore into the city, wreaking havoc on people and buildings alike. Then, on 17 April 1975, the guns fell silent and almost immediately after hopes for some return to normality were shattered as the victors drove Phnom Penh's inhabitants out of the city into giant agrarian work camps.

I followed these events and the slowly emerging details of the true awfulness of the Pol Pot regime at a distance, from the United States, Singapore and finally Australia. It had become clear that terrible crimes were being committed by the regime, even if putting an accurate figure on the number of deaths was impossible. It slowly also became apparent that Pol Pot and his associates were engaged in sending their troops across the border into Vietnam where they indiscriminately slaughtered men, women and children. Beginning on Christmas Day 1978, and in the face of this extraordinary provocation, the Vietnamese government finally turned on its erstwhile communist comrades, invading Cambodia and driving the Khmer Rouge from Phnom Penh, and then most of the country. I learned something of the human cost of the period of war and tyranny working on, and sometimes just over, the border between Thailand and Cambodia when, in early 1980, and again early in 1981, I worked as a consultant to the United Nations High Commission for Refugees. Most of the Cambodians whom I interviewed, with one notable exception whom I write about later in this book, were not linked to Phnom Penh. But the men and women whom I met at this time left me with an indelible impression of the true horror of the period when Pol Pot and his associates ruled over Cambodia and its capital.

When I was able to return to Phnom Penh in 1981 it was to a shattered city, with large sections still empty of people. Outside of the occupying Vietnamese and their protégés in the fledging Cambodian administration, those parts of the city that were occupied had the air of a vast, insanitary transit camp, as poorly nourished survivors of the Pol Pot tyranny returned to the city and sought to scrape a living. Many— probably at this stage most—of those living in the city did so as squatters. Like most visitors then and since, I visited Tuol Sleng, the outwardly banal school buildings that had been used as an extermination centre for those seen as enemies of the overthrown regime. I also saw the "Killing Fields" at Choeung Ek at a time when the mass graves were still being exhumed. Then it was a markedly different site from the now "sanitized" tourist destination it has become, and the smell of human decomposition hung heavy in the air over the lines upon lines of battered skulls lying on the ground besides the graves. Close to my old haunt at the Hôtel le

Royal, I realized with a shock that not only had the Khmer Rouge wrecked hundreds of cars and demolished some of Phnom Penh's markets as symbols of capitalist evil, but had also completely removed all traces of the city's Catholic cathedral. It, too, was seen as a reflection of western oppression and where it had once stood was an empty field.

TODAY'S PHNOM PENH

Much has changed in Phnom Penh since that 1981 visit, and both Cambodia and its capital have attained an apparent degree of normality. But it is a normality that includes a government that brooks no challenge, in a system where rampant corruption, including at the highest level of government, is a daily fact of life. The nature of society is such that the rich are powerful and powerful are rich. The word that is repeatedly used to sum up the character of contemporary Cambodia is "impunity". If you are powerful with links to the government you may act without concern for the consequences of your actions. It would all be unrelievedly depressing to contemplate were it not for the remarkable resilience of the people and their struggle to recapture something of the world that existed before Cambodia began its descent into chaos nearly forty years ago.

For if corruption and the impunity of the powerful are leitmotifs of contemporary Cambodia, these must be measured against the spirit of its people. Phnom Penh has come alive with a renewed commitment to commerce. Nowhere is this more apparent than in the innumerable cafés and restaurants that have re-emerged as a sign of better times. Those signs are also reflected in the bustling markets that once again teem with traders and their customers. But even more importantly, Phnom Penh is once more a city where the traditional festivals stamped out in the Pol Pot years, and muted or not honoured at all during the period of Vietnamese occupation in the 1980s, have been revived as joyous displays of its identity. Old royal ceremonies such as the "Ploughing of the Sacred Furrow", an event that associates the country's ruler with the opening of the planting season, have a renewed meaning since the accession to the throne of King Sihamoni in 2004. But it is the great popular festivals, and most of all the celebration of *Chaul Chhnam*, the Cambodian New Year, falling in April, and *Bon Om Tuk*, the November Water Festival, that are the truest reflection of the unbeaten spirit of Phnom Penh's population. And while I argue later in this book that the importance of

Ploughing the Sacred Furrow

monarchy has been much diminished in Cambodia, there is no doubt that Sihanouk's return to Cambodia as king in 1993 was important for the revival of the city's pre-Pol Pot identity.

Phnom Penh has done more than just survive the Pol Pot tyranny and the years of Vietnamese occupation in the 1980s, when a vicious guerrilla war continued to be fought in the Cambodian countryside. Since "the Cambodia problem", as it was known, was resolved at the beginning of the 1990s, and despite the many problems that its population must face on a daily basis, Phnom Penh has come back to vigorous life. At times that life seems chaotic and it remains marked by endless inequities of opportunity and reward. Yet there are other features of contemporary life that attest to hope in the face of the many negatives than can be listed. Phnom Penh is home to an active, if frequently irresponsible, press. It is, more than ever before, an international city, with one of the largest collection of resident foreign non-governmental organizations (NGOs) to be found anywhere in the world. And even more importantly, the city boasts its own, courageous domestic NGOs, which have repeatedly not hesitated to criticize the government on human rights issues.

The buildings that best represent Phnom Penh's traditional identity have survived the upheavals of the past fifty years remarkably well. This is true of the buildings in the Royal Palace compound. Surprisingly, given some of their other actions, the Khmer Rouge did little more than leave them untouched and neglected of regular maintenance, though the royal regalia and most importantly the *Preah Khan*, the kingdom's sacred sword and most cherished item of the royal regalia, disappeared. An uncertain number of the gold, silver and crystal Buddha images in the "Silver Pagoda", located next to the palace compound and so named since its floor is covered in 5,281 silver tiles, are said to have been stolen while the Khmer Rouge ruled, or possibly in the chaos that followed the arrival of the invading Vietnamese troops in January 1979. One guide book speaks of some sixty per cent having disappeared in this way. (This claim does not accord with my memory of what was housed in the pagoda in the pre-1975 period.) Certainly, a remarkable number of Buddha statues remain, including a 200-pound solid gold image, said to have been cast in the form of King Norodom I (reigned 1863-1904). And the "Emerald Buddha" itself, after which the pagoda takes its Cambodian name, is also still present. Reputedly made of Baccarat glass, its presence in the pagoda reflects the wish of Norodom I to match in his own capital the famed Temple of the Emerald Buddha found within Bangkok's Grand Palace.

Just as the Silver Pagoda escaped major damage, neither was there any attempt to desecrate the most important palace building, the throne hall, with its frescoed ceilings depicting scenes from the *Ramayana*. Possibly even more remarkably, the magnificent pre-Angkorian and Angkorian holdings—exquisite stone and bronze statues of priceless value—of the National Museum, just outside the palace walls, survived without major loss. What moved the Khmer Rouge to ensure this survival is still unclear. We must be grateful that this is what occurred, even if we cannot explain how it happened. The suggestion that it was part of a concern by the Pol Pot regime to honour Cambodia's past is unconvincing.

So Phnom Penh has been reborn. While tourists flock to the great temples of Angkor far too many forego visiting Cambodia's capital. This is a mistake and reflects a lack of knowledge of what Phnom Penh has to offer. It is, in many ways, a very different city from the one I first encountered in 1959. Yet, with all the changes that have taken place, there is much of the "old" Phnom Penh to discover beneath the overlay of the new. And both those old and new aspects of the city's character are what make the city and its people an object of endless fascination.

Chapter Two

DECIPHERING THE PALIMPSEST:
FINDING THE PAST IN THE PRESENT

From its earliest recorded existence as a capital city in the fifteenth century, Phnom Penh's orientation has been determined by its location at the confluence of the Mekong and its tributary, the Tonle Sap river (the River of the Great Lake). Fairly recent archaeological research has shown that there were small settlements established in the area around Phnom Penh perhaps as long ago as two thousand years, and so well before the foundation of the great city of Angkor, sited close to the north-eastern edge of Cambodia's Great Lake, in 802 CE. These early settlements, housed populations dependent on agriculture, fishing and hunting. They were located on land just above the high water level of the annual floods. One which has been revealed through aerial photography was laid out in a circular form and was established close to what are today the "Killing Fields" of Choeung Ek, about ten miles south-west of Phnom Penh's city centre.

By the fourteenth century CE, Phnom Penh's modern site was home to a small but growing commercial settlement. Its existence reflected the fact that the Cambodian court at Angkor was increasingly looking to trade with China as a way to maintain its prosperity, diversifying away from its previous heavy reliance on agriculture and the control of population as sources of its wealth. Just how many people lived in Phnom Penh at this time we do not know and it may be rash to draw the conclusion that the numbers later reported to live in the settlement by Iberian chroniclers in the sixteenth century—varying between 10,000 and 20,000—can be taken as indicating the size of the population a century and a half before. Nevertheless, it is reasonable to assume that in the first half of the fifteenth century Phnom Penh's population numbered in the thousands, perhaps as many as ten thousand. Although there is some scholarly uncertainty about the issue, it seems probable that the important present-day Buddhist pagoda, the Wat Unnalom, in central Phnom Penh and home of the Buddhist patriarch, is sited on the location of a foundation established before the Cambodian court abandoned

Wat Unnalom, Phnom Penh's oldest Buddhist Foundation

Angkor, some time after 1431. This is despite the fact that the foundation date for this pagoda is often given as 1443.

From Phnom Penh trading vessels could travel down the Mekong to the South China Sea to begin the long journey to China. But it was also a location that provided a strategic base giving access to trade with the distant regions far to the north in what is today modern Laos. Reached after many weeks or even months of travel, the petty states in those remote areas were a source of rare forest products, such as benzoin, the balsamic tree resin used as a fumigant, of semi-precious stones and of the feathers of exotic birds, all of which were valued in the Chinese market. The essential character of Phnom Penh's location is captured in the name by which the settlement was first known. It was called Chatomuk, (sometimes transliterated as "Chaktomuk") or "The Place of the Four Faces", a site open to the four quarters of the compass and a name that conjures up the distinctive four-faced towers of the Bayon temple at Angkor. It is a name still known to Cambodians today. And whether consciously or otherwise, the name bestowed by the French on the stretch of water where the Mekong and the Tonle Sap flow together and then divide, the Quatre-Bras, or the "Four Arms", holds an echo of the Cambodian toponym.

As for the city's more familiar name of Phnom Penh, there is a romantic legend accounting for its existence. Some time in the fourteenth century, the legend recounts, and not long before the Cambodian court left the great city of Angkor with its magnificent temples, a woman named Penh lived beside a small hillock close to the river bank and a little above the point where the Mekong and its tributary came together. One day, when the rivers were in flood, she saw a huge *koki* tree—a type traditionally planted only by royalty or Buddhist monks—floating in the current. When she pulled it to the shore, hoping to use it for firewood, she found to her amazement that wedged in the tree's branches were four statues of the Buddha and one of the Hindu god Vishnu. Penh recognized this as a sign that the gods had decided to leave the holy city of Angkor and to give their blessing to a new Cambodian capital.

Like women in contemporary Cambodia, Penh was energetic and determined. Calling on the people who lived nearby to carry the images to her home, she then organized them to pile earth on the hillock close to her home, so transforming it into a feature that could legitimately be called a hill, a *phnom* in Cambodian. When this was done, she built a temple on top of the hill to house the images of the Buddha and a stupa for other holy relics, while the statue of Vishnu was placed in a separate chapel. In memory of these events, the city took its name as Phnom Penh, the "Hill of Lady Penh".

Sadly, and charming though the story is, the record is clear that the settlement did not acquire its modern name until after the Cambodian court, led by King Ponhea Yat, left Angkor to settle briefly at the site of modern Phnom Penh. Despite some assertions to the contrary, we do not know exactly when this profoundly important event took place, although it occurred some time after 1431, possibly in the same decade, perhaps in the 1440s. It was a final act in a long drawn-out drama of the decline of the Angkorian empire's power in the face of a century of attacks from the emerging Siamese (Thai) principalities on Cambodia's western frontier. This decline did not mean that Angkor was totally abandoned, as is sometimes suggested. The temples, and most notably the greatest of them all, Angkor Wat, remained a place of pilgrimage after the court moved away. After spending about thirty years in Phnom Penh, the court moved again to one of a series of locations, all of them a short distance to the north of the modern city. From that time on, Phnom Penh remained as a commercial centre of fluctuating importance, enjoying brief periods as the site of the Cambodian king's court from time to time. It only came into European awareness in the sixteenth century, but at no time did it ever match the importance of such Southeast Asian trading settlements as Ayuthia, in independent Siam, or Batavia, the Dutch colonial predecessor of modern Jakarta.

PONHEA YAT'S CAPITAL

Nearly one hundred years ago, and on the basis of his vast knowledge of early Cambodian history, the great French scholar, George Coedès, sketched a map of Phnom Penh at the time King Ponhea Yat briefly established his capital there after leaving Angkor. To some extent the map is reliable; the dimensions of Ponhea Yat's settlement—an area surrounded by a dyke on three sides with the Tonle Sap river on the fourth—corresponds remarkably closely to today's central Phnom Penh. With the modern city divided into seven *khan*, or districts, of which four are strictly urban and three semi-urban, central Phnom Penh is designated Khan Daun Penh, the "District of Old Lady Penh". This is the area bounded by the Tonle Sap, Sihanouk Boulevard to the south, Monivong Boulevard to the west, and one of the east-west streets running away from the area of the Japanese Friendship Bridge across the Tonle Sap to the north. (Sihanouk Boulevard is named after Cambodia's most famous twentieth-century ruler, while Monivong Boulevard is named after the king who preceded him on the throne, reigning from 1927 to 1941.) Almost all the buildings that existed when Ponhea Yat moved from Angkor to Phnom Penh were located close to the river, or indeed constructed to float on it. For while the dyke at the settlement's perimeter would have kept at bay the floodwaters that cover so much of the low-lying landscape during the wet season, most of the area enclosed within the dyke was watery marshland. As modern Phnom Penh has expanded relentlessly, it has done so largely by a continuing process of pumping dry the surrounding marshes and reclaiming new land.

So the contours of the core area of modern Phnom Penh were laid down well before the French colonialists persuaded King Norodom I, at the end of 1865, to leave his capital at Udong, 25 miles to the north, and to establish his palace there. By then, and for centuries previously with its identity as a trading settlement, Phnom Penh consisted of little more than a single street of wooden houses straggling along the Tonle Sap. In some of the earliest maps of the nineteenth-century city this street was simply called the Grande Rue, colloquially rendered as the Grand' Rue. By the second decade of the twentieth century it had been given two names: Quai Norodom in the south where it was overlooked by the palace compound and named after the king who had died in 1904, and Quai Lagrandière in the north, named after an admiral who had served as an early governor of France's colony in southern Vietnam, then known as Cochinchina. By then, and indeed ever since the time when Phnom Penh resumed its status as Cambodia's capital in the 1860s, the city has expanded westwards from the Grand' Rue—slowly until the 1930s, increasingly rapidly from the 1960s to the present day. The built environment is almost entirely sited on reclaimed marshland and on filled-in canals that previously channelled minor streams and floodwaters to the Tonle Sap.

More recently, there has been major expansion to the north and south of the city's centre, so that urban settlement stretches for almost fifteen miles in each direction from the centre. The city now reaches out along the Tonle Sap to the north into areas that were previously the preserve of Cambodia's Islamic community, known by their collective name as Chams. To the south and running parallel to the Bassac, the Mekong's western arm as it flows towards southern Vietnam, settlement has expanded so that the once separate town of Ta Khmau has effectively become one of Phnom Penh's outer suburbs. Along with this rapid expansion the appearance of some sections of Phnom Penh's built environment has changed radically following the terrible years of war in the 1970s, the period of the Pol Pot tyranny, and the troubled years before peace finally arrived at the beginning of the 1990s. One of these radical changes has already been mentioned in the previous chapter. This is the complete demolition of Phnom Penh's sizeable Catholic cathedral, once located on Boulevard Monivong where the city's town hall now stands. This was not the only church to vanish while Pol Pot ruled. With the exception of a tiny convent chapel, all other Catholic churches, including a large church in what is today Street 126, were torn down as symbols of western imperialism.

Some of the radical changes also reflect the extraordinary growth of Phnom Penh's population since the early 1980s. The city remains home to a huge but uncertain number of squatters at a time when there has also been a post-conflict baby boom. Both of these developments have placed tremendous pressures on the city's services. Some major landmarks such as the Royal Palace and the National Museum have changed little over the past century. This is also true of the grandest of all Phnom Penh's boulevards, Boulevard Norodom, running from the *phnom* to the Independence Monument, which still retains much of the character it possessed in colonial times. But there are other parts of central Phnom Penh that are barely recognizable by comparison with the city that existed before civil war broke out. In some locations buildings that were conceived as housing for the country's emerging urban middle class have become the worst kind of squatter slums. To have a sense of the past in Phnom Penh's present it is necessary, figuratively, to decipher the urban palimpsest.

CENTRAL PHNOM PENH

Until the end of the 1960s, Phnom Penh's identity as a city shaped by its royal and colonial past was clear to see, and it is only in the very recent past that dramatic change has begun to transform its appearance. At the heart of the city was, and is, the Royal Palace compound, located in a prime geomantic position overlooking the point where the Mekong and the Tonle Sap rivers come together. Its buildings shelter behind a crenellated wall, with the Silver Pagoda located in the south of the compound. Next to the pagoda were the royal elephant stables. Today the beasts are only a memory, but in the past the elephants that occupied the stables could be seen each day making their stately progress along Street 240, which in earlier days was known as the Street of Okna Chhun. It was named after one of the first Cambodians to act as an interpreter for the French administration in Phnom Penh. As a young boy he had worked for the first French representative in Cambodia, Doudart de Lagrée. Later he rose to become a grand and rich official. Today the elephants which Chhun and so many others would have seen are now sadly evoked only by life-size models, and it is no longer possible to see the highly treasured "white" elephant whose disposition was so uncertain that a sign warned in French, *Attention, éléphant méchant*, with the delightful English translation, "Attention the naughty elephant".

Small by the standards of the Grand Palace in Bangkok, the palace compound dominates the buildings in its surrounding area, which boasts the National Museum, the great open space of the Men Ground, the site for royal cremations, and the quiet elegance of the French-built law courts. Not far away is the many-times rebuilt Wat Unnalom, thought to be the oldest Buddhist foundation in the capital and the residence of the head of the Buddhist *sangha*, and as we have seen, possibly standing on a site that was occupied by a Buddhist foundation before Ponhea Yat moved to Phnom Penh. Nearby, too, are buildings that once housed the parliament and the Buddhist Institute. Today these have been relocated further south along the Bassac. The outstanding Chatomuk Conference Hall, completed in 1961, stands in refurbished splendour on reclaimed land beside the Bassac. Designed by Vann Molyvann, it is said to be one of its architect's favourite works.

During the years of French rule the section of the city immediately to the south of the palace was the "Cambodian Quarter", the area where senior Cambodian officials and their families lived, particularly those linked directly to the royal court. The area retained this character in the years following independence. Strikingly enough, and at a time when power and prestige are no longer firmly linked to the palace, it remains the area of choice for many of the new power elite, the politicians of the ruling party and their commercial associates. Tellingly reflecting its status, it is the section of the city where, it is often snidely but correctly noted, there are never any power failures, a notable contrast to less politically favoured areas.

Moving to the north from the palace along the Tonle Sap, on what is now the Sisowath Quay—it takes its name from the king who ruled from 1904 to 1927—a visitor could be forgiven for thinking that this was an area created for its present purpose. What could be a better location for the succession of cafés, restaurants and small hotels than this stretch of river front? Here, indeed, is the popular Foreign Correspondents' Club and dozens of other moderately priced establishments that are a Mecca for visitors, whether comfortably funded or budget-conscious backpackers, and the many expatriates who now work and live in Phnom Penh. Few among these varied eating places offer Cambodian food, and in this practice they are following in a long-established tradition of neglecting local fare in favour of other cuisines. There are a small number of restaurants that offer traditional Cambodian food in the city, a cuisine that owes much to Thailand but is generally less spicy. But aside from snacks sold at market stalls, Cambodians of even marginally prosperous means have always looked to restaurants serving Chinese and French food if not eating in their own homes. Now the variety available is much greater than ever was the case before the 1970s, though just why, for instance, a visitor to Phnom Penh would choose to eat Mexican food is puzzling.

Hard though it is to visualize nowadays, until the 1970s the converted three- and four-storey shophouse buildings along the Sisowath Quay served a different purpose. They were linked to Phnom Penh's status as a river port that could receive vessels of up to 6,000 tons in the high water season. Here with coils of tarred rope spilling out onto the footpath were the ship chandlers selling the necessities for life afloat. Here, too, were the provision stores and the offices of the shipping agents. And until the mid-1960s the Sisowath Quay was home to the

The popular Foreign Correspondents' Club

dimly lit offices of Denis Frères, the agency house founded by Bordeaux merchants in 1862 that was French Indochina's equivalent of Hong Kong's leading *hong*, Jardine Mathieson, the great trading house founded on the sale of opium into China. An occasional break in the ranks of maritime commerce was provided by a few cheap eating houses, and a couple of coffin makers' shops, one of which has survived to the present day. With Phnom Penh's port no longer used by sizeable shipping, another, human element once so apparent on Sisowath Quay has also disappeared. No longer are there the groups of tough stevedores, with their handling hooks stuck in the waistbands of their shorts, waiting for work. Some were Cambodian and some were Chinese, the presence of the latter a testimony to the fact that not all Chinese immigrants into Southeast Asia are to be found in the ranks of the wealthy.

Not everyone is happy with the manner in which Sisowath Quay has developed. Cambodia's most distinguished architect, Vann Molyvann, who studied at the Ecole Nationale Supérieure des Beaux Arts in Paris after the Second World War, has condemned what he see as "rampant development" along the river. He and others have expressed their regrets that the built environment has been developed so much with the interests of foreign visitors in mind, as well as the profit motive that has driven local owners to respond to those visitors' interests. Yet at the same time as the buildings along the Tonle Sap have acquired their present character, there is no denying that locals have become the "owners" of the open spaces, especially in the gardens near and in front of the Royal Palace. This area has increasingly become a focal point for local traders in the evenings. Some are food vendors, who take up regular positions by the road side, while others sell their goods from small carts. There are also always men and women present to sell cheap toys or balloons to children brought to the riverside by their parents.

Stretching back from the river front up to Norodom Boulevard was the "Chinese Quarter". Until the 1970s, this was where all but the richest of Phnom Penh's ethnic Chinese population lived in an ambience of noisy commitment to commerce and the celebration of their festivals and funerals, particularly the latter. In the hot months of the year funerals became an almost daily affair, complete with wailing mourners and gong bands competing with out-of-tune renderings of Chopin's *Funeral March*, played on saxophones and cornets. Thirty years later the buildings remain much the same as they were before the Pol Pot regime took power, but the population mix is now very different. There are still many ethnic Chinese, but they are probably now outnumbered by the Cambodians who took up residence in this area once the regime fell and people began to return in large numbers to the capital. It is an area where the streets have only recently been sealed after years of neglect and where small-scale commerce spills out from the pavements to provide an obstacle course for any form of wheeled transport. Just as was the case before 1970, there is a busy market on the corner of Streets 29 and 110. Known as Psar Chaa (the Old Market), it is now, as one guidebook correctly notes, a "scruffy place", with no resemblance to the charming flower market that occupied much of this space in earlier times.

Moving further north, and having crossed the great open space running from the river to the city's railway station, the visitor reaches a little bit of France transplanted into Southeast Asia at the post office square. Many of the buildings around the square or close to it were damaged either in the last stages of the civil war or while Pol Pot was in power, but slowly these are being restored. Some like the post office retain their original identity. Others, like the building that once housed the powerful Banque de l'Indochine, at the corner of Streets 102 and 106, play roles that faintly echo the colonial past, for that building now

The city's main Post Office, built in 1910

houses an insurance company. La Taverne, alas, has not been among the establishments to be given a renewed life.

The heart of the colonial administration was built in the shadow of the *phnom*, from the post office to the buildings aligned along the wide avenue running west from the *phnom*, once called Avenue Daun Penh (Old Penh's Avenue), but now labelled more prosaically as Streets 92 and 96. Before Cambodia's independence in 1953, this avenue housed, on one side the headquarters of the French Protectorate, now in use as the Ministry of Economy and Finance. Beyond the ministry is the National Library, with the National Archives located immediately behind it, and continuing to the west is the Hôtel le Royal. Each of these three buildings continues to fulfil its original function. On the opposite side of the avenue, the intimidatingly austere new American Embassy is built on the site of the Cercle Sportif, the French and Cambodian elite's sports club, which provided tennis courts and a swimming pool beside its pleasant low-rise club house. Moving west towards Boulevard Monivong one came to the Lycée Descartes, the high school supported by the French government. No longer in its original building but still an essential part of this favoured area, it remains the high school of choice for children of the Cambodian elite.

For all of the sense of the past that may be found close to the *phnom*, there is also much to remind a visitor of the immediate present. Around the base of the *phnom* and under the shady trees nearby modern Phnom Penh declares itself in food and drinks stalls, souvenir vendors, fortune tellers and the men who have gained a franchise to offer visitors an elephant ride around Lady Penh's Hill. Nearby, but largely hidden behind a high fence, is the former residence building, the home of the most senior French official in colonial times. Built in the 1930s to replace a more modest building and constructed in a style that echoes the Palais de Chaillot buildings of the Trocadéro in Paris, it became the independent Cambodian government's Hôtel du Gouvernement, a state guesthouse and location for formal banquets. It now houses the Council for Cambodian Economic Development.

It is just as well that there are sights that evoke the present in the shadow of the past. As the visitor moves further north, away from the post office square and the gardens around the *phnom*, it is into the sadly transformed European Quarter. This was once an area of gracious villas, their steep roofs and decorative ironwork suggesting they had been plucked in their entirety from provincial France. Following independence they were sited close to the reassuring presence of the large French Embassy compound, a location which was to figure tragically in the dramas that followed the victory of Pol Pot's forces in 1975. Today, the embassy has been re-established and sits protected behind a vast wall, but the formerly elegant quarter houses a collection of jerry-built structures and villas transformed out of recognition into crowded slums occupied by squatters, with only a few buildings identifiable in their original form. The northernmost point of the European Quarter was occupied by the Convent of the Sisters of Providence, accessed from A Cha Xoa Street, the northern extension of Sisowath Quay. Today most of the site of the convent is unrecognizable, with only part of the chapel remaining and that being used as a home for squatters. Even to see this, a visitor must walk through a narrow, unpaved and rubbish-strewn lane to see the remnants of the convent's chapel, just identifiable from the still surviving concrete cross that crowns its roof.

Until very recently, there has been less change to the character of Phnom Penh's buildings in that section that lies between Boulevard

Norodom and Boulevard Monivong. But now, with construction under way in 2007, the area close to the railway station, inaugurated in 1932, has become the location for Phnom Penh's first high-rise developments. With a frontage on to Boulevard Monivong, Canadia Bank is constructing a building that will have thirty-two storeys and is set to be the highest in Phnom Penh. Close by, again on Boulevard Monivong, Vattanac Bank's new building when completed will rise to twenty-two storeys. On the same boulevard, opposite Street 88, construction has begun on what is planned to be a seventeen-storey building that will house a hotel and offices.

These new developments will dwarf the building, not far distant, which, after the Royal Palace and the National Museum, is the most distinctive in Phnom Penh. This is the remarkable Psar Thmei (the Great or Grand Market, not the central market as the name is sometimes translated). Constructed between 1934 and 1937 to a design by Jean Desbois and with Louis Chauchon as architect, the market building has been categorized as an example of art deco and, perhaps less appealingly, as an example of the Munich School's dedication to the need for form to follow function. Whatever the categorization, it is a triumph of reinforced concrete in the arches forming its central section, with its dome rising to a height of 150 feet. Criticized at the time of its construction as too big for the population of Phnom Penh, it is crowded each day from the early hours of the morning when the ice arrives for the vendors in the wet market to the evening when commerce is busiest around the gold shops and clothes stalls. Now under renovation, with its importance as a distinctive part of Phnom Penh's modern history, the Psar Thmei stands in striking contrast to its near neighbour, the newly erected Sorya Centre, Phnom Penh's first modern shopping mall with its six floors served by the city's first escalators.

Until now, the blue dome of the Sorya Centre and the six- or seven-storey buildings found along Boulevard Monivong, running south from the road to Pochentong airport, scarcely gave Phnom Penh any sense of being a high-rise city. In this it contrasted sharply with both Bangkok and Saigon. Phnom Penh left an overall impression of flatness, of a city that had been pasted onto the reclaimed marshland on which it is built and hesitated to rise too far above it. With the high-rise developments just described, and with suggestions that even taller buildings might be in prospect, the pace of change is increasing and with it a profound alteration to Phnom Penh's appearance.

AWAY FROM THE CENTRE

As Phnom Penh's urban footprint continues to expand, it is increasingly eliminating the quasi-rural identity that existed not far from the centre of the city until the 1970s. This is abundantly apparent along the southern continuation of Boulevard Norodom, from the traffic circle around the Independence Monument and as it heads towards the Monivong Bridge over the Bassac river or the provincial route leading south to Ta Khmau. Now a wide road, the boulevard is flanked by grand villas occupied by members of the ruling party and their associates who have grown rich as they have linked their fortunes to the government. It was in this area that Prince Sihanouk had his villa at Chamcar Mon, before he was deposed in 1970, and the name of its location makes the point about rural land being overtaken by settlement: it was located on what was once a *chamcar*, the word in the Cambodian language for an area used for agriculture that floods in the wet season.

Just south of Sihanouk Boulevard, with a frontage on to the Bassac river and reached by Samdech Sothearos Boulevard, are the two sets of buildings that were once known as the "white" and "grey" apartment complexes. Conceived and built in the early 1960s as housing for both lower-income workers and staff of Cambodia's National Bank, these buildings have become one of the city's most noxious slums. Even with the aid of photographs of this complex taken shortly after its construction it is difficult to believe that one is looking at anything other than a dirt-stained construction site. Total demolition seems the only answer for this monstrous eyesore, but with its limited means the government is not able to face the costs involved, not least in rehousing the squatters. Nearby stand the giant new Foreign Ministry and the ugly Naga casino, a large concrete box lacking any architectural distinction.

Much of the area lying within the Monireth and Mao Tse-tung Boulevards, which now form a kind of ring-road, was rural until the mid-1960s and used for market gardening. Settlement was light, though already expanding, so that a visit to Phnom Penh's most famous opium den, Mère Chhum's establishment, not far from the extension of Boulevard Norodom, no longer took place in an almost rural ambience.

con.
name\
Penh sh
with shop.
every kind in .
as a normal mai
foreigners, unless t.
pepper grown in the c

AND THE FUTURE?

As Phnom Penh grows eve.
linked as it is to the city's ea,
outside the centre are of interest
the road to the airport and .
constructed for the 1964 Southeast .
Molyvann, there is little reason to thi
going to change in any significant fas
fundamental questions in terms of the w
to take one fundamental issue that is of gre
upwards of ninety per cent of central Phnom
down when the French controlled the city
replacement.

At the same time, Phnom Penh's population continues to expand—the population of "greater" Phnom Penh was estimated at just over two million in 2005, but was probably larger. This raises questions about the city's urban character. Will there be further infilling, perhaps with additional reclaiming of land around the remaining three *boeng* (ponds) within the city limits? If so, will Phnom Penh follow in the footsteps of other cities in developing countries, growing ever larger with a consequent strain on services? And what will be done with the squatting communities, now numbering tens, and possibly hundreds, of thousands? The answer to this last question, if developments in 2006 are a guide, is that the government will increasingly look to resettle squatters in rural regions, as it sells off areas occupied by them to developers and then forcibly trucks the former occupants to unoccupied land many miles distant from the capital. As for other aspects of the future, deciphering the palimpsest reveals a past different in many ways from Phnom Penh's present, but it tells us little about the shape of things to come.

Chapter Three
IBERIAN ALARUMS AND EXCURSIONS

All but forgotten today by Cambodians as well as foreigners are the years in the sixteenth and seventeenth centuries when Phnom Penh was briefly linked to the remarkable seaborne expansion of the Spanish and Portuguese empires. Even today a visitor will encounter occasional Iberian names among contemporary Cambodians—names such as de Monteiro, Diaz or Fernandez. It is difficult to know whether these date back to those earlier centuries or come from a later era. Only occasionally, as is the case with the de Monteiro family, can we be certain of when the first Iberian ancestor reached Cambodia: in their case in the seventeenth century. Probably the ancestors of most contemporary Cambodians with Iberian names came to Cambodia later, from the Spanish Philippines, including those whom the local rulers employed as gunners to man their artillery. Few descendants of these Iberians remain today, and those who do are completely assimilated into the general population except, importantly, for their Catholic faith in a nation that is overwhelmingly Buddhist in religious character. In the nineteenth century the first Frenchmen to spend time in Phnom Penh found that the descendants of long-ago Iberian settlers proudly remembered something of their ancestry. Little of this memory remains among the men and women who still bear Iberian names in contemporary Phnom Penh.

Extraordinary though it seems today, at the beginning of the sixteenth century Europe knew nothing of Cambodia. The country was truly *terra incognita*. The great city of Angkor had risen to power after its foundation in the early ninth century and had flourished as it extended its power over all of modern Cambodia, as well as large sections of modern Laos, Thailand and Vietnam. And then it had declined, with the ruler moving his court to Phnom Penh, as described in the previous chapter, in the first half of the fifteenth century. Yet none of this was known in Europe, as no European traveller ever visited Cambodia, not even Marco Polo, before the sixteenth century. It was not until after the Portuguese navigator, Vasco da Gama, rounded the Cape of Good Hope in 1488 and laid the way open for Affonse de Albuquerque's seizure of

Goa in India, in 1510, and then Malacca in modern Malaysia the following year, that Europeans slowly became aware of Cambodia.

Albuquerque's goal was to control the seaborne commerce of Southeast Asia from Malacca and so to monopolize the rich trade in spices, particularly cloves and nutmeg. With this aim, using both treaties and ruthless force, he sent vessels to the spice-bearing islands of the Moluccas, the Maluku region of modern Indonesia. At the same time he opened trade with the Siamese court at Ayuthia for products from the interior of mainland Southeast Asia, such as deer skins, *lac* (the resin used in varnishes and sealing wax) and other rare forest products. We know that the new rulers of Malacca were soon aware of Cambodia, for Tomé Pires, a Portuguese apothecary turned trader who lived in the great trading city between 1512 and 1515, wrote of the country in his *Summa Oriental.* This was a compilation of political and geographic information that he collected from the merchants, both Asian and European, who traded in Malacca. In his *Summa* Pires recorded that Cambodia's king and population were warlike and that the country was a source of various tropical products. It was also a country, he wrote, that "possesses many rivers." The largest of these, which he did not name, was, he stated erroneously, a branch of the Ganges.

The limited knowledge that Pires recorded did not initially lead to any effort by the Portuguese to establish contact with the ruler of Cambodia. By the standards of other countries, Cambodia did not seem to warrant an effort to seek its trade. For at least three decades after the capture of Malacca there seems to have been no knowledge of where the Cambodian court was located or how it might be reached by travelling up the Mekong, let alone a mention of the name Phnom Penh. Indeed, it was not until 1563 that the first map was published in Europe that showed Cambodia with a river running through it given the name "Mecon". By the time this map was published the first European visitor to record his impressions of Cambodia had already reached the court at Lovek, a location reached by travelling upstream from Phnom Penh on the Tonle Sap. It is from Spanish and Portuguese records, most prepared by missionaries and assembled by Bernard-Philippe Groslier with assistance from Charles Boxer in *Angkor and Cambodia in the Sixteenth Century* (1958) that we have a remarkably rounded picture of the period of Iberian endeavour in Cambodia. It is from these chroniclers we glean almost all our knowledge of the dramatic and ultimately failed efforts of men from Portugal and Spain to shape the course of Cambodian history.

The first chronicler of the Iberian link with Cambodia was a Portuguese Dominican, Father Gaspar da Cruz. He reached Lovek in 1555 and remained there for two years. Without providing a date for the event, da Cruz makes clear that he was not the first of his countrymen to reach Lovek. His predecessors, who had reached the Cambodian capital some little time before, had been, he recorded, the cause of "troubles". Indeed, troubles of various kinds were an almost constant feature of the hundred years or so of an Iberian connection with Cambodia.

Trouble for the missionary priests who came to Cambodia lay above all in their almost total failure to convert the Buddhist population to the Catholic faith. If we can believe da Cruz and his successors, the Buddhist monks simply reacted passively to their presence, apparently secure in their belief that the population would not welcome the salvation the missionaries claimed to offer. With the court brahmins, it was a different matter. They actively campaigned against the missionaries. These priests were survivors from the time when the court religion at Angkor was Hinduism, before Theravada Buddhism, the religion of modern Cambodia, became dominant in the thirteenth century. Despite this national embrace of Buddhism, the brahmins remained an essential part of the court, casting horoscopes for the king and playing a part in state ceremonies, as they do even today. With the combination of general apathy towards the Christian message and the active opposition of the brahmins, Cambodia proved a barren field for the missionaries' evangelism.

ANGKOR'S TEMPLES AND IBERIAN HIGH ADVENTURE

After Father da Cruz left Cambodia in 1557 there is no certain evidence of any European visitors until the early 1580s, though it is possible, even likely, that Portuguese traders could have reached both the trading settlement at Phnom Penh and the court at Lovek in the intervening period. Finally, in 1583, there is firm evidence of missionaries returning, both Dominicans and Franciscans. Their evangelizing was no more successful than da Cruz's and by the end of the sixteenth century their efforts were almost at an end. It would scarcely be worth dwelling on their activities except for two things. They were the first to see and report on the existence of the great temples at Angkor. And they were to record the short but remarkable, and finally bloody, part played by Diogo Veloso and Blas Ruiz in Cambodia's and Phnom Penh's history. For a brief time these two men—the first Portuguese, the latter Spanish—held the fate of the kingdom in their hands. They were characters who showed the same ruthless courage as the better known conquistadors of Latin America, men such as Hernán Cortés and Francisco Pizarro. But their fate was different and today, in Cambodia, their exploits are almost totally forgotten.

So far as references to Angkor are concerned, the earliest reference to the famous temples appeared in a book published in Barcelona in 1603 and was based on reports sent back by the missionary priests to their orders' headquarters in Spain and Portugal. The Barcelona publication was rapidly followed by other accounts, all expressing wonder at the size of the temples and at the great wall which surrounded many of them and which we now know is the wall that encloses Angkor Thom. Yet as they expressed their amazement at this collection of largely abandoned temples, none of the missionaries could believe that they had been built by the ancestors of the Cambodians they now encountered. Perhaps, they speculated, these great buildings were the work of "Alexander the Great or the Romans", or even "the Jews" whom they believed were "numerous in China", where they had later emigrated. With the passage of years these early accounts of Angkor, confined as they were to the obscurity of the books published for a small Iberian audience, were forgotten. It was not until the nineteenth century, and particularly through the writings of the French naturalist Henri Mouhot, that the Angkor temples were to emerge from the historical shadows into which they had fallen.

These accounts of the temples at Angkor are much more detailed than the brief descriptions the Iberian missionaries and adventurers left of Phnom Penh in the fifteenth century. Given its location, sited beside the Tonle Sap and without any nearby source of stone for building materials, it is not surprising that its houses were constructed in timber and bamboo. As for the numbers who lived there, the adventurer Christoval de Jacque, who saw the city in the final years of the sixteenth century, put the total number of "households" at 20,000, of which 3,000 were Chinese. These figures would suggest a total population of upwards of 50,000, which seems much too large. On the basis of what we know of settlements elsewhere in Southeast Asia, and the estimates of the size of Phnom Penh's population in the nineteenth century, a figure of around 10,000 inhabitants seems much more likely. One point Jacque and other chroniclers record is the presence of "two pyramids", which we can take to be stupas, with one surely the stupa crowning the *phnom*.

As for Diogo Veloso and Blas Ruiz, without the record of their actions left to us by the missionary priests, it would be difficult to credit that two men could have achieved what they did. Unquestionably, their brief lives may be taken as examples of the worst aspects of rapacious imperialism. But they were surely something more. Almost unbelievably they prefigured the actual deeds of the White Rajahs of Sarawak and the fictional exploits of Conrad's Lord Jim, though scarcely with Jim's hopes for personal redemption as the reward for his actions in "Patusan". They were men of reckless courage and extraordinary energy. To survive and overcome tropical heat and humidity, dressed in unsuitable clothing and often wracked by tropical diseases, speaks of men who were grittily determined if nothing else. And they met their end in Phnom Penh.

In 1593 the Portuguese Diogo Veloso was thirty-four years old, and had been living in Cambodia for about ten years, becoming fluent in the Cambodian language and living at the court in Lovek with a woman of high status, though probably not a "princess" as suggested by some sources. As Veloso found favour with the Cambodian ruler, King Satha, he also provided assistance to his missionary and trader compatriots. Most of the latter group were part of the polyglot population who lived in Phnom Penh. By the latter years of the sixteenth century, and building on its role that had developed even before the fall of Angkor, Phnom Penh was Cambodia's main trading settlement. It was a cosmopolitan but rough-and-ready place, where different nationalities—Portuguese and Spanish, Chinese, Malays and Japanese—lived in ethnically defined quarters. We have no certain knowledge of the ethnic breakdown of these inhabitants, though, as already noted, one Portuguese chronicler put the number of Chinese "households" at 3,000. Whatever their nationality, this motley group of foreigners lived cheek by jowl with one another along the river in a ramshackle collection of huts, or on boats moored to the bank.

The royal court to which Veloso had become linked was a fractious place, with its ruler fearful both of potential internal enemies and the

nore powerful Siamese kingdom
'ᵉ overtures to the Portuguese
ᵘp Cambodia's security, but
Ruiz de Hernán González
ᵘu, he had travelled to
for Cambodia only to
ᵑgly weak state on
ʹietnam. Escaping
and soon fell in
fluence foreign
ᵓeriod, Veloso
ʹᵔis rule from
ᵓnt to the
o returned
vasion of
Iberian
is way
ᵑgue,
nish
no
his

of
ʅ

The Chinese in the junks were spoiling for a fight after having recently been treated in a high-handed fashion by Spanish officials in Manila. The small numbers in Phnom Penh's Iberian quarter seemed to offer a chance for revenge, which the Europeans quickly realized was the Chinese intention. For a short time there was a tense stand-off. This brief delay gave the Portuguese and Spaniards time to organize, and grasping the advantage they had through possessing better weapons they took the fight to the Chinese. They seized the Chinese vessels and killed not only many of those who had arrived on the junks but also members of the Chinese trading community in Phnom Penh. Then, for good measure, they burned down the houses in the Chinese quarter. This was not the first nor the last occasion that Phnom Penh witnessed violence, but it was the first in which men from Europe were undoubtedly culpable.

Now Veloso and Ruiz faced a dilemma, for in attacking the Chinese they were damaging the king's control of trade and his capacity to profit from it. In these circumstances they decided they had no choice but to seek an audience with the king at Srei Santhor. But once there the new ruler refused to see them and it became clear that their position was hazardous. Rather than retreat, they saw only one course of action open to them, an attack on the king's palace. So, in May 1596, and blessed by the missionary priests accompanying them, they stormed the palace, killed the king and blew up his powder magazine, before sailing down the Mekong to Phnom Penh.

This was not the end of their adventures. In Phnom Penh they came under the control of a more senior Spanish figure, General Juan Xuarès Gallinato, who was angered by their actions. With the two men now under his command, Gallinato made reparations to both the Cambodian court and the Chinese merchants who remained alive in Phnom Penh. Then he ordered Veloso and Ruiz to accompany him back to his base in Manila, leaving Phnom Penh in June 1596. But when Gallinato's vessel stopped at the Vietnamese port of Faifo (modern Hoi An), the incorrigible pair persuaded him to let them disembark so that they could travel overland through Vietnam to Vientiane in Laos. This was where their former patron, the deposed King Satha, had taken refuge. Leaving Faifo in late June, Veloso and Ruiz reached Vientiane in October, having made a remarkable journey across rugged terrain at the height of the wet season.

Once in Vientiane their hopes were dashed when they found that Satha had died. Undeterred, they then decided to accompany his son back to Srei Santhor, where he was accepted as Cambodia's new ruler and took the reign name of Barom Reachea in May 1597. The court to which the two Iberians now attached themselves was beset by jealousies and resentments at their influence with the king, whose own authority was being questioned. When Ruiz killed two senior officials, whom he claimed were plotting to overthrow the king, resentment of his and Veloso's role increased. In this fevered atmosphere Ruiz and Veloso briefly fell out, only to be quickly reconciled and to receive as a mark of Barom Reachea's favour appointment as governors of two key provinces. These were lucrative appointments, for they now had control over the provinces through which trading vessels had to pass to reach Phnom Penh.

This was the high point of Iberian influence in Cambodia, and the time when, finally, Veloso and Ruiz overreached themselves. Reinforced by the arrival of more missionaries and soldiers from Manila, and joined in their endeavours by a ship's company of Japanese commanded by a freebooter of mixed Portuguese and Asian ancestry, the two men sought further concessions from the Cambodian court. Now they wanted to play a part in the affairs of the kingdom as a whole, not just to hold control over two provinces. In making this additional bid for power they crystallized the resentment felt against them by most of the court officials. As they were soon to find out, this was a fatal mistake.

It was now 1599 and as Veloso and Ruiz pursued their ambitions at Srei Santhor, backed by a Dominican priest, Father Maldonado, unrest was growing downstream in Phnom Penh. Living dangerously close together in their separate trading quarters, relations between the various national groups were strained at the best of times. When trouble flared between a Spaniard and a group of Malays the commander of the Iberians did not hesitate. Aided by members of the Japanese community, the Iberians attacked the Malay quarter. It was an ill-judged decision since the Iberians were outnumbered by the Malays who repulsed the attack and in turn laid siege to the Iberians.

When this news reached Ruiz and Veloso, who were still at Srei Santhor, they chose to travel back to Phnom Penh, ignoring the advice of the king who urged them to go into hiding. It was a brave but foolish act, since shortly after the two men reached Phnom Penh the Malays were

joined by Cambodians from the ruler's court who were now ready to
on their resentment of Ruiz and Veloso. Around the middle of 1599 t.
besieging Malays and Cambodians overwhelmed the Iberians and put
them to the sword. The Iberian dream of souls saved for Christ and of
riches flowing to their distant homelands from Phnom Penh was almost
at an end.

It is probably no surprise that this period of Cambodian and of
Phnom Penh's history represented an aspect of the kingdom's slow decline
with its interests ill served by many of its rulers. Indeed, if some of the
royal chronicles can be trusted, shortly after Ruiz and Veloso were killed
the Cambodian king who came to the throne so offended the leading
figures in the court that he was seized and trussed up in a bag before
being thrown into the river at Phnom Penh. An execution carried out in
this manner avoided the prohibition against spilling royal blood.

PHNOM PENH AND CAMBODIA SLIP FROM EUROPEAN SIGHT

In the centuries that followed this brief "Iberian period" of Phnom Penh's
history, there are occasional references to Spanish and Portuguese
missionaries passing through the settlement but, as with their
predecessors, success eluded them. There were still Portuguese traders,
some of whom were as ready to fight as to trade, at a particularly complex
period of Cambodian history in the 1640s. During this decade, and in
circumstances that are still a matter of debate, the country's ruler
embraced Islam, in either 1642 or 1643, and took the notably un-
Cambodian reign name of Ibrahim. Some chronicles suggest that he
succumbed to the charms of a Malay woman who subsequently
reinforced her hold over him with magic water. Other sources lead to the
conclusion that he saw the opportunity by embracing Islam to gain the
backing of the growing number of Chams and Malays, who were
followers of Islam, living near his capital. If nothing else, this event
underlines the important presence in Cambodia, at this time, of a
community made up of both Chams and Malays whose villages were
located along both the Mekong and the Tonle Sap, with many grouped
around Phnom Penh.

From a confusing jumble of evidence it seems possible that in the
decade before this event Iberians had acted as mercenaries in support of
one of the claimants to the Cambodian throne. And we know that the

Portuguese resident in Phnom Penh had difficult relations with the Dutch, who had established a post there in 1636. Whether these traders-cum-freebooters participated in the Cambodian massacre of the Dutch traders in Phnom Penh that took place in 1643 is not clear, but it is possible given the hostilities that existed between the Iberian powers and the Dutch fighting for their independence in Europe. Perhaps all that can be said is that as Portuguese power in Southeast Asia declined, so Portuguese and Spanish traders in Phnom Penh faded from prominence. Yet, as noted earlier, a small Catholic community remained in Phnom Penh linked through ancestry and the occasional infusion of men from the Spanish Philippines with the earlier Iberians. Traders from other European nations, including the English, appeared for short periods but to little effect. Despite the massacre in 1643 the Dutch maintained trading posts in the Cambodian capital, which had now moved to Udong, and in Phnom Penh, before leaving in the 1670s. They left their mark in the name of a church sited by the Tonle Sap, a little north of the modern Japanese Bridge. Known as the Eglise Hoalong, the Church of the Hollanders, it was sited in a location where the Dutch had once had a trading factory. (As already mentioned, I came to know it and its remarkable priest, Father Paulus Tep Im, in 1966.) Today the only signs of the church are a few *ex voto* tablets set on a rock near to what was the entrance to the churchyard. As with the other churches, except the convent chapel, it too was destroyed during Pol Pot's rule. As for Father Tep Im, translated from Phnom Penh to be the Vatican's Apostolic Vicar in Battambang, he was murdered by the Khmer Rouge shortly after Pol Pot's victory in April 1975.

With the departure of the Dutch, European interest in Cambodia was almost totally eclipsed. Before the end of the seventeenth century Vietnam had gained control over the areas of today's southern Vietnam that had once formed part of Cambodian territory, and in doing so they effectively blocked the Cambodian court's access to the sea down the Mekong. We know that by the nineteenth century Cambodia's only significant port was at Kampot on the Gulf of Thailand, a location reached in four days of travel on elephant-back from Udong.

It is not until Henri Mouhot, the man credited with bringing the Angkor temple ruins to the world's attention, visited Cambodia in 1859-60 that there is anything like a detailed description of Phnom Penh

M. Henri Mouhot. — Dessin de H. Rousseau d'après une photographie.

Henri Mouhot, "rediscoverer" of Angkor

before it fell under French control. Stopping there briefly, he described the town as "the great bazaar of Cambodia", with a population of 10,000 persons living on land, "almost all Chinese", and estimated that double that number, Cambodians and Vietnamese, lived on boats on the Tonle Sap. Singularly unimpressed by what he saw, Mouhot found Phnom Penh "long and dirty". The *phnom* and its pagoda he dismissed as "possessing neither beauty nor interest". At the extreme southern end of Phnom Penh he found a collection of upwards of five hundred boats forming a "floating town". These, he was told, were used both for commerce and as residences by merchants, who grouped together on the water so that they could, at a time of any trouble, quickly slip away into the safety of the stream. Patriot though he was, we have no sense from Mouhot's writings that he imagined that within six years the French tricolour would be flying over this "great bazaar" which had become Cambodia's new capital.

Chapter Four
ROYAL CITY, COLONIAL CITY

Modern Phnom Penh is the urban child of a colonial paradox. While its slow growth through the second half of the nineteenth century—growth which accelerated from the beginning of the twentieth—depended on French "protection", it is also beyond dispute that its character as Cambodia's royal city reflected the course of the country's modern history. This, at least, was true until the overthrow of Norodom Sihanouk in 1970. Since that date and the years of war and tyranny the power of royalty has greatly diminished. However dedicated the present Cambodian king is to his lonely job as the country's monarch, there is no doubt that the power of royalty in contemporary Cambodia is merely a shadow of what it once was.

Whether Mouhot's estimate of its size was strictly accurate, there is no doubt that at the beginning of the 1860s Phnom Penh was a minor settlement by comparison with other major urban centres in Southeast Asia, such as Saigon and Bangkok in neighbouring Vietnam and Siam. While all population statistics at this time must be viewed with reserve, it seems certain that both Saigon and Bangkok in the 1860s had more than 100,000 inhabitants. With Cambodia's capital still at Udong, Phnom Penh was indeed, as Mouhot termed it, the country's "bazaar", a commercial settlement as opposed to a seat of government. While the first Frenchman to represent France's interests in Cambodia, the splendidly named Ernest Marc Louis de Gonzague Doudart de Lagrée, was perhaps more restrained after his first view of the settlement in 1863, he was nevertheless succinct in terming Phnom Penh *misérable*—a word perhaps best translated as "wretched".

THE CITY SURVIVES
That Phnom Penh existed at all as a *Cambodian* settlement at the beginning of the 1860s—rather than as a Vietnamese or Siamese city—has to be explained. And this requires a brief summary of Cambodia's tortuous history of decline over the previous one hundred years. By the closing years of the eighteenth century Cambodia was steadily being squeezed between its stronger neighbours, Siam in the west and Vietnam in the east. Both of

these states were slowly absorbing territory that once had been ruled by Cambodia. The agriculturally rich area of western Cambodia around Battambang and the region close to Siem Reap in which the temples of Angkor are located had come under Siamese control before the end of the eighteenth century. And well before the mid-1700s Cambodia had lost control of Prey Nokor, the settlement that we know today as Saigon (Ho Chi Minh City).

Despite having to deal with its own challenges from Burma, Siamese influence in Cambodia was stronger than that of Vietnam up to the end of the eighteenth century. This reflected the fact that Cambodia and Siam shared a common culture, influenced by India and devoutly Theravada Buddhist in character. But after Vietnam was united under the Emperor Gia Long in 1802, the court at Hue, with its attachment to Chinese culture and Confucian values, showed an increasing readiness to seek a measure of control over its weak neighbour to the west. An important opportunity to advance Vietnam's interests came in 1811 when the Cambodian king, Ang Chan, appealed to Hue to come to his aid against a rebellious brother. This was too much for the Siamese who, having long regarded the Cambodian ruler as their vassal, now marched against the Vietnamese. As the Vietnamese sought to assert their position by taking the king with them to Hue and as the Siamese took the king's brothers, Ang Im and Ang Duang, to Bangkok, there seemed real doubt as to whether Cambodia would continue to exist as an independent state or whether its territory would be divided between Siam and Vietnam, with the Mekong as a border between them. In the event, the rulers in Bangkok and Hue concluded that their interests were best served by allowing Cambodia a semi-independent existence as it paid tribute to both—to Bangkok each year and to Hue every three years. Despite the appearance of Siamese primacy in these arrangements, it was the Vietnamese who propped up Ang Chan and who persuaded him to move his capital from Udong to Phnom Penh.

In this state of heightened rivalry between Siam and Vietnam the Bangkok court found the degree of control that Hue now exercised over the Cambodian king deeply offensive. In 1834, and led by the renowned General Bodin, with the Cambodian princes Ang Im and Ang Duang accompanying him, the Siamese marched to Phnom Penh, burned its buildings to the ground and filled their wagons with whatever loot they could find. Quoting French missionaries who observed the event, John Tully records in his *A Short History of Cambodia* (2006) that the Siamese sack of Phnom Penh was so complete that "even the dogs were loaded onto wagons." Then, in the face of a Vietnamese counterattack, the Siamese withdrew, leaving Ang Chan still under Hue's control. The next year Chan died and Cambodia was plunged even deeper into misery.

As Chan had left no sons to succeed him the Vietnamese seized the opportunity to assert their control over Cambodia and its royal family by placing his daughter Ang Mei on the throne and embarking on a wholesale programme to "Vietnamize" Cambodia and its institutions. Phnom Penh was renamed *Tran Tay*, or "Western Commandery". Cambodian officials were expected to wear Vietnamese dress and Vietnamese administrative models were substituted for Cambodia's traditional practices. According to some reports, the Vietnamese even went to the extent of trying to construct a citadel in Phnom Penh that would diminish the importance of the *phnom* by being higher than that monument. No trace of this building remains, nor did any of the early western observers who came to Phnom Penh in the 1860s refer to it. As a sign of just how determined the Vietnamese were to transform Cambodia, when they did allow Ang Mei to have her position validated by a coronation ceremony, it was one that followed Vietnamese royal forms and not those of Cambodia.

The next decade was the nadir of Cambodia's post-Angkorian existence. As Hue's officials in Phnom Penh sought to transform the country and its population in a fashion that would make them conform to Vietnamese models, they met solid resistance from a society deeply attached to its traditional ways. When a six-month-long revolt, apparently led by resentful provincial officials, broke out in 1840-41, the Vietnamese spirited Ang Mei away to Vietnam, taking the royal regalia with them. Cambodia was now effectively without a ruler. Even before the revolt the Vietnamese had, as the distinguished historian, David Chandler, points out in his *A History of Cambodia* (1992), demoted Ang Mei and her sisters to "low ranks in the Vietnamese civil service".

For the next five years the Vietnamese and Siamese marched and countermarched across the open plains of central Cambodia, wreaking death and destruction but with neither managing to achieve a knockout blow. Finally, in 1845, with the Vietnamese concluding that they could not, after all, succeed in imposing their control over Cambodia, the rival contestants reached an agreement that ended their hostilities. The Hue court gained a face-saving acknowledgement from the Cambodian court that it had the status of a tributary, but in reality it was the Siamese who were in the driving seat. It was they who clearly exercised control over the new Cambodian king who now occupied the throne. This was Ang Duang, who had been a hostage-guest in Bangkok for decades and whom the Siamese now chose to occupy the throne. When Ang Duang was crowned at Udong in April 1848, Siamese as well as Cambodian court brahmins took part in the ceremony. He chose Udong for his capital rather than the shattered settlement at Phnom Penh, though he maintained a small palace there, sited beside the Tonle Sap, a few hundred yards north of the modern Royal Palace compound. In a telling gesture that repudiated previous Vietnamese influence, he took bricks from the fortifications that the Vietnamese had built in Phnom Penh to use in the construction of monasteries in Udong.

From his accession to the throne until his death in 1860 Ang Duang sought to revitalize the kingdom, passing new laws, promoting literary endeavour and minting coins showing a stylized façade of Angkor Wat on a coining machine imported from Birmingham. According to some accounts, he also acted as a patron of the Thommayut Sect of Buddhism, introducing this reformed and austere sect closely linked to the Siamese court into Cambodia. In later years his reign was looked on as a "golden age", a curious foreshadowing of how Norodom Sihanouk's rule would come to be remembered one hundred and fifty years later. Whatever the justice of this view of Ang Duang's time as king, there is one matter on which we can be certain. In 1853, almost certainly under the influence of French missionaries, he sent a letter to the French emperor, Napoleon III, seeking to establish some form of relationship with France and offering gifts and "homage" to the French ruler. Some French historians, writing with nationalist zeal, have argued that this was a clear case of Ang Duang asking for "protection" against his "traditional enemies", the Vietnamese. As long ago as 1891 a French scholar convincingly demolished this view, though there seems little doubt that the patriotic French Bishop Jean-Claude Miche, who advised Ang Duang, thought in these terms. But whether or not Ang Duang fully recognized the implications of his actions, his letter played a part in a slowly developing French policy that finally saw Cambodia declared a French protectorate ten years later. Ironically, the final decision to extend French protection over Cambodia came as much as a result of French fantasizing about supposed British intentions as from clear-eyed understanding of what was happening in the Cambodian court at Udong and the Siamese court in Bangkok.

FRANCE COMES TO CAMBODIA

In 1856 a French envoy, Charles de Montigny, travelled to the Cambodian port of Kampot in response to Ang Duang's letter. He never saw the king, since in circumstances that had many farcical elements, the Siamese officials who played a major part in Ang Duang's court refused to let the king travel to see Montigny. After the French envoy's aborted visit and again guided by Bishop Miche, the king sent another letter to Napoleon III seeking the emperor's assistance in regaining Cambodian control over lands lost to the Vietnamese in past centuries. He did not ask for French protection.

Two years later, in circumstances that combined missionary zeal, a thirst for imperial grandeur and the commercial hopes of Bordeaux's merchants, France sent an invasion force to central Vietnam. This, it must be remembered, was the heyday of European colonialism, a time when a French naval officer would write without embarrassment that "countries without colonies are dead." But in 1858 Cambodia was still not in France's sights. It became so in the unsettled circumstances the followed Ang Duang's death in 1860. In the two years that followed this event the fractious Cambodian royal family came close to tearing the country apart. Ang Duang had named his eldest son, Norodom, as his successor in 1856, but this choice was deeply resented by Norodom's half-brothers, Sisowath and Siwotha. Sisowath made clear his resentment, but peacefully. Siwotha went further and opted for open rebellion. Bandits roamed the countryside looting and destroying property, including some of the buildings of the Catholic mission station headed by Bishop Miche, at Pinhalu—now known as Ponhea Lu—not far from Udong. Facing these problems, Norodom retreated first to Battambang, a region under Siamese control, in 1861, and then to Bangkok, in 1862. Miche, meanwhile, seized on the damage done to the mission station to advance his case for some form of French intervention in Cambodia.

Miche's appeal came in changed circumstances for the French forces that had begun their invasion of Vietnam in 1858. Failing to make progress against the Vietnamese defending Tourane (the modern Danang), the French had moved their expeditionary force to lay siege to Saigon, which they finally seized in February 1861. This did not end resistance to the French by Vietnamese guerrillas, some of whom operated from areas along the ill-defined border between southern Vietnam and Cambodia. This was complication enough and a reason for the French to think about some form of action in relation to Cambodia. Now, as they turned their minds to Cambodia, the French began to take account of the reality of Siamese influence over the Cambodian court. But to this reality they joined a fantasy that Britain, perfidious Albion, was playing an influential role in Bangkok. In their minds they conjured up images of British officials secretly advising the Siamese court with the hope of gaining some ill-defined control over Cambodia. In reality, the most senior British official at the Bangkok court at the time was a bandmaster. But fact was becoming less important than belief, however erroneous. What is more, some of the most enterprising of the French officers now in Saigon had begun to think in terms of using the great Mekong river as a route to the presumed riches of China. If France was to make future use of the river in this way, it could scarcely accept a situation in which the Siamese court, probably manipulated by the British, might be able to act to deny it free navigation of the Mekong.

In the end, Norodom himself opened the way for the French to establish a protectorate over Cambodia. This is a charge that has been repeatedly used by Cambodian critics of their country's monarchy to denigrate the institution, and it has been a proposition steadfastly and angrily denied by Norodom Sihanouk. Yet the facts are clear. At the end of 1862 Norodom I returned from Bangkok to Udong with an assurance from the Siamese court that it supported his claim to the Cambodian throne. But Bangkok wanted to keep Norodom on a tight rein, so despite his being permitted to return to Cambodia he was not allowed to bring back the royal regalia with him. Angered by this slight, Norodom opened negotiations with the French, who were now ready to respond to the king's overtures as they sent him suitably lavish gifts. In August 1863 Norodom agreed to sign a treaty with the French that gave them special trading rights within the kingdom in return for their protection. A French representative was to be appointed to the Cambodian court with rather ill-defined responsibilities, though clearly the French saw his role as ensuring the primacy of French interests in the country.

There were two final acts to this drama. More than the French ever realized until almost the end of the nineteenth century, Siamese influence within Norodom's court remained extremely strong, however much he resented this fact. Moreover, for all his resentment of the Siamese retention of his regalia, he was a firm believer in tradition, and so worried about a situation in which he was acting against the wishes of his suzerain, the Siamese king, Mongkut. These considerations led him to conclude a secret treaty with the Siamese court in December 1863 which, in effect, negated the French claim to protection over the kingdom. Even before the French learned of this secret treaty, months later, they had found that Norodom was playing a double game as they found him seeking to slip away from Udong with the intention of travelling to Bangkok for a Siamese-sponsored coronation. In terms that Lagrée would have understood, a "whiff of grapeshot" was sufficient to carry the day for the French, as a small detachment of French troops took control of Udong. For when Norodom heard the cannons on French gunboats moored near Udong being fired he turned back. Then, after heated debates between French and Siamese representatives over who had the right to crown the king, Norodom accepted that it could be done by both and his coronation finally took place in Udong in June 1864.

Eighteen months later, in December 1865, and urged on by Doudart de Lagrée, Norodom agreed to move Cambodia's capital from Udong to Phnom Penh. He was leaving behind a town of about 12,000 people with a palace that an English visitor in 1858 described as "a rambling wooden structure". When Henri Mouhot came to Udong a year later, in 1859, he spoke of the king's residence as being surrounded by "houses built of bamboos and planks" with the nearby market filled with Chinese and "as dirty as all the others I have mentioned." Certainly, the palace that Norodom began to construct in Phnom Penh, when he moved there in 1866, differed sharply from what had existed at Udong, a symbol of the fact that the modern history of Cambodia's capital had begun.

CAMBODIA'S CAPITAL AGAIN

It is not hard to see why Lagrée and his superiors in Saigon wanted the king to live in Phnom Penh and for this settlement to be Cambodia's capital. Commercial considerations were never far below the surface when decisions were made in what was eventually to become French Indochina, and Phnom Penh, Mouhot's "great bazaar", offered more prospect of meeting at least some of the costs of maintaining a colonial presence in Cambodia. This was important at a time when the expenses of running the newly established French administration in southern Vietnam, based in Saigon, were a matter for concern in Paris. Strategically, too, Phnom Penh was a much better location than Udong. With growing interest in the possibility that the Mekong might offer a trade route to China, a position at Phnom Penh meant that the French could command all travel up and down the great river. At the same time, and however imperfectly, men like Lagrée recognized the vital role played by the king as *the* necessary element in preserving the concept of a Cambodian identity. As such, his presence was essential to the city's status as the country's capital.

All early visitors to Phnom Penh at the beginning of its renewed existence as capital commented on the extraordinary diversity of its population, numbering perhaps 10,000 in total in the 1860s. Without exact census figures we must guess at the ethnic breakdown of this population, but there is enough evidence to gain a fairly reliable picture. Cambodians did not form the majority of the city's population. Gregor Muller, whose book *Colonial Cambodia's "Bad Frenchmen"* (2006) has ably broken much new ground in providing a picture of Phnom Penh's polyglot society in the second half of the nineteenth century, suggests that the number of Cambodians living there towards the end of Norodom's reign, in the 1890s, was somewhere between 5,000 and 15,000—the wide range of the estimate is due to the lack of reliable statistics. So the numbers would have been smaller in the 1860s. Louis de Carné, a member of the French Mekong River Expedition which visited Phnom Penh in June 1866, estimated the total population to be no more than 5-6,000, though this estimate is probably too low. Cambodia's capital, he wrote, "is only a crowd of petty wooden and bamboo houses, most of them raised above the ground on posts, round which pigs and chickens live in a familiarity which brings the inhabitants inconvenience of more kinds than one."

Both at this time and well into the twentieth century, a large proportion of Phnom Penh's Cambodians would either have lived in the

Royal Palace or worked directly for the monarch while living outside it. The palace compound was, in effect, a town itself, populated by the royal family and the king's female establishment, high court officials and those who occupied roles as hereditary servants, or bondsmen, sometimes and wrongly described by the French as slaves. (There were "real" slaves in nineteenth-century Cambodia, too, most of them drawn from the ranks of minority hill peoples.)

The largest group in 1860s Phnom Penh, and for decades after, were the Chinese. They were composed of at least four, and maybe five, main dialect groups, with the Hokkien and Cantonese speakers, initially at least, the largest. They ranged from the richest inhabitants of the city to some of the poorest. Of the utmost importance was the fact that they had commercial links with their ethnic counterparts and extended family members in Cholon, Saigon's essentially Chinese twin city. Already existing before the French seized Saigon in 1861, Cholon was steadily assuming the position it occupied throughout the French colonial period as the powerhouse of Indochinese commerce, particularly for the export of rice.

As for other ethnic groups living in Phnom Penh at this time, it is easier to list their identities than to provide accurate numbers or proportions. In addition to Cambodians there were, as the French explorer Francis Garnier recorded in 1866, Vietnamese, Siamese, Malays—a term which probably incorporated the Cham community—and Indians. To which list we can add Filipinos, who provided the personnel for one of Norodom's orchestras, and occasional visitors from faraway Burma and Laos, as well as rare representatives of the hill people who lived in the uplands of Cambodia's north-east. At a rough estimate, it seems we should envisage Phnom Penh's population in the late 1860s as being upwards of half composed of Chinese, with Cambodians at most a quarter of the total, and the remainder made up of these diverse ethnic groups.

Then there was the floating population of Europeans. As was the case in British colonies, there was a clear division between the senior officials and those Europeans whose reason for being in Phnom Penh was to make money. A fairly detailed picture of the men who made up the senior ranks of French officialdom has been available for some time. For the first twenty years after Phnom Penh's promotion as capital they were drawn from the military, or men who had previously served in it. Now, aided by Gregor Muller's research, we have a remarkably detailed understanding of the "unofficials" as well, and in particular of their dealings with King Norodom. Although, as de Carné recorded, most of the buildings strung out along Phnom Penh's Grand' Rue in 1866 were built of timber, with the city's new capital status masonry constructions began to appear, as did a rough apportioning of areas according to ethnic identity along the lines already described. The clearest of these ethnically linked neighbourhoods were the area around the palace, for Cambodians, and that close to the French representative's residence a short distance to the north of the *phnom*, for Europeans. Further north again was where the Iberian Cambodians clustered together, close to a newly constructed Catholic church. But at this stage there was still a remarkable intermingling of ethnic groups in the slowly expanding city. Only in the late nineteenth century did more rigid town planning take hold and begin to impose the firm, ethnically-linked character on districts that lasted until the 1970s, and still has echoes today.

AN "ANIMATED AND INTERESTING SCENE"

There is more than enough commentary on Phnom Penh in its early stages under the French that is disdainful in tone (as we have seen in Mouhot's and de Carné's remarks). Against this generally negative picture it is striking to find the positive views of a Scottish visitor, John Thomson, who came to Phnom Penh after spending some time photographing the Angkor temples. As with the observations of Auguste Pavie on the Cambodian court, noted later in this chapter, Thomson's record of what he saw underlines the extent to which prejudice, or a lack of it, played a large part in the tone of European commentators.

Visiting the city in 1866 and recording his impressions in the journal of a London learned society, Thomson found the "Pnomb Pinh bazaar... the most interesting and animated in Cambodia". Noting the overwhelming preponderance of Chinese among the merchants in the market, his description goes on to provide a picture of a market full of life:

> ... Buyers and sellers are busy everywhere, and a keen spirit of competition is observable in the attractive display of merchandise in the line of shops and stalls. Long trains of produce-bearing elephants and buffalo wagons, with their Cambodian drivers are passing to and fro, or

have halted to discharge at some Chinese store. Light and elegant conveyances flit past, in which women in picturesque costumes are seated, driving fleet pairs of bullocks covered with jingling bells.

Already, Thomson went on to observe, a new market was being constructed under the direction of the same architect who was overseeing a palace built for the king.

Six years later there is another detailed description of Phnom Penh—Panompin as he called it—by an American traveller, Frank Vincent, in his book, *The Land of the White Elephant*, published two years later. He was coming downstream from the Great Lake after visiting Angkor, so his description begins with a reference to the Catholic mission at the northern end of Phnom Penh's settlement pattern and then to the barracks and French resident's house near the *phnom*. The city then extends, he continues:

> along the bank of the river for a distance of about three miles, and perhaps [stretches] no more than half a mile at the farthest into the interior... There is no wall about Panompin, not even around the palace. The main road runs north and south along the river, there are a few

The *Phnom*, seen from the Tonle Sap River in 1866

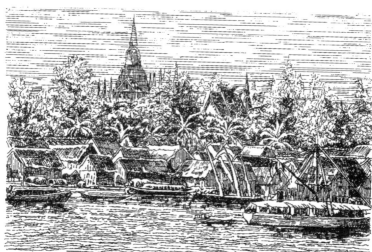

cross-roads, but this is the street. It is about thirty feet wide macadamised with broken brick and sand, and lined throughout its entire length with little bamboo shops, the greater part owned by Chinese, many by Klings [Indians], and the remainder by Cambodians and Cochin Chinese [*Vietnamese*]. Many of these shops are "gambling hells"; some are used by opium-smokers... The population of Panompin is about 20,000, and embraces Chinese, Cochin Chinese, Klings, and Siamese, besides Cambodians.

Although Vincent's book gives the impression of his being a careful observer throughout his travels, there seems good reason to adjust his picture of Phnom Penh as still little more than a collection of "little bamboo shops" by 1872. Apart from the masonry constructions in the Royal Palace that Norodom had begun as soon as he moved there, there were other buildings of a more solid construction built in the years immediately after 1866. Writing about Phnom Penh's cityscape ten years later, Louis Delaporte, who as a young naval officer had been the French Mekong Expedition's official artist, remarked on the fact that there were an ever-growing number of brick buildings. Nevertheless, it was clearly the case that a great many wooden buildings remained until a great fire swept through these in May 1894, an event that was seized on by the French to ensure that henceforth buildings constructed in central Phnom Penh had to be in masonry.

NORODOM I'S PHNOM PENH

We know little about Norodom's views of the transfer of Cambodia's capital from Udong to Phnom Penh. Although it is clear that the initiative for the move came from the French representative, Doudart de Lagrée, we have no records to suggest that the king felt strongly about the move, one way or the other. Norodom's mother, one of Ang Duang's wives and by all accounts a formidable figure, chose to remain in Udong where she maintained a strictly traditional establishment. In terms of his view of his own role as king, Norodom was no less a believer in tradition, a fact that successive French officials failed fully to grasp. Yet he was also open to new ideas, new technology and new, if sometimes troubled, relationships with foreigners. Indeed, an understanding of Phnom Penh's transformation over nearly forty years between 1866 and Norodom's death in 1904, is to be

King Norodom I entertaining members of the French Mekong Expedition in 1866

found as much in an account of the king's ultimately unsuccessful efforts to rule as well as reign as in a bald account of which buildings were built where and when.

With a site selected for his palace compound overlooking the *Quatre-Bras*, Norodom quickly set work in progress for his new palace. By the middle of 1866 Norodom was living in a European-style building, though he received visitors in another large, hangar-like building, constructed in wood, where banquets took place and the court dancers performed for the ruler's pleasure. Louis Delaporte, the Mekong Expedition's artist, drew an evocative picture of Norodom entertaining the explorers with his traditional dancers and their orchestra, while his servants crawled along the floor to serve the king and his guests. Throughout the nineteenth and into the twentieth century new palace buildings were constructed as others were demolished to be replaced by grander edifices. Set among these buildings with their exotic architecture is the Empress Eugénie's prefabricated palace, constructed of cast iron, which she used at the opening of the Suez Canal in 1869, after which it was shipped to Cambodia as a gift to Norodom. French officials congratulated themselves on their cleverness in sending this gift, since it was adorned with the initial "N" for Napoleon, but which equally could be taken to stand for Norodom. Whether true or not, those same officials maintained that it became his favourite residence within the palace compound for some time. With so much building and reconstruction, today's Royal Palace compound only achieved its present form around 1920. (For a detailed description of the buildings forming the modern compound, see Appendix: The Royal Palace.) In addition to Norodom's early concern to construct his palace, we also know that once he had moved from Udong to Phnom Penh he gave orders for the foundation of an important Buddhist *wat* (pagoda) a little distant from the palace, the Wat Botum Vaddei, as the headquarters for the Thommayut order that his father had imported from Bangkok.

Whatever the importance of the palace buildings, it was the king within it who lent to Phnom Penh's physical location its great symbolism. For the Cambodian population he was more than a mere human being. Finding the right words to describe his status is difficult, and perhaps we can do no better than say he was looked on as "semi-divine". Horsemen dismounted as they passed the palace wall and when, on one occasion, Norodom fell to the ground from a carriage no Cambodian dared go to help him to his feet, as to touch him would have been an act of sacrilege. The French might refer to Norodom dismissively as a *roitelet*, a "kinglet", but this was not how he was seen by his people or by himself. In his traditional titles he was the "Great king with heavenly feet, better than all others, descendant of angels and of the god Vishnu, excellent heart, supreme earthly power, as full of qualities as the sun, born to protect men, supporter of the weak, he who knows and understands better than all others, eternally precious like the angels..." and the admiring encomiums continue.

Norodom as Cambodia's king was central to the nation's great calendrical festivals, and most particularly the ceremonies marking the New Year, *Chau Chnam*, which occurs in April; the annual Ploughing of the Sacred Furrow, *Chat Preah Nengkal*, which depending on the lunar calendar may take place in April or May; and what today is probably the most important festival for the population in general, the Water Festival, *Bon Oum Tuk*, which takes place in November. While the New Year ceremonies were celebrated by the king within the palace, his presence was vital outside its walls in the Ploughing of the Sacred Furrow and the Water Festival. Ploughing a furrow to signal the start of the planting season drew on ancient traditions that invoked the blessings of the gods of the Hindu pantheon, and the same or similar ceremonies are found elsewhere in Asia. In Norodom I's time we should imagine it taking place in a real field, not (as it was later to become) a ceremony held close to the palace itself, with the plough pulled by oxen but without a furrow actually being turned. After the king had turned a furrow in this ceremony, the oxen which had drawn the plough were taken to seven bowls to play their part in casting the horoscope for the country's fortunes over the next twelve months. In the bowls were water, alcohol, rice maize, sesame seeds, beans and grass. If the oxen chose to drink from the bowl containing water, this was a prediction that there would be bounteous rains, just as their eating rice predicted a good crop. But consumption of alcohol foreshadowed disaster, as did consumption of beans.

The Water Festival over which Norodom presided was part of another long tradition celebrated in a similar fashion along the Mekong over many centuries. But in Phnom Penh it had a special character since it marked not only the end of the rainy season, at the very end of October or in early November, but also the remarkable reversal of the Tonle Sap. With the signs that the river was about to reverse its flow preparations were made for the festival. It was the king's role and duty to cut a symbolic string stretched out across the water that sanctified the reversal. But for the population the festival was also a time for boat races taking place over three days. Boats were brought from all over the kingdom to race down the now-reversed river, their crews straining to wield their paddles in time to the beat of a drummer in the boat, and with a clown or buffoon in each boat roaring out ribald commentaries as each of the boats made their way upstream against the current. The scholarly French official, Adhémard Leclère, who worked in Cambodia in the 1880s, recorded some of these:

It has rained a great deal this year, the river has broken its banks. There will be much rice and joy. All the women are pregnant, either by their husbands or by their lovers. It doesn't really matter. Aya!

Cambodians make love all night; the Vietnamese all day. They say that the French only make love in the evening. Aya!

Oh you women, lift up your sarongs, so that I can tell who amongst you pleases me the most. Aya!

Within the palace compound Norodom's will was law and he enforced that will over his sons as well as over his officials, beating them or confining them in chains when they transgressed the rigid protocols of palace behaviour. He was, as Doudart de Lagrée once described him, "a tiger" when it came to maintaining his absolute rights over the members of his female household. French officials slipped too easily into describing these women as members of a "harem". That many were the king's sexual partners is true enough, just as it was true for a later king, Monivong (reigned 1927-41), who, amazingly enough, had Pol Pot's sister as a member of his female household. And there is convincing evidence that through the efforts of an Indian agent in Bangkok Norodom was supplied with the Siamese women whom he particularly favoured after having spent many of his youthful years as a hostage-guest in the Siamese court. But many of the women in the establishment were something more, the daughters of senior officials whose presence cemented relations on both sides of an equation of respect and service.

With senior male members of the royal family each having their own female establishments, there were many dozens of children who could claim a royal connection. In the case of the male children this did not matter much, though it was seldom the case that there was much fraternal feeling among the male children of a single father and different mothers— as exemplified by Norodom and his two best-known brothers. For the female children it was indeed a problem since Cambodian tradition decreed that princesses could not marry men who were of lesser status than themselves. This led, in the words of censorious French officials, to royal princesses seeking to smuggle "men of the people" into the palace to relieve their sexual frustrations. It was not until after Norodom's death, in 1904, that the rule against princesses marrying men with a lower status than their own was finally relaxed.

It is possibly true, as some observers have suggested, that the French who wrote about Norodom in the early years of the period of French "protection" were too ready to highlight the more sensational and sanguinary aspects of the punishments meted out to those who transgressed his wishes. Yet there is no doubt that *lèse-majesté* in the form of daring to have sexual relations with the king's women was to court death by beheading, with the heads of those who were executed exposed on bamboo poles outside the palace. On one occasion in the 1870s, having learnt for the first time of the European practice of using firing squads to execute criminals, Norodom immediately arranged for a squad of his soldiers to be assembled to despatch by this new method four women of his household and two men accused of infidelity. As late as 1884, twenty years after the French had first sought to inculcate something of their "civilizing mission" into Cambodia, Norodom was only with difficulty dissuaded from punishing one of his sons by having him dragged to his death behind horses through the streets of Phnom Penh.

THE KING AND THE FRENCH

For nearly two decades, from 1866 to 1884, the city's existence revolved around two poles. The first centred on Norodom and the palace. At one level this was a bastion of tradition, where sacred rites were observed, traditional entertainments that could last for days took place, and Norodom jealously guarded his rights, whether over the raising of taxes or the strict control of his female household. Yet the palace was also a place where the king was remarkably ready to deal with a motley cast of self-interested foreigners who were usually of dubious character and often out-and-out carpetbaggers.

The other pole revolved around the French representative, whose official residence was sited close to the *phnom*. Whether this choice of location reflected much thought on the part of the French and so an effort to link their presence with an important symbol of the city's identity it is hard to say. In many ways the French representative was an isolated figure, conscious of his responsibilities and of his dignity, but not above quietly maintaining a Cambodian concubine. This was at a time when the near total absence of European women meant that there was not yet a barrier to this form of common, if unequal, relationship between Frenchmen and local women. Above all, the French representative was able to advance his country's interest by deploying troops to combat Norodom's enemies, for at various times the king faced rebellion from pretenders to his throne and the armed enmity of his half-brother Siwotha. Norodom welcomed this aid, but his gratitude did not extend to accepting the various French attempts to have him "reform" the traditional practices of the kingdom. Through the 1860s, 1870s and into the early 1880s a pattern developed in which the French representative pressed changes to the kingdom's administration on the king—changes such as a less oppressive tax system

The French Residence in Phnom Penh built in the 1890s

and the elimination of slavery—and Norodom would agree to implement them. He would then fail to act. Angered and frustrated, French officials more than once considered removing Norodom from the throne, knowing that his half-brother Sisowath was a more than willing replacement ready to toe their line. Then they, too, pulled back, as they ruefully concluded that to depose Norodom would probably cause them more trouble than the action was worth.

We have many descriptions of Norodom. We know that he was a small man, barely five feet tall, with pockmarked skin. In the early years of his relations with the French he appears to have readily adopted a style of dress modelled on European military fashions, with tunics draped in gold lace. He liked western alcohol, with sherry and brandy apparently his preferred choices, and he was an opium smoker. His heavy indulgence in this habit in the final years of his life was undoubtedly to deaden the pain of the cancer that finally killed him. Despite the condescending terms in which the French so often described the king, we are indebted to a perceptive French observer for some sense of Norodom's majesty in the eyes of his people, a majesty which colonial officials so often did not understand. Writing about Norodom returning from an excursion outside

Norodom I as a young man

Phnom Penh, the remarkable French explorer Auguste Pavie, who lived in Cambodia for several years, recorded in 1881 that:

> To meet in one's travels the Asian monarch and the Cambodian court returning from an excursion in oriental style, with disorder adding to its curious character, is really good fortune. Two hundred elephants, rolling the ancient seats, gilded or black, which they support, carry the king and the princes under roofs of scarlet bamboo screening, and pass like a parade, filled with women of the harem and with dancers half naked beneath their scarves. They disappear with the horsemen, the carriages, and those on foot, in a cloud of dust, leaving the impression of an unforgettable enchanted picture.

Pavie was a perceptive and unusual observer of Cambodia who had lived contentedly in Kampot, a small, isolated coastal settlement as a telegraphic officer. He had initially served in Indochina as a sergeant in the marine infantry in southern Vietnam, in 1869, and then returned to Cambodia in 1871. Acquiring a deep knowledge of the country and its language he was called on in 1879 to supervise the construction of a telegraph line between Phnom Penh and Saigon and then between Phnom Penh and Bangkok. For these tasks he became a resident of Phnom Penh and his writings make clear the pleasure this afforded him. When not engaged in official tasks he visited nearby villages and above all observed life on the rivers that flowed by the Cambodian capital. As an interesting comment on the urban services available to residents at this time, he wrote of how he would take a barrel out in a boat to fill it with the clear water to be found in the Mekong, as opposed to the turbid water drawn from the Tonle Sap that was usually distributed in the city. He would then return with the barrel and the water it contained for his domestic use.

With French protection afforded to him, Norodom prospered as no Cambodian king had done for centuries. We know this through an indictment drawn up against him in 1882 by the Governor of Cochinchina, Le Myre de Vilers, which lists the material benefits that had accrued to Norodom and which allowed him, as the governor put it, "to join the refinements of European comfort to the luxury of Asia." Under French protection he had Filipino and Cambodian court orchestras; a flotilla of steam boats; two hundred and fifty elephants; Filipino and Cambodian bodyguards, infantry, cavalry and artillery; and "finally, and to crown everything, a harem made up of four hundred women, which becomes larger each year through the recruitment of young girls carried on in Siam through the intermediary of an Indian, Ibrahim, who is an English subject."

In these early years of the French presence Norodom's adherence to tradition was no barrier to his court being remarkably cosmopolitan in character. To French distress there were still men who regarded themselves as Siamese citizens occupying positions within the court. Wealthy Chinese were welcome as, perhaps most curiously, were the Europeans already briefly mentioned. With the insights provided by Gregor Muller's book they have now become three-dimensional figures, where once they tended to seem little more than shadowy bit players. In a sense, they too drifted between the two poles of Phnom Penh society. French officialdom despised them, but could not utterly ignore them because of their nationality. Norodom, on the other hand, was ready to meet them in a camaraderie that mixed joining them to play billiards—he had his own table—with using them as his agents to import goods from Europe and as a source of loans when he was temporarily short of funds. With their readiness to flatter him, he found them a comforting relief from the often hectoring tone used by French officials when they dealt with him.

Frédéric Thomas-Caraman, who falsely claimed to be a French count, was one of the earliest French settlers in Cambodia. He lived for decades in partial amity with the king, now supplying him with European luxuries, now in dispute with him over the non-fulfilment of a contract. Paul le Faucheur was another quasi-intimate. He had come to Cambodia even before the capital shifted to Phnom Penh, dealt in timber and pepper and sustained a long association with the king despite periods of estrangement after the failure of business deals that he had negotiated for him. In the 1870s the widow Marrot and her son moved to Phnom Penh from Saigon, where she had run a hotel. Importing French goods and selling them to the king on credit, she appears to have maintained an amicable relationship with him despite being his creditor over long periods. Other names from this group of Norodom's foreign associates include the Creole magistrate and journalist Henri Ternisien, the lawyer Jules Blanscubé and Félix-Gaspard Faraut, originally a public works employee in Saigon, who advised Norodom on everything from architecture to politics. Remarkably enough, these "unofficial" associates of the king represented a substantial proportion of the Europeans actually resident in Phnom Penh. For while exact figures are uncertain, it is probable that the city's resident European population did not exceed forty by the end of the 1870s.

The surprisingly free and easy relations between the Cambodian king and these individuals reflected a degree of tolerance, or for some resigned acceptance, of social mores that would not have been contemplated in the bourgeois world of France itself, whatever might have been the moral standards of the wealthier members of French society. In circumstances in which European women were rarely present the practice of maintaining concubines was widespread. This was true even of Jean Moura, the French representative for eleven years from 1868 to 1879. It seems that Phnom Penh in these early years was no different from other colonial settings in which an absence of European female company "changed the rules." In the French colony next door, in southern Vietnam, the Vatican's apostolic vicar complained in 1872 that fifty-eight out of sixty senior French officials were living with "native" concubines.

On the surface, and despite official French concerns about Norodom's intransigent refusal to institute the various administrative changes he had agreed to, Phnom Penh by the end of the 1870s appeared to be a capital at peace. This was particularly the case as Norodom's half-brother Siwotha had failed in yet another effort to turn his long-standing opposition to the king into territorial success. His attempts to seize government outposts in the north-east of the country had been defeated by French-led troops. In 1876, in what they regarded as a gesture of benevolence, the French even provided Norodom with a life-sized equestrian statue, in which he bestrode the horse dressed in a French general's uniform, and which now stands in the grounds of the Silver Pagoda. The best evidence is that the statue was a "stock model", to which only Norodom's head had to be added to give it a "personal" character. This background to the statue's origin became lost in the years that followed, so that it became prized possession for the modern royal family, particularly as Norodom Sihanouk promoted his ancestor in the 1950s and 1960s as a model of Cambodian nationalism.

As the 1870s drew to a close, the French in Phnom Penh could look to other signs that their rule and the city's future were acquiring an increasingly settled character. A particularly important basis for this outlook was the agreement reached with the Siamese government in 1879 for the construction of a telegraph line between Phnom Penh and Bangkok, one that would also link Phnom Penh and Saigon. Constructed under the supervision of the energetic Auguste Pavie, the line was completed in 1883.

For the French, this period of apparent calm and largely amicable relations with the Cambodian king seemed as good a time as any to insist that Norodom finally honour his promise to embrace reforms. The French were mistaken, and in the events that unfolded between 1877 and 1886, Phnom Penh's future was decided in a manner that reinforced French control of the king, of the city, and of the country, until the years of the Second World War.

Rebellion: Phnom Penh under Siege

Commencing in 1877, and as the king appeared to accept French advice and then failed to act, Norodom secretly sought to open negotiations with Spain, with the apparent aim of diluting French influence over his position and that of the country. A treaty was actually signed, though it was later disavowed by Spain, which would have at least given Norodom the right to receive a Spanish consul at his court. French fury when they became aware of the treaty was incandescent. Whether either side realized it, they were now set on a collision course.

The first step towards a rebellion that, for a period, became a small-scale but serious colonial war, and which at one stage threatened to drive the French from Phnom Penh, came five years later in 1882. Determined to bring Norodom to heel, the most senior French official in Indochina, Governor Le Myre de Vilers, demanded that the king agree to meet the cost of the French protectorate. At the last moment the governor drew back, seeking some limited changes from Norodom, but not pressing his original demands to a conclusion. Le Myre de Vilers' successor, Governor Charles Thomson, took a different attitude when he took up his post in Saigon in 1883.

At the beginning of 1884 Thomson demanded that Norodom should give up his control of the country's customs service. This was Norodom's sticking point, an issue on which he felt deeply; as he wrote to Thomson: "The Cambodian Government and the Cambodian people are not accustomed to giving up their ancient ways in order to adopt new ones." Moreover, he went on to tell the French: "It will be thought that the king has lost all authority over his subjects." There was no meeting of minds as Thomson continued to demand Norodom's acquiescence and the king would not budge. With both sides' *amour propre* now engaged, Thomson decided that the impasse could not be allowed to continue.

Summoning three gunboats and an extra detachment of troops from Saigon, and sure in his own mind that Prince Sisowath was ready to take his brother's place on the throne, Thomson proceeded to act out one of the truly dramatic episodes in Phnom Penh's colonial history. On 17 June 1884, with the gunboats visible from the palace in the waters of the *Quatre Bras*, Thomson strode into the palace, accompanied by a detachment of soldiers. Penetrating into Norodom's private quarters and waking the king, Thomson issued an ultimatum. If the king did not accept a new convention redefining France's protection over his kingdom and implementing the reforms for which the French had long called, Norodom would be dethroned. Initially refusing but faced with this threat, Norodom reluctantly signed the new convention as Thomson congratulated himself that he had brought real change to Cambodia.

He had indeed, for under the arrangements in the new convention the French representative in Phnom Penh was to have a predominant position over the king's own advisers and the right to private audiences with the monarch. In the provinces French officials were to assume new positions that reinforced French control over the country. A new system of land ownership was to be introduced and slavery was, finally, to be abolished. It was six months before the illusory nature of Thomson's victory became clear.

The first act in what was to become a major rebellion took place on 8 January 1885, when a French army post in the remote north-east of the country was attacked with the loss of the French commander. This was the signal for a general uprising that spread throughout Cambodia and which, by the end of the year, left only Phnom Penh and a few isolated posts under French control. On one occasion the capital itself came under attack. As a reflection of the French administration's concern that it might be necessary to protect its headquarters against the insurgents' attacks, the stupa sited on top of the *phnom* was used as an observation point.

As France deployed 4,000 troops to confront an armed challenge to their control of the country, all of the classic aspects of guerrilla war came into play. French-led troops found that they were fighting an elusive enemy that only attacked in conditions that favoured it. In their frustration at being unable to bring about a decisive victory, French officers resorted to summary executions and mass punishments of villagers. More and more French troops fell seriously ill to tropical disease and to a surge in venereal disease as prostitution in Phnom Penh flourished—and still the rebellion dragged on through 1885 and 1886.

Although some of the rebel leaders were clearly identified, in particular Siwotha, the big question the French asked themselves was whether the king himself had orchestrated this challenge to their control. He repeatedly denied this was the case, though it may be observed that if he wanted to stay on the throne he could do little else. A review of all of the evidence suggests that the reforms that the French had forced from the king were resented by provincial officials, as they were of course by Norodom. In these circumstances, Norodom may have indicated to these senior officials that he would welcome acts of rebellion. This was never proved, despite the best efforts of the French to do so, but the important point is that it was only when Norodom called on the rebels to lay down their arms that the rebellion finally petered out at the end of 1886. Norodom acted as he did with promises from the French that some of the major demands for change that Thomson had placed before him would, at the least, be deferred. The last real challenge to French control until after the Second World War gave way to fifty years of largely untroubled colonial calm. This judgment is not contradicted by the notable events of 1916 discussed in the following chapter.

Norodom's was a pyrrhic victory, with the French determined to impose change with only a minimum of delay. And this they did, piecemeal, as they wore the Cambodian sovereign down. They were aided in their aims by a change in the attitude of the most senior Cambodian officials below the king, through whom they increasingly worked. By the mid-1890s these officials had sensed the direction in which the winds of change were blowing and, not without hesitations, increasingly showed themselves ready to make decisions that favoured French interests rather than those of the king. Moreover, Norodom was growing tired. He had turned fifty in 1886 and his health was no longer robust. More and more he found solace in the traditional aspects of life in the palace and in the company of his female establishment. We do not know what he thought of the physical changes occurring in Phnom Penh from the late 1880s onwards. For as the king's power slipped even further from his hands he would have been aware that the city was steadily changing in appearance.

BUILDING A NEW CITY

With Cambodia again at peace in 1889, France appointed a new representative in Cambodia, the *Résident Supérieur* Huyn de Vernéville, who remained in his post until 1897. Forty years ago I met members of the Cambodian royal family who remembered his name with bitterness, as he fought a relentless and largely successful administrative battle with Norodom to reduce the king's prerogatives. Today that fact is forgotten in Phnom Penh. Indeed, more broadly, the history of the country and the city before Norodom Sihanouk came to the throne in 1941 has largely been forgotten by a population traumatized by decades of suffering. Certainly, there is no memory of de Vernéville's unconventional private life— unconventional, at least, for a senior official by this period, in which he maintained a Cambodian mistress. But if de Vernéville is forgotten except by a few historians, his heritage can still be found in a number of buildings constructed during his time in office and which still stand. These include the treasury building at the corner of Street 106 and Boulevard Norodom, the central prison on Street 154, and what was the central police station at the corner of Streets 13 and 96 near the central post office.

During the 1890s much of the pre-independence street pattern was fixed in place. De Vernéville oversaw the construction of two major canals in the areas now bounded by Streets 92 and 96 and 102 and 108 and which, in the 1930s, were filled in to create the open spaces seen today. (The reliance on numbers instead of names for most streets reflects both political considerations and the rapid expansion of the city in the past two decades. Under the period of Vietnamese occupation a number of streets were named after international communist heroes, such as Lenin, today's Sisowath Quay, and past Cambodian communist leaders, such as Tou Samouth—now Boulevard Norodom. Such names are no longer seen as appropriate by a government seeking to stress its modernity and to bury the links with the communist past of its leaders. Most French and Cambodian street names that existed before 1975 have been discarded and are today seen as carrying too much colonial baggage. There are exceptions in the names of Cambodian monarchs and a French figure such as Louis Pasteur, and names from the Sihanouk era were restored in 1993.)

It was during this period that the street pattern of the European quarter north of the *phnom* was laid out in grid form. Of symbolic importance, a new residence for the head of the French administration was completed a little north of the area of the modern post office. During the same period, as Penny Edwards describes in her *Cambodge: The Cultivation of a Nation, 1860-1945* (2006), the French town planner Daniel Fabre provided the inspiration for a wholesale renovation of the hillock formed by the *phnom* with the construction of a great staircase incorporating Angkorian details, most obviously the rearing, seven-headed *naga*, or sacred snakes, at the base of the stairs which can still be seen today. Importantly for Phnom Penh's contemporary appearance, de Vernéville widened the Grand' Rue and decreed that apart from some port buildings there should be no construction on the side of the street adjoining the bank of the Tonle Sap. This decision set in place the essential urban landscape that remains to the present day along Sisowath Quay.

With Phnom Penh's population increasing in size its river port grew in importance so that docks were constructed and the banks of the river revetted. According to figures cited by a French geographer Michel Igout in his book *Phnom Penh Then and Now* (1993), the city's population nearly doubled between 1889 and 1897 while de Vernéville was at the administration's helm, from 25,000 to a little less than 50,000, of whom 16,000 were Cambodians, 22,000 were Chinese, 4,000 were Vietnamese, and 400 French (this last figure seems too large). The balance was made up of other Asians, mostly Indians and Chams. The numbers of Chinese and Vietnamese in the country at large, and particularly in Phnom Penh, were to increase sharply in the following decades.

END OF AN ERA

By the end of the nineteenth century Norodom was a diminished figure in his own eyes, if not in the eyes of his subjects for whom his growing number of palace buildings and range of material possessions were taken as a sign of his high kingly status. Opposing almost every change the French demanded, he consistently lost out as his senior officials increasingly sided with the colonial power. These officials had sensed the way in which power had shifted in the kingdom, devoted though they were in their own way to traditional values. Their readiness to side with the French administration was not disinterested, for the record is clear that the best known of the senior Cambodian officials benefited significantly from their positions in monetary terms. At the urging of the colonial power Norodom had sent two of his sons to whom he had shown favour into exile. Contracting cancer in 1902, he held true to the kingdom's old ways, concerned to see the completion of the Wat Preah Keo Morokat (Temple of the Emerald Buddha) immediately to the south of the main palace compound and widely known today as the Silver Pagoda because its floor is paved in silver tiles. He presided over its inauguration in 1903.

Norodom's death in April 1904 was truly the end of an era and it was one that finished with all the pomp of a royal funeral such as had not been seen for centuries. After the king's body had lain in a gilded urn filled with mercury for nearly two years his bones were reverently removed by his daughter, Princess Malika, in a solemn ceremony described in great detail by an official French observer, Paul Collard, in his book *Cambodge et Cambodgiens* (1925). The occasion later became a set-piece in Roland Meyer's autobiographical novel, *Saramani, danseuse khmer* (1919), one of the few French novels from the colonial years that offers a realistic picture of life within the Royal Palace. In January 1906, the late king's bones were transported in a vast procession that included over two hundred elephants

The "Silver Pagoda"

to a great funeral pagoda, a *men*, set in the empty ground to the north of the palace wall, in front of where the National Museum now stands. Then, following the cremation and according to custom some of Norodom's ashes were consigned to the river, while the remainder were placed in a stupa erected in the grounds of the Silver Pagoda.

While Norodom's death ended an era it preserved kingship as an essential feature of Cambodian life. At his death he was a richer monarch than any who had preceded him since the fall of Angkor. His palace compound stood in Phnom Penh as the most obvious symbol of his wealth, a fact that was to be of continuing importance until the overthrow of his great-grandson, Norodom Sihanouk, in 1970. He died in a city that was unrecognizable from the collection of poorly constructed wooden buildings stretched out along the banks of the Tonle Sap at the time he came to the Cambodian throne. Much of the modern Royal Palace was completed before his death and it now sheltered behind an encircling, crenellated wall. He had lost almost all his temporal power but he had seen Phnom Penh become a settlement worthy of the name "city".

Yet within that same city the French who now lived there did so in an ambience far different from that of the first two decades of the protectorate. From the late 1880s onwards it had become commonplace for French officials to come to Phnom Penh accompanied by their wives. "Respectable" single French women came to Phnom Penh and married there. The colonial flotsam and jetsam of the early years, so clearly represented by the bogus count Thomas-Caraman and his associates, were slowly passing from the scene. Phnom Penh now had a French mayor and the city was run along the same lines as a provincial town in metropolitan France. Although dubious adventurers were never totally absent from the city's twentieth-century history, "bad Frenchmen", to appropriate Gregor Muller's term, no longer formed the core of the "unofficial" expatriate community. Those few who remained were seen by their bourgeois compatriots as a stain on France's reputation, an embarrassment to a great European power committed to the goals of its "civilizing mission".

At the turn of the century it was still less than fifty years since Phnom Penh had assumed its status as Cambodia's capital and the French administration's headquarters. Yet following the burst of construction that took place in the 1890s it already had the air of a long-established colonial settlement. Even so, it was far from boasting a large European community. Muller lists a total of some seventy Frenchmen in positions as traders over the thirty years between 1861 and 1890, though it is unclear how long many of these men stayed after their arrival. Charles Meyer pointed out, in his book *La Vie quotidienne des Français en Indochine, 1860-1910*, that apart from officials and military personnel there were a mere twenty-one Europeans, of the "better kind" employed in the city in 1904. He lists them as four insurance agents—a surprisingly large number—two bankers, a newsagent, a hairdresser, a manufacturer of bottled drinks, two contractors, a café owner, a hotel owner, an ice maker, a pharmacist, a mechanic, a hardware store owner and four men dealing in import and export. Their diversions were few: drinks at the café or at the city's tiny European club, and a few practice rounds at the shooting range. For the rest, Meyer suggests there may have been a few dozen other non-official Europeans in the city, living from hand to mouth and dreaming of riches that never came their way.

The stage was now set for another four decades of colonial rule, which saw the continuing transformation of Phnom Penh's built environment. This took place in circumstances in which it appeared both to the country's traditional leaders, or at least most of them, and to the French that they had found a formula for coexistence without any obvious terminus. For the

French, of course, the years of the First World War were a time for deep concern, not least because it was then that the remarkable "1916 Affair" took place, a series of mass demonstrations that showed the extent to which the Cambodian king remained central to the population's sense of their identity. But this event, which is discussed in the following chapter, came to be regarded by the French as a puzzling anomaly, ultimately a minor matter when it was compared to the bloody challenges to French rule that took place in neighbouring Vietnam.

Phnom Penh, and Cambodia as a whole, seemed to slumber in political apathy even as new buildings changed the capital's appearance. When the British Admiralty's Naval Intelligence Division compiled its *Geographic Handbook for Indo-China* at the beginning of the Second World War, it captured the received sense of colonial somnolence as it felt able to observe in a patronizing tone that the French administration in Cambodia was lavish in its distribution of decorations to Cambodian officials. These, the handbook recorded, "are widely appreciated and by conferring them generously the French have created a body of loyal officials who are an important stabilising influence in native affairs." There is more than a hint, here, of "decorations" being a twentieth-century equivalent of "beads for the natives". But was this how those "loyal officials" thought of things? Perhaps not, for relations between the king and his senior officials in Phnom Penh were rather more complicated than the British commentators suggested.

Chapter Five

TRANSFORMATION: BUILDING THE NEW PHNOM PENH IN AN ERA OF COLONIAL GOOD FEELING

Many of the major buildings to be seen in present-day Phnom Penh date from the years between King Norodom's death in 1904 and the onset of the Second World War. To list only the most prominent, they include the throne hall of the Royal Palace, the central post office and several of the administrative buildings grouped close to its square, the Hôtel le Royal, the former headquarters of the French administration (now the Ministry of Economics and Finances), the railway station, the town hall (now a commercial building), the National Library and the National Museum, and perhaps most architecturally distinctive of all the Psar Thmei, the Grand or New Market. Although the novelist, Pierre Loti, thought Phnom Penh old beyond its years in appearance when he visited in 1901, it was during the following four decades that the centre took on much of the appearance that is still observable today. At the same time, improved infrastructure underpinned the city's increasingly modern appearance. Electric street lighting was installed in central Phnom Penh in 1912, and after 1927 the water pumped from the Tonle Sap passed through a filtration system in an effort to minimize waterborne diseases.

There are three striking aspects to what happened in the city during the reigns of King Sisowath (1904-27) and his son King Monivong (1927-41). The first was the fact that there was no challenge that came close to undermining French control for nearly forty years. Associated with this was the general pattern of mutual acceptance of the nature of their relationship that existed between the king and his senior officials and the French administration. And the third notable aspect was the extent to which even the Great Depression did little to slow the steady development of Phnom Penh's built environment during the reign of the second of these two kings.

With the exception of the 1916 Affair, described later in this chapter, colonial calm prevailed in Cambodia to a remarkable degree. It is true that there were repeated instances of banditry in the countryside, characterized in the more colourful French term as *piraterie*. But this was never a threat to France's colonial control and reflected a long history of rural lawlessness, often including homicide. Mention must also be made of the resistance to the extension of French control over the western provinces that were returned to Cambodian sovereignty in 1907. In the grander scheme of things this, too, was an annoyance and not a real challenge to the colonial power. The contrast with the French colony in next-door Vietnam could not have been sharper. In that country resistance to French control never really stopped and was marked by repeated outbreaks of violence against the colonial power that were then savagely repressed. A notable example of this repression occurred with a major revolt against French control in the central Vietnamese provinces of Nghe An and Ha Tinh in 1930-31. As thousands of Vietnamese in these desperately poor provinces formed primitive soviets to challenge the administration's control, French Foreign Legion troops were called in to put down the revolt. As they did so, they were given orders authorizing them to kill nine out of ten of any prisoners they took. Compared to such a background of challenge and violence in Vietnam, Cambodia was a different and—in all ways that mattered to both the Cambodian and French administrations—an essentially peaceful place. This state of affairs does not accord with received views that characterize all colonial relationships simply in terms of exploitative domination, but it is a correct judgment, nonetheless.

SISOWATH ON THE THRONE

When he came to the throne in 1904, King Sisowath was 64 years old and a proven friend of the French. He had coveted the throne all his adult life, making clear as early as 1877 that should the French depose Norodom he was ready to take his brother's place and accede to any and all of their wishes. During the years of rebellion in 1885-86, Sisowath had worked tirelessly with the French and he now had his reward. Part of that reward was an annual allowance of 250 pounds of high-grade opium, since Sisowath, like his brother Norodom, was a heavy user of the narcotic.

It is not hard to make patronizing fun of Sisowath, as some French observers were certainly ready to do. He was a portly old man who, when he went to France in 1906, immediately after Norodom's cremation, was an object of fascinated interest to the French public. He had travelled to

France to view the Colonial Exposition, where members of the court ballet were to perform, and in many ways the visit was, indeed, a *succès de théâtre*. Rodin sketched the dancers and Sisowath, clad in Cambodian dress topped by a bowler hat studded with diamonds, was cheered wherever he went. Summing up his own feelings at the time of the visit, he spoke of France as his "adoptive mother". But to view him simply as an amiable puppet is highly misleading, even if his later successor, Norodom Sihanouk, spoke of both Sisowath and the next king, Monivong, as being nothing more than "parrots" ready to say yes to whatever the French wanted. Certainly, Sisowath was a classic Herodian, a man and king ready to cooperate with the colonial power in a relationship that he saw as suiting his interests. And he was ready to do this at a time when the monarch's temporal power had been eroded in the closing years of Norodom's reign, and as the country's most senior officials saw their own best interests linked to the French rather than the king. But whatever choice his officials had made as to whom they were serving, for the population at large, living in a period of peace unequalled for centuries, Sisowath continued to be revered as their monarch, a figure who, with his semi-divine status, was someone and something more than a man.

Difficult though it may be to imagine in a world that has turned its back on colonies and all they stood for, it was possible for the Cambodian royal family and the country's senior traditional officials to find comfort in the colonial relationship. As Phnom Penh grew into a city that would be regarded as among the most attractive in Southeast Asia, Sisowath and his officials could, in their different ways, reflect on the contrast between the comparative peace and stability that now existed and the time, within living memory, when the very survival of Cambodia was uncertain. Sisowath, after all, could readily see the contrast between the city in which he now reigned and the unimpressive set of wooden buildings that had been the Royal Palace while the capital was still at Udong.

Under French protection there was no prospect of invasion by the neighbours to the east and west, Vietnam and Siam. Not only that, for in 1907, and to Sisowath's great delight, the French succeeded in having the Siamese government in Bangkok give up its control over the western provinces of Battambang and Siem Reap and return them to Cambodian sovereignty. This event is commemorated by a monument on the southern slope of the *phnom*, above the floral clock which was added much later, and with a statue of King Sisowath as its principal feature. These were provinces which, although ethnically Cambodian in character, Siam had controlled since the late eighteenth century. There could hardly be clearer testimony to the fact that French protection could work in Cambodia's interests. The traditionalist Norodom had never been able to look at the French presence in his country as other than regrettable, except perhaps in the early years of his reign. His negative view of the colonial relationship was then embraced by some of his sons, two of whom were sent into exile for speaking out against French control. But with Sisowath on the throne, there was no longer any resistance to the French that had the king's sanction. Instead of being a focus for discontent, two of Sisowath's sons went to France, apparently willingly, to study at French military academies.

Peasant Discontent and the "1916 Affair"

If the French presence was welcomed by the small Cambodian elite in Phnom Penh, it was a different story in the countryside. There peasant discontent with the system of personal taxes and demands for *corvée* (forced) labour had been growing over a number of years. This development reflected a paradox, for although the countryside had been at peace ever since the rebellion of 1885-86, this peace had meant that local officials were able to enforce demands for *corvée* labour in an ever more efficient fashion. Although the demands that taxes be paid and *corvée* obligations honoured, particularly for road construction, were requirements of the French administration, it was local Cambodian officials who were responsible for seeing that they were met. In response, the peasants turned to their king in Phnom Penh, following a long-established right that every Cambodian had, the right to appeal to the ruler in the face of injustice. And this they did, spectacularly, in the "1916 Affair".

Even today there are gaps in our understanding of this episode, but the broad outlines are clear enough. Starting at the end of 1915 but growing quickly over the following two months, crowds of peasants made their way to Phnom Penh and to the Royal Palace to tell the king of their discontent with the taxes and labour demanded of them. At times the number of peasants massed in front of the palace was as many as ten thousand, and estimates of the total number of protesters were as high as one hundred thousand. On at least one occasion the crush of the crowd was so large that they broke through the palace gates, scattering the palace guards, to Sisowath's considerable annoyance. During the entire period of the "affair" the peasants simply ignored the French. It was the king whom they came to see, and it was the king who, having listened to their complaints, promised to review the tax and *corvée* system, and sent the protesters on their way back to their villages.

Throughout 1916 there was no violence in Phnom Penh. This was not the case in the provinces, where deaths did occur. Just how many deaths were a result of the demonstrations, whether on the part of the peasants or the forces of order, is one of the many uncertainties associated with the protests. The lowest number recorded was eight, but it is clear that there were more; something of the order of fifty seems more likely. As the French puzzled over the event, with some seeing it as part of a plot involving German espionage, one clear lesson emerged. The king in Phnom Penh remained the central figure in the kingdom for the Cambodian population. The French may have robbed him of his temporal power, but his symbolic importance was as strong as ever, perhaps even more so. Moreover, the paradox involved in this situation goes even deeper, for including the last king to reign before the institution of French control, Ang Duang, no Cambodian monarch for centuries had exercised power other than with the assistance of other rulers. Yet now the Cambodian monarch rejoiced in greater symbolic riches in the eyes of his subject than had ever been the case since the abandonment of Angkor.

THE "CIVILIZING MISSION"

Efforts to find out how Cambodians below the elite felt about the presence of the French in their country face great difficulties. If, as suggested, the events of late 1915 and early 1916 are a guide, the French were almost an irrelevant factor in the daily lives of most Cambodians. This conclusion is borne out by the fact that only one French official was ever killed in the pursuit of his official duties during the years up to the Second World War—the assassination of the *résident* of Kompong Chhnang, Félix Louis Bardez, in 1925. The details surrounding this event and the trial that followed are discussed by David Chandler in one of the collection of his articles in his book, *Facing the Cambodian Past*. (The killing of the *conservateur* at Angkor, Jean Commaille, in April 1916, was a case of banditry, pure and simple, not an attack related to colonial policies.)

Violence directed against the French was simply not part of life in the capital.

This does not represent an apologia for French rule in Cambodia, or throughout Indochina more generally. There was much that was done in the name of the French administration throughout Indochina in the 1920s and 1930s that deserves the sharpest criticism, and the vicious methods used in the suppression of the rebellions against French rule in Nhge An and Ha Tinh provinces in Vietnam in 1930-31 have already been mentioned. The employment conditions for workers on French-owned plantations in both Vietnam and Cambodia were a matter of scandal and condemnation in both Indochina and in France in the 1930s. But the fact was that virtually none of the labourers employed on the plantations was Cambodian. Rather, they were almost entirely Vietnamese. And the earlier grandiose construction in the 1920s of a hill station retreat at Bokor, a site overlooking the ocean in Kampot province, involved the use of harshly treated convict labour, much of it Vietnamese again.

To take these examples of French disregard for those whom they had colonized as a reflection of how Cambodians were treated, and how they felt about their situation, would simply be misleading, particularly in relation to those Cambodians who lived in Phnom Penh. Notwithstanding Marguerite Duras' memories of what her mother had witnessed at Bokor, where she claimed to have seen convicts being punished by being buried up to the necks in the ground, Cambodia in the 1920s and 1930s was scarcely the colonial hell of leftist polemics. The essential criticism to be levelled at the French administration lies in the inherent inequality of a colonial system in which the interests of the colonizing power overrode all other considerations. This meant the French officials at the head of the administration in Phnom Penh disregarded, or chose to minimize, the problems associated with widespread rural poverty and unsatisfactory health services. And, above all, they made far too little effort to provide education for the population, a fact made clear by the number of Cambodians who had successfully completed the *baccalauréat* examination by the Second World War totalling barely a dozen.

Yet it would be misleading not to add one further and rather particular comment about education, in the broadest sense, in this attempt to draw up a scorecard of French legacies in Cambodia. The establishment in 1900 of the Ecole Française d'Extrême-Orient (French School of the Far East) dedicated to a wide range of cultural research in the Indochinese region was to have profound importance for the retrieval of Cambodia's past.

What is more accessible is the view the French held of Cambodians. While there was a range of attitudes held about the *indigènes*, it is striking that even the most sympathetic French men and women looked on the general Cambodian population as a diminished race in a country that had "fallen from its antique splendour." Such a country could, in the genuinely held, if self-deceiving, views of the period, be rehabilitated as France played its role charged by history with a *mission civilisatrice*, a civilizing mission. What today seems like unbridled arrogance was a much more complex set of attitudes. In a phrase that was still to be heard in Phnom Penh in the 1960s, many French spoke of the Cambodian population as having *la mentalité d'esclave*. But they were slaves who should be freed from their cultural and historical fetters. And the idea of a fallen, diminished people came to be an element in the formulation of a national history which took the greatness of Angkor as its central theme.

Among those who sought to evoke the greatness of the past no one was more sympathetic to the Cambodian population than George Groslier, who designed the Phnom Penh Museum, with its striking evocations of traditional Cambodian architecture, and was its director until 1942. Construction of the museum began in 1917 and it was inaugurated three years later, taking its name from a former Governor General of Indochina, Albert Sarraut. (For additional details on the National Museum, see Appendix B.) Groslier was an artist and writer who worked tirelessly to rehabilitate the traditional Cambodian arts and crafts. Yet this man, for whom the study of Indochina was both a vocation and a love affair, could still look at Cambodians and write about the population and the country in which they lived in terms of a contrast with the greatness of the Angkorian period: "The gods have disappeared, and ironic Death has left only slaves."

The head of the French administration in Cambodia at this time, François Baudoin, certainly thought along these lines. A pivotal French administrator in the early twentieth century, first as a provincial *résident* and then for eight years between 1914 and 1922 as *résident supérieur*, Baudoin acted swiftly in relation to the "1916 affair" in his position as head of the French administration. He oversaw the arrest and jailing of those identified as leaders of the peasant protesters and had them brought to trial. But just as importantly, he enlisted Sisowath's support in overcoming the protest movement, making sure that the king travelled widely to areas of disaffection to promise relief at the same time as he called for laws to be obeyed and order to be re-established.

By the time Baudoin assumed his duties as the *résident supérieur*, a curious form of reverse social acculturation was taking place at the senior levels of the French administration in Phnom Penh. Mostly conservative in their personal and political inclinations, it is clear that the French officials enjoyed their association with the royal court. There was nothing in republican France quite like the exotic pomp of the Cambodian court, with the king's brahmins blowing ceremonially on their conch shells and the assemblage of Cambodian officials prostrating themselves before the monarch in time with the deeply reverberating tones of a giant gong. French officials participated in traditional court ceremonies, their white colonial uniforms contrasting with the colourful silk *sampots* (sarongs worn looped up between the legs) of the Cambodian courtiers. There were royal orders and medals to covet, above all the Royal Order of Cambodia. The wickedly perceptive account of his compatriots vying for decorations from the French colonies in Roger Peyrefitte's satiric novel about the French diplomatic service, *Les Ambassades* (1951), could readily be transferred to Phnom Penh in the reigns of Sisowath and Monivong.

Nothing better characterizes the process of reverse acculturation than the lengthy and intense discussions found in the French archives when issues of succession to the throne in Phnom Penh were under review. This had not been an issue of importance when Sisowath succeeded Norodom, at least not for the French. It was a different story among members of the Norodom branch of the royal family, for however much they may have coveted the throne there was never any likelihood that Sisowath would be passed over. But as Sisowath grew ever older the question of who should succeed became a matter of the greatest interest to the French, as well as to the Cambodian elite.

The Cambodian monarchy had a long tradition of being elective rather than a simple matter of primogeniture. This fact was a further encouragement for French involvement in the decision as to who should be the next king once Sisowath died. Sisowath had made clear his own wishes, but much French ink was spilt in cables and despatches between Phnom Penh, Hanoi where the French Governor General of Indochina had his headquarters, and the Colonial Ministry in Paris reviewing alternative possibilities. Ultimately, the French chose Sisowath's preferred candidate, his son Monivong, whose education in a French military academy and apparent devotion to the metropolitan power seemed to make him ideal for the throne. Once installed, Monivong showed little interest in affairs of state. In terms of implementing their policy, the French relied not on Monivong but rather on the Minister of the Palace, Thiounn, whose long service and dedication to French interests made him invaluable to the colonial power. Monivong's eventual successor, Norodom Sihanouk, has left us with his memory of the king as a man more concerned with the pleasures he could find with his female household than with affairs of the state, and who scribbled assent to documents placed before him without bothering to read them.

CONSTRUCTING CAMBODIA'S PAST

The reigns of Sisowath and Monivong were of fundamental importance for the construction of a received view of Cambodia's past, one that to an important degree was shared by elite Cambodians and French alike. This was a process that had started almost from the beginning of the establishment of the protectorate in the nineteenth century. Senior French officials such as Jean Moura, Adémard Leclère and Etienne Aymonier had combined serious scholarly endeavour with their administrative duties in particular to establish an "authorized" version of the kingdom's royal chronicles. But it was in the last decade of the nineteenth and the first four decades of the twentieth centuries that a vision of Cambodia's past was settled upon as a result of both French and Cambodian efforts, a vision that sought to establish an unbroken cultural link between contemporary Cambodia and the period of Angkorian greatness. Not the least of the motivations behind French actions was a concern to minimize memories of Cambodian royalty's close links with the Siamese court in Bangkok. There were not only links directly involving members of the royal family, for even in the last decade of the nineteenth century French administrators were disturbed to find that some senior officials within Norodom's court still thought of themselves as Siamese rather than Cambodian. Perhaps even more importantly, the monasteries of Bangkok remained a magnet for Cambodian Buddhist monks seeking to pursue higher studies.

The desirability of establishing a view of the Cambodian state that was both closely linked to the Angkorian past and distinctively separate from the influence of Siam was also embraced by important Cambodian actors in search of an official state identity. This is a subject examined in detail in Penny Edwards' recent book, *Cambodge*, and by the Japanese scholar Sasagawa Hideo, particularly as it relates to the dance forms of the royal ballet. In an impressive article, Hideo describes the manner in which French and Cambodian writers alike sought to downplay the influence of Siamese culture on the court dancers and the works they performed, instead linking them to what were supposed to be the dance forms of Angkorian times. This was a particularly striking example of what came to be described as a proper definition of *khmerité*—the fact, for individuals and the state, of being Khmer or Cambodian.

The subject is complex, and what follows here involves a degree of simplification. An important starting point are the arguments presented by George Groslier in his 1911 book *Danseuses cambodgiennes anciennes et modernes* [Ancient and Modern Cambodian Dancers]. The essence of Groslier's argument was that while it was true that Norodom I had Siamese dancers in his court troupe, the dances they performed, and the gestures used in them were directly descended from what one could see in the bas-reliefs of the Angkorian temples. This was not the only example of Groslier's concern to establish the unique character of Cambodian culture. In his book *A l'Ombre d'Angkor* [In the Shadow of Angkor, 1916], he argues vigorously against any suggestion that the temples at Angkor should be seen as essentially an Indian architectural and artistic form in a Cambodian setting. Yes, Groslier argued, those who built Angkor drew on Hindu and Buddhist legends and religious beliefs, but they transformed them into something that was uniquely Cambodian—a view broadly accepted today.

Bound up in the question of whether or not the court dances were influenced by Siam was the broader question of France's role as protector of Cambodia, a power that had rescued Cambodia from extinction. To see France's establishment of its colonial relationship in these terms was, of course, reassuring to colonial officials, and not without a substantial measure of intellectual justification. Although history can only ever be about what actually happened, French officials were not simply being self-serving in suggesting that without their country's intervention in the

Indochinese region, Cambodia could well have been a prey to its neighbours and have been eliminated as a state.

For the French it thus became important to argue that they had saved Cambodia from disappearing and that they were also playing a role in assisting Cambodians to assert the primacy of their cultural identity stretching back to the Angkorian period. In doing so they received important assistance from a powerful figure at the Cambodian court, the Minister of the Royal Palace, Thiounn. Not only did Thiounn prove a loyal *collaborateur* with the French for decades, arguably the most important official for the entire period of a French presence in Phnom Penh, but he also played a significant part in promoting the view that the dances performed by the royal ballet troupe in the twentieth century drew on Angkorian models.

Yet both Cambodians, with Thiounn at their head, and the French were misrepresenting Cambodian history. Despite the fact that in modern times Sihanouk has held up his great grandfather, Norodom I, as a prime example of Cambodian nationalism, it is beyond dispute that he was a man deeply influenced by the culture of the Siamese court in which he had lived for many years. To write the Siamese (Thais) out of Cambodian history suited the French and the Cambodians in the 1920s and 1930s, but it was, and is, an a-historical gloss on Cambodian history. Just as importantly, indeed even more so, it was an approach to the Cambodian past leading to a glorification of Angkor, and this formed part of Sihanouk's political credo, as it also did for Pol Pot.

Sihanouk's encomiums of the Angkorian past were, it is true, more nuanced than Pol Pot's. He was ready to say that "we have reason to be proud of the Angkorian kings," but to the extent he gave much thought to history it tended to be in terms of defending his more immediate predecessors against the charge that they had sold out to the French. In contrast, as both David Chandler and Philip Short, his astute biographers point out, Pol Pot could state, in 1977, "If our people were capable of building Angkor, we can do anything."

At another level, there is no doubting the important role French research played in reconstructing a history of the Angkorian past. From 1907 the temples at Angkor became accessible for research of all kinds, and continued to be so through the protectorate period and beyond, when Cambodia gained independence. It is not an exaggeration to say that the

Ecole Française gave their past back to Cambodians. How much this meant for the Cambodian elite in Phnom Penh in the 1930s it is difficult to say, though the choice of the name *Nagara Vatta* (Angkor Wat) for the newspaper discussed in this chapter is surely significant.

URBAN TRANSFORMATION

The other immediately striking aspect of Sisowath's and Monivong's reigns is the extent to which the First World War and the Great Depression had remarkably little effect on the steady pattern of building in Phnom Penh, including the filling in of major canals. Both the war and the Depression certainly did have effects in all French colonies, and Cambodia was not immune from the global downturn which led to a major reduction in the demand for rubber and rice. But even so, the colonial budget continued to permit the transformation of the city to continue, even during the worst years of the Depression, between 1931 and 1935.

Even before the onset of the Depression, one of modern Phnom Penh's long-standing landmarks had been built. This was the Hôtel le Royal, which opened its doors to custom in 1929—the date given by Michel Igout in his book. *Phnom Penh Then and Now*, of 1932, is incorrect. When the prolific French writer of the interwar period, Guy de

The Hôtel le Royal which opened in 1929

Pourtalès, visited in 1930, shortly after it had opened, he recorded in his travel book, *Nous, à rien n'appartient: voyage au pays khmer* (1931), that he was the only guest in the hotel. But by the end of the 1930s it was widely accepted as the city's premier hotel, and it was where Charlie Chaplin, accompanied by Paulette Goddard, stayed for a night on their way to Angkor in 1936.

During the 1930s two of the largest public buildings still standing were completed, the railway station and the Grand or New Market, the Psar Thmei. Both are striking examples of construction in reinforced concrete with their visible character dependent on the repeated use of arches. One of the architects of the market building was Victor Chauchon, a French practitioner who was highly regarded in the interwar period. Some architectural historians believe that he was also involved in the design of the railway station, which makes similar use of reinforced concrete arches behind its undistinguished façade. It was also at this time that the National Library that stands today next door to the Hôtel le Royal was also completed, in 1932.

The 1930s saw, too, the emergence onto Phnom Penh's streets of the distinctive *cyclopousse* bicycle rickshaw. Usually referred to simply as *cyclos*, they remain an important form of transport to the present day even though they are less visible now than only a few years ago after being banned from some major streets. Moreover, the number of men prepared to ride them is slowly diminishing, for it requires great physical effort and is an almost certain path to debilitating disease. The idea of constructing a *cyclopousse*, with a passenger sitting in a form of "armchair" between two wheels while the rider sits behind over a single wheel and pedals the *cyclo* forward, was conceived by a French engineer, Maurice Coupeaud, in 1937. Three years later they began to be used generally in the city, following Coupeaud's publicity stunt of riding one himself from Phnom Penh to Saigon—a distance of some 125 miles—in a time of seventeen hours.

A *cyclopousse* rider

STIRRINGS OF NATIONALISM

As central Phnom Penh took on an appearance readily recognized today, the first tentative stirrings of nationalism became apparent. Phnom Penh was slowly developing an educated nucleus of people who might, rather loosely, be described as forming a Cambodian intelligentsia. This was a development that came much later than in neighbouring Vietnam. Those who made up this small group were the product of the secondary education system introduced after the First World War in the form of the Collège Sisowath, which was transformed into the Lycée Sisowath in 1935, together with perhaps a dozen Cambodians who had received a form of tertiary education outside the country and veterans who had served overseas with the French during the First World War. Their numbers were small, reflecting the shameful neglect of public education, particularly above the primary level, throughout the whole period of the French presence in Cambodia.

While the development of secondary education system remained painfully slow, a further factor in the emergence of both a small intelligentsia and a reinforcement of the concept of *khmerité* came with the founding of the Buddhist Institute in 1930. With the Cambodian and Lao kings as patrons, the institute was seen by the French as a necessary vehicle to counteract the readiness of monks from both Cambodia and

The classic colonial architecture of the Lycée Sisowath

Laos to travel to Bangkok for higher religious studies. While it had a substantial measure of success in this aim, the institute also provided a further focus for the still small number of Cambodians—including those who were born in southern Vietnam, *Kampuchea Krom* to use the Cambodian designation—who looked for ways to emphasize a sense of their Cambodian identity.

It was men in this group who provided the readership for the Cambodian-language newspaper *Nagara Vatta* (Angkor Wat). Edited by a veteran who had served in France, Pach Chhuon, it was a publication forever associated with a man who was to become the bitter enemy of Norodom Sihanouk in later years, Son Ngoc Thanh. By the standards of anti-colonial attitudes present in Vietnam, the contents of *Nagara Vatta* were tame indeed and directed essentially against the Vietnamese who had been brought into Cambodia by the French to staff their administration. In no sense did the publication of *Nagara Vatta* and the emergence of a small number of men who later became prominent, either in opposition to French rule, or as later critics of Norodom Sihanouk, lead to any significant change in the essential colonial facts of life as the 1930s came to a close.

Whatever the importance of these early nationalists in subsequent years, their existence at the beginning of the 1940s was overshadowed by other momentous events: Nazi Germany's invasion and defeat of France in the summer of 1940; a brief border war with Thailand in the same year, which led to the loss of the western provinces Cambodia had reclaimed in 1907; the positioning of the Japanese to become the de facto controlling power throughout Indochina by the end of the same year; and the death in April 1941 of King Monivong. Expected by the French to be a devoted supporter of their rule, given his education at a French military academy, this was a role he had largely played until the late 1930s by adopting a disengaged view of his duties. But by the end of that decade his detachment from issues of government became even greater, possibly reflecting a final recognition that he was, after all, no more than an instrument of the French. There are also suggestions that he had a particular problem in his dealings with the head of the French administration at the time, Achille Silvestre. Possibly, too, his withdrawal from public life was a symptom of his advancing age. Whatever the case, he spent more time in his country villa than in the palace, and when

French forces were defeated by the Thais this event put an end to his former feeling of closeness to the colonial power. His death, when it came, appeared to be followed by a master stroke for the French administration, which now expected that it would be ruling in Indochina at the pleasure of the Japanese. Beset as they were by the defeat of France, and fearing for their control of Indochina, the French decided that the next king of Cambodia was to be a shy *lycéen* then studying in Saigon. This was Norodom Sihanouk, a youth of eighteen, who at no stage had had an expectation of succeeding to the Cambodian throne.

At the time of Sihanouk's elevation to the throne, the French made much of the fact that he was chosen because, with his father a member of the Norodom branch of the royal family and his mother from the Sisowath branch, he could be seen as reconciling the tensions between these two branches. There was probably a trace of truth in this rationale, for there was a degree of rivalry between the two branches; the Norodoms were resentful that they had missed out twice from having one of their princes succeed to the throne after Norodom I died. Sihanouk himself referred to his parents' marriage as a "Romeo and Juliet" affair. And, as we have seen, there was a distinct readiness among the most senior French officials in Phnom Penh to develop a preoccupation with the intricacies of royal family politics. But it certainly was not a major consideration, any more than the fact, according to Sihanouk, that part of the reason for his selection resulted from the wife of the Governor General of Indochina, Madame Decoux, finding him *mignon*. He wept when he heard the news of his elevation and neither he, nor anyone else, could have guessed how much the years that followed his coronation would indeed be the Sihanouk years.

Chapter Six

PHNOM PENH BEFORE THE SECOND WORLD WAR: A LITERARY WAY STATION FOR THE ANGKOR TEMPLES

At the end of the 1920s, Albert de Pouvourville, a French writer long associated with Indochina, estimated that from the time France established a colonial presence in the region in the 1860s his compatriots had published some three thousand books on the countries of Cambodia, Laos and Vietnam, of which about a third were novels. A few years later, and limiting his observations to novels alone, another French writer and scholar, Louis Malleret, bluntly noted that most of the novels that de Pouvourville referred to were virtually unknown in France, with their existence barely guessed at in Indochina itself. These are observations to be kept firmly in mind when it comes to discussing Phnom Penh as a literary subject.

Throughout the entire period that Cambodia was under French control, even in the years after the Second World War, Phnom Penh remained an out-of-the-way location, scarcely known by comparison with the two much larger cities in Vietnam, Hanoi and Saigon. Most writers who did visit Phnom Penh came there only to pause, using it as a brief stopping place before travelling on to the Angkor ruins. Only Luang Prabang and Vientiane, in Laos, were subjects for fewer writers, whether they were novelists, travel writers or resident officials. So it is not surprising that the number of authors who have provided extended descriptions and impressions of Phnom Penh is limited. What is more, during the years of French colonialism Phnom Penh only rarely appeared as a setting in novels by French writers, or indeed writers of other nationalities. Moreover, few other than those written by Roland Meyer and George Groslier, both discussed later, deserve mention in terms of literary merit. These two men were exceptional in having lived in the city they wrote about for sustained periods. The much better known writer, André Malraux, does mention Phnom Penh, briefly, in his novel *La Voie royale*, published 1933, but the essential setting of the book is not the city but a half-imagined, half-realistic version of upcountry Cambodia and Laos.

All but two of the writers mentioned in this chapter were transients, men for the most part, who spent a few days or at best a week in Phnom Penh before travelling on to Angkor. There is, it must be noted, a question mark hanging over the amount of time André Malraux spent in Phnom Penh in 1924. It appears to have been a period of some months, but we have no literary evidence of this extended sojourn.

Typical of many visitors who passed rapidly through Phnom Penh in the period between the two world wars was the French diplomat, aesthete and poet, Paul Claudel. Travelling from Saigon by road in 1925, he reached Phnom Penh one day and left for Angkor the next. Yet he managed in this brief period, as he records in his *Journal*, to call on the king, visit the Silver Pagoda and the National Museum, and meet the French *résident supérieur* and George Groslier. With few exceptions, those who did visit and write about Phnom Penh have largely been forgotten in the modern world despite some having been well known, even famous, in their own time. Sadly their visits produced nothing to match Somerset Maugham's short stories, such as "The Letter" or "The Yellow Streak", no novel of towering importance such as Conrad's *Lord Jim*, and—moving to more recent times—no fictional rendering of social criticism to stand alongside J. G. Farrell's *Singapore Grip*. What does exist, and is treated in another chapter, is a body of reportage dealing with the civil war period from 1970 to 1975, the terrible onset of the Pol Pot regime and its ghastly nature. It is from this period that one unquestionably fine novel has emerged in which Phnom Penh receives extended focus. This is Christopher Koch's 1995 *Highways to a War*.

PIERRE LOTI, SOMERSET MAUGHAM AND OTHER LITERARY TOURISTS

The first extended descriptions of Phnom Penh after its establishment as Cambodian capital in 1866 came from French officials and from travellers, both French and of other nationalities, at a time when Cambodia and Vietnam were slowly opening up to contact with the European world. Thus we owe our descriptions of Phnom Penh in the early years of a colonial presence to men such as Francis Garnier and Louis de Carné, both members of the French Mekong Expedition of 1866-68; to Louis

Delaporte, a member of the same expedition who returned again briefly in 1873 and 1881 to survey temple sites away from the Angkor region; to occasional travellers such as the American Frank Vincent; and to the comments of French officials such as Jean Moura, Auguste Pavie and Etienne Aymonier, all of whom lived for varying periods in Phnom Penh. It was not until the beginning of the twentieth century that we can record a visit to the city by the first recognized literary figure, Louis Marie Julien Viaud, the immensely popular writer, naval officer and member of the French Academy, who wrote under his better known *nom de plume* of Pierre Loti.

At the turn of the century, and although it was still less than fifty years since Phnom Penh had assumed its status as capital and French administrative headquarters, the burst of construction that had taken place in the 1890s meant the city already had the air of a much older colonial settlement. This was a fact that Loti remarked on when he reached Phnom Penh in November 1901 on his way to the temple ruins at Angkor. He arrived at the time of the annual Water Festival, but not even the raucous gaiety of that event served to modify what he saw as Phnom Penh's melancholic character. Writing in his book *Un Pélerin d'Angkor* [An Angkor Pilgrim, 1911], he saw the city as "lost in the interior of the region, possessing neither great ships, nor sailors, nor a liveliness of any kind." The French he met were, he believed, condemned to a life of exile. Visiting the Royal Palace, the newly constructed Silver Pagoda, and encountering royal elephants and members of the court ballet did little to dissipate his ennui. In his characteristic world-weary style, Loti summarized his feelings, observing:

> ...already all we have built in Phnom Penh appears old under the effects of the burning sun; the fine, straight streets we have constructed are devoid of any human presence and overgrown with grass; one could believe that this is one of our old colonies whose charm is found in their desuetude and silence.

Loti's visit to Cambodia was a forerunner of a slow but steady development of tourist interest in Angkor. The return of the western provinces to Cambodian sovereignty in 1907 meant that the temples at Angkor were more readily accessible to visitors, though it seems likely that most of those who travelled to the ruins through Phnom Penh in the years before the First World War were members of the French administration in Indochina who had come either from Vietnam or from their postings in Cambodia itself. In the dry season of 1907 there were no fewer than two hundred visitors to Angkor, a tiny number by comparison with the growing flood of visitors in the present day, but a sudden increase from the years immediately before.

Pausing briefly at Phnom Penh en route to Angkor was to become the standard procedure for tourists. After boarding a ship of the Messageries Fluviales line such as the *Mékong* or the *Jules Rueff* in Saigon or in Mytho (in southern Vietnam), visitors stopped at the Cambodian capital before continuing on to the ruins by boat along the Tonle Sap to the Great Lake itself. Landing on the eastern shore of the lake they then travelled by ox cart to the tiny provincial settlement of Siem Reap and then to a rest house or "bungalow" constructed by the French administration and located near Angkor Wat itself. Travel by road from Phnom Penh to Siem Reap and the Angkor ruins did not become an option until after the First World War. It is suggestive of how little impact Phnom Penh had on many visitors who passed through that in travel books of the 1920s and 1930s it is not uncommon for writers like Claudel to fail to mention it in more than a sentence or two, if at all. The temples at Angkor were what brought travellers to Cambodia. Phnom Penh was, at best, an afterthought.

By the second decade of the twentieth century, and separate from the slow growth of tourist visitors, the two French novelists already mentioned, Meyer and Groslier, had already begun their association with Cambodia. Indeed, Groslier had the distinction of being the first child of French parents to have been born in Cambodia, in 1887. Both were associated with the promotion of the fine arts, Meyer as Director of Fine Arts and Groslier, finally, as Director of the Phnom Penh Museum. This background gave them insights into the country and its capital that were reflected in their novels. Yet until they were reprinted recently, these were extremely difficult to find and they remain untranslated into English. Neither is written in an easily accessible style for anyone but a reader with a solid mastery of the French language.

At one level both Meyer's novel *Saramani, danseuse khmer* [Saramani, Cambodian Dancer, 1919] and Groslier's *Le retour à l'argile* [Return to the Clay, 1928] border on caricatures of the themes so often treated in colonial novels, no matter which nation's colony is the setting of the story. In Meyer's story the protagonist is a Frenchman who falls in love with a court dancer but ultimately chooses to abandon her. In Groslier's the outcome is reversed, with the Frenchman choosing to leave his French wife and "go native". But to judge the novels only in these terms would be unfair. Meyer's association with the royal court while he served in Phnom Penh gave him insights into life in the Royal Palace and its occupants, from the ruler himself down to the young women who danced in the court ballet, and were often the king's concubines. The picture that emerges from his account of the court is far from glamorous. He depicts the last days of Norodom I's reign as replete with conspiracies and betrayals as members of the royal family jockeyed to take advantage of the death of one king and the accession of another. The new king, Sisowath, Meyer portrays as an opium-soaked sensualist—an assessment that undoubtedly has some truth. The palace he describes is dirty and insanitary, with its female occupants wracked with jealousy as they strive for the king's favour, enter into lesbian relationships and live in cramped quarters almost totally lacking in privacy. Even the clothing of the court dancers comes in for criticism, having been worn hundreds of times by different dancers but never washed nor cleaned.

One problem with *Saramani* as a novel is its tendency to offer all of Meyer's knowledge of Cambodia to its reader. The result is overwhelming, with its more than eight hundred pages of text, in the words of a French critic, rather like a river into which the author has indiscriminately tipped his knowledge and impressions of the country in "bucket loads" of detail. Nevertheless, the descriptions Meyer provides of the ceremonies associated with Norodom I's death and cremation, and of festivals such as the Ploughing of the Sacred Furrow and the Water Festival, have real worth as an eyewitness account of palace life at the beginning of the twentieth century. Since the book was sharply critical of Cambodian royalty, it was not until after Norodom Sihanouk was turned out of office in 1970 that, a year later, a Cambodian translation of *Saramani* finally became available in Phnom Penh. Both the French and later the independent Cambodian government considered the picture Meyer provided of the royal family and the palace as far too close to the bone to have widespread circulation.

George Groslier's *Le retour à l'argile* is the best known of the novels he wrote with a Cambodian setting, and one that is set, essentially, in Phnom Penh. Another novel, *La route du plus fort* [The Hardest Road, 1926], has French life in the provinces of Cambodia as its theme, though it does contain some reflections on what life was like for Cambodians in the settlements found on the outskirts of the capital. *Le retour à l'argile* is a less ambitious, much shorter work than Meyer's. It traces the slow absorption of Claude Rollin, an engineer sent to Cambodia to build a bridge, into the country's indigenous society as he responds with growing warmth to its ambience, and finally to a Cambodian woman who becomes his mistress. This is the "return to the clay", an abandonment of the falsities and vanities of the western world, as Claude comes to see them. The Phnom Penh in which this story takes place is largely the city of the Cambodians, of bamboo huts and boats on the Tonle Sap, rather than that of colonial society. It is portrayed with sympathy by Groslier in contrast to what he had written fourteen years earlier, in his first non-fiction book about Cambodia. Then, in *A l'Ombre d'Angkor*, he had stated that he had no wish to write about Phnom Penh, which "offered so little of interest" by comparison with the country's ancient temples. This novel is a testimony to his change of outlook.

By the 1920s the Angkor temple complex was attracting visitors in increasing numbers, among them Somerset Maugham. In contrast to most visitors, who travelled up the Mekong from Saigon, he reached Phnom Penh after boarding a boat in Bangkok, landing at Kep on Cambodia's southern coast and finally travelling by road to the capital. He recorded his 1922 visit in his travel book *The Gentleman in the Parlour*, which was not published until 1930. Phnom Penh, he wrote, was "a hybrid town built by the French and inhabited by the Chinese; it has broad streets with arcades in which are Chinese shops, formal gardens and, facing the river a quay neatly planted with trees like the quay in a French riverside town." He found his hotel "large, dirty and pretentious", while the Royal Palace afforded him the opportunity to amuse himself "with sundry reflections upon the trappings of royalty, the passing of empire, and the deplorable tastes in art of crowned heads." But, as noted at the beginning of this chapter, and unlike the Malay world or the Pacific, Cambodia was never to become part of Maugham's stock in trade. Nevertheless, he obviously found the Angkor temples interesting enough to make a return visit many years later, in 1959, at the age of eighty-five. Enjoying his role as a "grand old man" of literature as he paused in Phnom Penh at the end of that visit, I heard him deliver the observation that: "No one should die before they see Angkor."

Yet if Maugham's comments at the time of his first visit seem to share much with Pierre Loti's reserved reactions, he was unqualifiedly admiring of some of the sculpture he saw in today's National Museum, then known as the Musée Albert Sarraut. It had been inaugurated in 1920, only a little before he came to Phnom Penh. In the museum, he wrote, a visitor would see:

> among much that is dull and commonplace, examples of a school of sculpture that will give him a good deal to think about. He will see at least one statue that is as beautiful as anything the Mayans or the archaic Greeks ever wrought from stone. But if, like me, he is a person of slow perceptions, it will not for some time occur to him that here, unexpectedly, he has seen come upon something that will for the rest of his life enrich his soul.

While it is not possible to be sure, since he does not identify the "examples" in any more detail, it is difficult not to think that Maugham was referring to the pre-Angkorian statues in the museum such as the sixth-century Vishnu from Prey Veng (sculpture no.1597) and the Rama from Phnom Da (no.1638), both slim, almost androgynous representations of male divinities.

By the time Somerset Maugham visited there was still only limited hotel accommodation in the city. As early as 1881 an enterprising French couple had set up a bar and hotel which, after they sold it to a new owner, enjoyed a period of passing prosperity during the 1885-86 rebellion as French troops became a source of eager custom. There continued to be hotel accommodation of varying quality in the years that followed, mostly situated in or close to what is today the post office square. (It is noteworthy that Loti returned to sleep on board the vessel that brought him to Phnom Penh.) Yet Maugham's critical comments on the hotel he occupied in 1922 were not echoed by an American visitor, Harry Foster, who arrived at much the same time, recording his experiences in *A Beachcomber in the Orient* (1923). He found that there was only one hotel in the city, the Grand Hôtel de Madame Duguet. The hotel was large and comfortable, he recalled, but he did grumble that it was expensive. Perhaps as a comment on the honesty of some of the previous guests, Foster found that he had to pay his bill in advance. Complaints about the prices of accommodation in Phnom Penh are scattered through the accounts of visitors in the interwar period. Writing of his visit in 1925 in his book *East of Siam* (1926), Harry A. Franck, an American traveller, observed that his hotel could have been in Paris both in terms of its physical appearance, and not least because of the "tourist prices" it charged.

ANDRÉ MALRAUX

Of all the literary visitors who came to Phnom Penh in the 1920s and 1930s, none was to have a more notorious association with Cambodia than André Malraux, the writer, French Resistance fighter and Gaullist Minister of Culture in the 1960s. Already something of an *enfant terrible* in the hothouse artistic world of Paris, Malraux in 1923 was still only twenty-two, married and short of money. As he contemplated his future, he saw an opportunity to be seized in Cambodia's temple ruins. We do not know if he had read Pierre Loti's meditations on Angkor, though given their popularity in France it is possible he had. But he undoubtedly did have a genuine interest in Asian art, probably developed through his association with a renowned German dealer and scholar, Alfred Salmony. What we do know is that he had read an account, by an eminent French scholar, Henri Parmentier, of the recent discovery of a small, previously unknown temple distinguished by particularly delicate carving. This was the temple of Banteay Srei, located some twelve miles from Angkor Wat and the main temple complex.

With the pressing need to improve his finances, Malraux concluded that a great deal of money could be made by removing sculpture from the Angkor temple complex and shipping it to New York, where it would sell for high prices. Matching action to inspiration he sailed for Indochina in 1923, with his wife Clara and friend Louis Chavasson. After a brief visit to Vietnam, they passed through Phnom Penh on their way to steal statuary from the temple of Banteay Srei. Once in Siem Reap they set off to go about their nefarious task in early December 1923. Reaching Banteay Srei, and with the assistance of Cambodian workmen, they cut statuary from the temple using stone saws, in exactly the same fashion that Malraux describes in *La Voie royale*. This done, with some difficulty, and clearly aware that they were acting outside the law, they packed the stolen material in wooden cases falsely marked as "chemical products", loaded them on a vessel on the Great Lake and consigned them to Saigon. But unknown to Malraux and his companions, their activity had been observed and when they reached Phnom Penh, on Christmas Eve 1923 Malraux and Chavasson were arrested by the colonial authorities and the items they had stolen were impounded.

The detailed story of this affair was only told for the first time in 1966, and by an American writer, Walter Langlois, rather than a French author, in his book, *André Malraux: the Indochinese Adventure*. After their arrest Malraux and Chavasson appear to have spent some seven months in Phnom Penh, allowed to move about but forbidden to leave the city as they waited to come to trial. The trial and their conviction surely played their part in Malraux's short and disdainful reference to Phnom Penh in *La Voie royale*, the book born of his attempted theft. His protagonist, Claude, uses the image of a blind man in Phnom Penh singing the story of the Indian epic, the *Ramayana*, as he accompanies himself on "a primitive guitar" to describe Cambodia. "What better personification of Cambodia, of this land of decay, could he have found," Malraux writes, "than that old singer whose heroic strains had ceased to interest any but the beggars and coolie-women squatting around him?"

Malraux's trial in July 1924, remains a controversial affair, with his conviction and three-year jail sentence (and the requirement to return the stolen sculpture to the state) seen by his admirers as the reaction of a mean-spirited and philistine colonial administration. It was, they argued, an attack by officials who could not come to terms with a talented young man who had already cut a swathe through Paris' literary circles. There was no doubt that he had taken important sculptures from the temple of Banteay Srei in Angkor without permission, but was this really theft since the temple from which they had been taken had not yet been gazetted as property of the state? Ultimately, in the eyes of his supporters in Paris, the question of his guilt or innocence did not really rest on the technical issue of whether he was breaking the law but rather on the "right" of someone with Malraux's talents to be above the law. As Malraux and Chavasson appealed against their sentences, famous cultural figures in France, many of whom had never met Malraux but led by André Gide, circulated a petition calling for his release. It had an effect, as I found when looking through material in the Phnom Penh archives in 1966. For there, in an official letter book, as a tribute to French culture, if not necessarily to French justice, support from the *métropole* was enough for a functionary in Phnom Penh to scrawl across official correspondence in 1924 that his colleagues "should take care," as the matter had "become a political affair."

Despite detailed reporting in the Indochinese press of the trial itself we know next to nothing of how Malraux filled his time in Phnom Penh before he came to court and was convicted—Malraux to three years and Chavasson to eighteen months in jail. Nor do we know much of his activities in Saigon, where he moved for the next stage of the case and where his appeal was heard in October 1924. When the appeals court handed down its judgment, Malraux and Chavasson both had their sentences reduced, but they were still facing the prospect of a year and eight months in prison respectively, and their claim to ownership of the sculptures they had taken from Banteay Srei was again rejected. Undaunted, they announced that they would appeal to the Cour de Cassation in Paris, the ultimate court of appeal in France. To this end Malraux left Saigon for France on the *Chantilly* in early November 1924.

From this point on the legal record becomes murky and the best evidence is that Malraux's appeal was never heard. Certainly, the sentences handed down against him and Chavasson were never enforced. What is apparent is that Malraux had become convinced during his time in both Phnom Penh and Saigon that the whole colonial administration in Indochina was corrupt, more concerned to advance the interests of the French and the French state than those of the inhabitants of the countries that made up the political union. By the time he left Saigon for France he had agreed to become involved in the establishment of a newspaper to be published in Saigon that would promote the interests of the colonized peoples of Indochina. Walter Langlois, the biographer of Malraux's "Indochina Adventure" offers as detailed a picture as possible of the course of events that took place and of the individuals who worked with Malraux to found the newspaper *Indochine* (later to be known as *Indochine Enchaînée*) in Saigon, and these details are of interest for anyone concerned with Malraux's career as a whole. They are also relevant for the study of colonial politics in Cochinchina, the designation given by the French to the southern section of Vietnam that, in contrast to the central and northern parts of the country, was administered as a directly ruled French colony. Of more immediate interest for a book dealing with Phnom Penh is the role Malraux played in another court case in Cambodia, the trial of a group of Cambodians arrested and charged with murder following the assassination of the French official, Louis Bardez, in 1925, an event already mentioned in Chapter Five.

It appears that Malraux attended the trial of those accused of killing Bardez in Phnom Penh, although it is not certain that he was present throughout its course, possibly writing some of his reports from Saigon. Whatever the case, his important contribution was the series of articles, in turn bitingly satirical or deeply ironic, that he wrote about the trial. These highlighted the extent to which the French administration stopped at nothing, from physical abuse of the defendants to a disregard for legal procedures, in order to achieve its verdict, which involved one man being sentenced to death and others to terms of imprisonment. Quoting from an article by Malraux in the *Indochine Enchainée* newspaper, Langlois records how he summarized the way the case had been handled with the observations that the following principles had been followed during the trial:

1. Every defendant will have his head cut off.
2. Then he will be defended by a lawyer.
3. The lawyer will have his head cut off.
4. And so on.

For all Malraux's arrogance and self-promotion, there is no reason to doubt the strength of his feeling about the injustices he observed and commented on while he was in Indochina. Whether he deserves to be categorized, in Langlois' words, as a man "transformed by his time in Phnom Penh and Saigon into a deeply committed anti-authoritarian agitator" is open to question, as are some of his own accounts of the life he led in Asia and later in Europe. But of all the well-known literary figures to have visited Phnom Penh before the Second World War Malraux, without question, was the one who moved beyond observation to an effort to change the system. And the attitudes he showed towards the colonial system in Indochina as a whole were to permeate much of his writing in the 1930s, particularly so in the novel set in China, for which he best remembered, *La Condition humaine* (1933).

BROUGHT TO BOOK

Few among the writers who left a record of their visits had much to say of Phnom Penh that was admiring. They may not have sneered at the city as Malraux did in *La Voie royale*, but it seldom received more than a few passing words, and these were often dismissive, if not outwardly critical. But there were exceptions to this way of looking at the city. The prolific American author Sydney Greenbie, who like others mentioned in this chapter is almost totally forgotten, visited Phnom Penh in 1929 and wrote warmly in his book, *The Romantic East*, of the bustle and energy of the shops along the Tonle Sap waterfront, where a visitor "can get anyone to do anything for you, from making a pin to order to rearing a fantastic pagoda." And his enthusiasm did not stop there as he lauded the museum and described the Royal Palace as a place to be regarded "with awe and reverence".

The once immensely popular French novelist, Pierre Billotey, came to Phnom Penh in 1928, having travelled over much of Vietnam and Laos before he reached the city, where he paused before going on to visit the Angkor ruins. He, too, in his book, *Indochine en zigzags* (1929), records finding a lively place, though in contrast to Loti's view, and writing nearly thirty years later, he was struck by the fact that, apart from the *phnom*, nothing of Phnom Penh was "old". With introductions to the French administration he was able to participate in King Monivong's fifty-second birthday celebrations at the Royal Palace. It was a set of buildings reminding him of what a visitor saw at one of the "universal exhibitions" that were popular in Europe in the early decades of the twentieth century. He almost certainly had in mind the Colonial Exposition held in Marseille in 1922, which had featured a huge model of Angkor Wat to house the exhibits brought from all the countries of Indochina. He found too much in the palace was built in cement and reinforced concrete. But most of all he deplored the "gaudy" paintings decorating the walls of the throne hall, the product of some "French artists' salon". These are the renderings of the Hindu epics, such as the *Ramayana*, still to be seen in the throne hall today by those who are permitted to enter it. And they were, indeed, executed by French rather than Cambodian artists.

A scene from the *Ramayana* murals in the cloisters of the "Silver Pagoda"

Proudly French, but clearly one with the firm outlook of a "republican", Billotey saw the absurdity enshrined in a representative of the French state participating in the king's birthday celebrations and offering a congratulatory address to Sisowath in terms that had long been banished in France itself. "Just imagine," he wrote, "how strange it was to hear the king addressed as 'your majesty' and 'sire' by a Frenchman." He had, with a novelist's perception, picked up the curious reverse acculturation that had led to French officials readily becoming part of the Cambodian king's court. But he was unreserved in his admiration for the dancers of the court ballet and praised the role that George Groslier was playing in rejuvenating Cambodian arts of all kinds. It was Billotey who quoted another of Groslier's pessimistic views of Cambodians: "An excellent people, but immensely tired. They are too old a people. They have suffered too much…"

Guy de Pourtalès, whose solitary occupancy of the newly opened Hôtel le Royal has already been mentioned, also heard Groslier's assessment of Cambodians when he reached Phnom Penh in 1930. More than that, he went out of his way to meet the distinguished linguist and scholar of Buddhism, Suzanne Karpalès, and recorded his admiration for her understanding of Cambodian culture. It was scholars and artists such as Karpalès, Groslier and the *conservateur* of Angkor, Victor Goloubew, he judged, who best served French interests, rather than members of the French administration. These latter, he observed, "tended to create a barbed defensive zone around themselves." Unlike Billotey he found much in Phnom Penh that was pleasing. It was "a modest capital that suited this pastoral country. It pleased me as much as I disliked Saigon. It was a city of avenues, of gardens and flowers." The account he provides of his regulation tour of the palace compound is largely factual in tone, and interesting for his detailed remarks on the members of the royal ballet, including yet another reference to the way in which their isolation led to the dancers forming passionate lesbian relationships. Entertained at the Protectorate's *résidence*, he found the assembled officials uncomfortably dressed in their "monkey jackets", while the most at ease was the Bishop of Phnom Penh in his purple soutane.

Whatever sympathy Pourtalès displayed in his account of the city, it was an American travel writer, Robert J. Casey, who visiting at same time as Billotey put his finger on a characteristic of Phnom Penh that still strikes many visitors today. In his book, *Four Faces of Siva: the Detective Story of a Vanished Race* (1929), Casey observes that there "is a fascination about Phnom Penh that one does not realise from descriptions of it given by casual travellers in the days when the Messageries Fluviales boats were the only transport to the North [to Angkor]. It is a town of wide, well-shaded streets with a Royal Palace, a pretty park, and a vast and pictureful array of markets." But these alone are not what set Phnom Penh apart from other Asian cities, in Casey's eyes. It is the fact that it is "part of the country". In short, in Phnom Penh a visitor was aware of being in Cambodia.

It is an interesting observation that Casey develops in some detail. He does not deny the presence of the French and of their buildings, and he appears to take too little account of the Chinese and Vietnamese elements in the population. Certainly, he does not suggest that the Cambodian king can act other than with the approval of the colonial administration. Rather, he paints a picture, perhaps overly romantic in tone but still evocative to the present day, of a city in which daily life is marked by the vigorous presence of Cambodians. They are there in the streets and in the markets, and as Buddhist monks "trailing the flame of their yellow robes through the twilight of the shaded streets." This latter image can still be captured today when the visitor sees a group of Buddhist monks walk through the shadows cast by the tall tamarind trees of Street 240.

When night falls, Casey continues, the visitor listens to "the heartbeat of the tomtoms, the plaint of pipes and the weird melody of the bamboo xylophone as the spirit of the Khmers is conjured out of the dead ages by the necromancy of unseen dancers." Overblown though his prose may be, it is a refreshing change from the frequently dismissive comments on Phnom Penh that were common among western visitors in the interwar period. Casey's appreciation of the city reflected the possibility of its being seen in a different and exotically striking way.

If Billotey's assessment of Phnom Penh mixed admiration with criticism, and Casey found much to please him, there was nothing good to say about the city in the eyes of Geoffrey Gorer, the author of *Bali and Angkor* (1936). A British writer and anthropologist, he was a man who received high praise in his time—the 1930s—but is mostly forgotten nowadays despite being described by the *New York Herald Tribune* as the equal as a travel writer of Evelyn Waugh, Osbert Sitwell and Peter Fleming. For Gorer, who arrived in 1935, the *phnom* was "a nasty little wart", while the town was:

> the usual colonial mixture of spacious European quarters, and crowded and filthy native slums; it contains, besides two or three not unpleasant Buddhist temples, the palace of the present emperor, where with considerable ingenuity is combined all that both Europe and Asia can offer of tawdry, gimcrack, flashy and pretentious taste. It is so ghastly that it has a sort of morbid fascination.

Obsessed with drugs, and having experimented with mescaline and hashish himself, Gorer struck an all-too-common note of the superiority assumed by the "white" races of the time in describing Cambodians as an "ugly, dull looking people, diseased and under-nourished, cowed and frightened, drably dressed in dingy black; with Buddha as their god, and opium as their way to Him."

In 1939 Alan Houghton Brodrick came to Phnom Penh. He was a man, like Gorer, with an already well-established reputation as a travel writer, however much he, too, has been forgotten today. His book, *Little Vehicle: Cambodia and Laos*, only finally published in 1948, is distinguished by a degree of seriousness and respect for scholarship going far beyond most of the works that we have seen. Just as importantly, as he wrote in the foreword to the book, it was "clear that never again will any traveller see Indo-China as I was lucky enough to see it on the eve of the last world-war." Brodrick had seen the end of an era, for in Cambodia, as everywhere else in Southeast Asia, the Second World War changed the entire equation of colonial relationships in a fashion that could never again be re-established.

Just how much changed after the Second World War, and how rapidly, is apparent from Brodrick's description of his arrival in Phnom Penh. He writes of how "insensibly you slip into Phnom Penh. There are no grubby suburbs. No ring of misery encircles the place." It contrasted sharply, he observed, with Saigon, a contrast that extended both to the Cambodians in the capital and to the senior French official to whom he had an introduction. The city Brodrick describes is uncrowded, deeply attached to traditional ceremonies and worshipful of its king. In a brief but perceptive passage he notes the manner in which the French have treated the Cambodian monarch in a manner that has enhanced his prestige, whatever his lack of temporal power.

Some of the history he recounts has become outdated, though his retrospective pen portrait of King Norodom I is probably closer to the mark than many offered by French writers. Norodom, Brodrick writes, "was all for wine, women and song-and-dance. He was cunning, parsimonious and an excellent politician." The style of the book, with quotations from Goethe, Descartes and Valéry interspersed through the text, reminds the reader that the prose of the interwar period could be very mannered. Yet much of the picture he presents rings true, as twenty years later it was possible to sense much of the magic that he found in the city. Nor, more than forty years on, has that magic completely disappeared. It is still possible in the quieter quarters of Phnom Penh to recapture the moment Brodrick describes, in almost the same words, and certainly with the same sentiment as Robert J. Casey when, "as dusk falls, the flame of the yellow robes dulls into a blur while the monks stroll back to their monasteries…"

Left to last in this survey of writing that deals with the period before the Second World War is Vannary Imam's *When Elephants Fight: a Memoir*. The author, a member of a family which, unusually, combined Vietnamese and Cambodian ancestry, offers interesting insights into life in both Phnom Penh and the provinces before and after the Second World War. Her concentration is on events rather than on the city itself, but with a grandfather and father who went to high school in Phnom Penh, and with the latter rising to senior status within the Cambodian administration, the book is well worth reading, though its character as a memoir, with seemingly endless family detail, does not always make it easy to digest.

With the onset of the Second World War, Cambodia ceased to be a subject for literary endeavour, or even for thoughtful travel writing or journalistic reportage. With the exception of Norman Lewis' account of Phnom Penh in the early 1950s, discussed later in this book, it is not until after Cambodia attained independence in 1953 that the way again opened for writers to take an interest in this exotic country. Even then, both the country and its capital were largely neglected until the shadow of war began to loom over Cambodia.

Chapter Seven

WATERSHED YEARS, 1939-1953

Writing of the complex events that took place in Cambodia during the Second World War, David Chandler has observed in *A History of Cambodia* that they were "important... but they are difficult to study." What applies to the country as a whole is certainly true for developments in its capital. Much the same may be said of the years following the war and leading up to Cambodia's achievement of independence from France in 1953. To tell the story of these years in detail would be a mistake in a book concerned with Phnom Penh as a city, given all that happened subsequently. Moreover, it is noteworthy that despite the political importance of developments between 1939 and 1953 the cityscape remained essentially unchanged. This was not a period that saw the construction of new buildings or the undertaking of notable infrastructure. On the contrary, it was a time when maintenance of public buildings was at a minimum so that the once-attractive inner city lapsed into prevailing shabbiness.

The war years and their immediate aftermath up to 1953 were a prelude to five decades of change, drama and tragedy. In the years that followed independence, and while Norodom Sihanouk was Cambodia's dominant politician in the 1950s and 1960s, Phnom Penh's cityscape was transformed. But the apparently successful period of Sihanouk's rule was followed by the chaos of the civil war between 1970 and 1975, a time when refugees flooded into the city, doubling its population to perhaps two million. It was this population which suffered the first, terrible decision of the Pol Pot regime as it took power, for as the guns fell silent the bulk of Phnom Penh's inhabitants were herded into the countryside, leaving the total number of those living in the city at about 50,000. The defeat of Pol Pot's forces in 1979 did not end Phnom Penh's tribulations. Not until 1993 did something approaching normality return to the city.

Looking back at the years between 1939 and 1953 two vital observations may be made. First, as was the case throughout Southeast Asia, at the end of the Second World War it was clear that there could be no turning back to the arrangements that had governed life in the 1930s. The French were able to return to an uncertain control of their Indochinese possessions in 1945, but although they were not prepared to admit the fact, they were on borrowed time. And, secondly, once the war had ended the stage was set for Norodom Sihanouk to emerge as Cambodia's dominant leader. These were watershed years, but it was a watershed that must be traversed quickly in this book. In doing so one point must be recognized. From the point of view of an outside observer looking at Phnom Penh before the Second World War, the role of the colonial power tended to overshadow the city's Cambodian element. This was so, even allowing for the importance of the king. Following the war and with the achievement of independence Cambodian figures and issues dominate Phnom Penh's story.

SIHANOUK AND THE VICHY REGIME

By the time of Sihanouk's coronation ceremony in October 1941, the leaders of the French administration in Indochina had well and truly come to terms with the Nazi victory in their homeland and the establishment of the Vichy regime. Indeed, the Governor General of Indochina, Admiral Decoux, was a passionate supporter of the Vichy leader, Marshal Pétain. From the French administration's point of view—and there were few senior officials who did not share Decoux's feelings—Sihanouk was a tool to be used to maintain the fiction that nothing had changed in Indochina. Throughout the period of the Second World War the French administration continued to act as patron for the concept of *khmerité*.

Yet of course there was change, some of it fundamental. This was a fact made clear once the Japanese established a presence in Cambodia, and in particular in Phnom Penh from the beginning of Sihanouk's reign. The coronation parade through the streets of Phnom Penh had all the elements of a traditional event, with Sihanouk in his rich robes passing before the crowds mounted first on a horse and then on an elephant. But by the time the parade took place there were 8,000 Japanese troops in Cambodia, and Cambodian schoolchildren assembled to cheer the new king waved both French flags and pictures of Pétain.

By his own admission to the French journalist Jean Lacouture in the book *L'Indochine vue de Pékin*, Sihanouk was ill-prepared for his new role as king. He was ready to spend much of his time, as he told Lacouture in 1971, in "horse riding, the cinema, the theatre, water skiing, basket ball, without speaking of my amorous adventures." (As regards the latter, he was, as he put it himself, *un chaud lapin*, a term which can be accurately rendered as "randy as a rabbit".) Indeed, between 1941 and 1946 he fathe political sniping and opposition that he encountered from politicians in Phnom Penh.

Perhaps as testimony to his aesthetic instincts, which were a genuine part of his complex personality, shortly after he mounted the throne he acted to clear the Royal Palace of the seemingly innumerable members of the royal family and their servants and retainers who had turned the buildings within the compound into something resembling a vast transit camp. While many years had passed from the time described by Roland Meyer in his novel about the dancer Saramani, we are left with the sense that not much had changed behind the palace walls before Sihanouk came to the throne and acted as he did. This indeed is the impression to be gained from Guy de Pourtalès' account of his visit to the palace recorded in the previous chapter.

Politics did not entirely vanish during the war while Japan exercised its effective control over Cambodia. With Japanese encouragement, the embryonic Cambodian nationalists associated with Son Ngoc Thanh seized on the French administration's arrest of two Buddhist monks, Hem Chieu and Nuon Duong, in 1942 for distributing anti-French pamphlets to mount a demonstration in Phnom Penh. The demonstration ended with a crowd attacking the French administration's headquarters, a notably symbolic event. The demonstration's leaders, Pach Chhoeun and Bunchan Mol, were arrested and imprisoned on the prison island of Con Son off the Vietnamese coast. Son Ngoc Thanh, who did not take part in the demonstration, was taken under the protection of the Japanese and did not return to Cambodia until after March 1945. To use a phrase much beloved of French colonial administrators, "calm returned" to Cambodia, only to be shattered by the Japanese *coup de force* in March 1945 when they seized power from the French throughout Indochina. But brief though this 1942 episode was, it foreshadowed one of the main elements of politics in Cambodia once the country attained independence: the clash between those who supported the king and his conservative advisers and those, exemplified by Son Ngoc Thanh, who wanted to undermine the old order's dominance.

For the moment the true test of just how ready Sihanouk was to play a political role came in March 1945, when the Japanese mounted their *coup de force* and removed the last vestiges of French control throughout Indochina. When this occurred, Sihanouk was unprepared for the role the

the political sniping and opposition that he encountered from politicians in Phnom Penh.

Perhaps as testimony to his aesthetic instincts, which were a genuine part of his complex personality, shortly after he mounted the throne he acted to clear the Royal Palace of the seemingly innumerable members of the royal family and their servants and retainers who had turned the buildings within the compound into something resembling a vast transit camp. While many years had passed from the time described by Roland Meyer in his novel about the dancer Saramani, we are left with the sense that not much had changed behind the palace walls before Sihanouk came to the throne and acted as he did. This indeed is the impression to be gained from Guy de Pourtalès' account of his visit to the palace recorded in the previous chapter.

Politics did not entirely vanish during the war while Japan exercised its effective control over Cambodia. With Japanese encouragement, the embryonic Cambodian nationalists associated with Son Ngoc Thanh seized on the French administration's arrest of two Buddhist monks, Hem Chieu and Nuon Duong, in 1942 for distributing anti-French pamphlets to mount a demonstration in Phnom Penh. The demonstration ended with a crowd attacking the French administration's headquarters, a notably symbolic event. The demonstration's leaders, Pach Chhoeun and Bunchan Mol, were arrested and imprisoned on the prison island of Con Son off the Vietnamese coast. Son Ngoc Thanh, who did not take part in the demonstration, was taken under the protection of the Japanese and did not return to Cambodia until after March 1945. To use a phrase much beloved of French colonial administrators, "calm returned" to Cambodia, only to be shattered by the Japanese *coup de force* in March 1945 when they seized power from the French throughout Indochina. But brief though this 1942 episode was, it foreshadowed one of the main elements of politics in Cambodia once the country attained independence: the clash between those who supported the king and his conservative advisers and those, exemplified by Son Ngoc Thanh, who wanted to undermine the old order's dominance.

For the moment the true test of just how ready Sihanouk was to play a political role came in March 1945, when the Japanese mounted their *coup de force* and removed the last vestiges of French control throughout Indochina. When this occurred, Sihanouk was unprepared for the role the thered three sons and three daughters by three different women. This is not to suggest that Sihanouk's amatory activities mattered much to his subjects. They did not. If anything, they would have applauded his royal potency. But the list he gives of his various activities, amatory or otherwise, confirm that he was not much interested in affairs of state during the wartime years. Certainly, he was ready to take part in the rituals that paid homage to Marshal Pétain. He attended Sunday football matches at the Phnom Penh stadium where, before the match began, the crowd was required to chant the Pétainist slogan, *Maréchal, nous voilà* (Marshal, we are with you). He was excused from actually shouting the slogan, Sihanouk tells us, but he had to stand to attention with the rest of the spectators as the ceremony took place.

With two important exceptions, Sihanouk did what the French asked of him during the war. The first exception related to the administration's demand, instituted at the orders of the Japanese, that Cambodia's peasantry sell all the fish oil and kapok they produced to the government so that it could be exported to Japan. Hearing bitter complaints about these demands as he travelled about the country, Sihanouk took the peasants' protests to the administration, but to no avail. He was equally unsuccessful in his efforts to block French plans to introduce a romanized form of the Cambodian language to replace its traditional script and to substitute the western Gregorian calendar for the traditional calendar. These were changes that the French had been trying to institute for years, and were bitterly opposed by the Buddhist clergy as traditional guardians of Cambodian culture. In the event, Sihanouk's failure to sway the French to his position was overtaken by the end of the war and the defeat of the Japanese, and the changes did not take place.

Yet there was one development during the wartime years that did play a part in Sihanouk's slow emergence as a skilful, if erratic, politician. In another effort by the French to try and prevent their control being even further eroded by the Japanese, Sihanouk was encouraged to travel widely through Cambodia. He was urged to show himself to his people and to make speeches intended to rally the population to their colonial masters. There is good reason to judge that this early experience of dealing with crowds and making speeches served the young king well when he did come to political maturity. He also appears to have been confirmed in his developing conviction that he was loved in the countryside as opposed to

Japanese now wanted him to play, the role of king in an "independent" country. The March 1945 coup was the final act in the script that the Japanese had followed from mid-1941. The French administration had been a hollow presence as Japan turned the screws to demand more and more of the agricultural products grown in the country. With their headquarters near the Phnom Penh post office square, and their contingent of 8,000 troops, the Japanese maintained a parallel security presence in the country, including a detachment of the *kempetai*, the feared equivalent of the German Gestapo.

"INDEPENDENT" CAMBODIA

As the war began to turn clearly against the Nazis in Europe and Japanese forces in Asia and the Pacific, sections of the French administration began to reassess their position. For French officials in Phnom Penh the reality of how misguided their faith in Vichy had been was given sharp emphasis by an allied bombing raid on Phnom Penh's suburbs in February 1945, which killed one hundred Cambodians and wounded several hundred more. No clear reason for this raid has ever been given, though it seems likely that it was intended as a demonstration to the Japanese forces based in the former French Indochinese countries of the capability of allied aircraft to strike at will against the enemy. Well aware of the changing mood among the French, but hiding their hand until the last moment, the Japanese struck in March 1945, overturning the French administration throughout Indochina and interning its officials. Among those taken away at this time under suspicion of a readiness to rally to Gaullist forces was George Groslier. He was taken into custody as a suspected spy because of his hobby as an amateur radio operator. He appears to have been tortured before being executed in June 1945, after which his ashes were returned to his family in a wooden box.

Having overthrown the French administration in a desperate effort to stave off what was increasingly looking like inevitable defeat, the Japanese next oversaw the establishment of "independent" states in Cambodia, Vietnam and Laos. So, on 13 March 1945 and at the behest of the Japanese, King Norodom Sihanouk proclaimed Cambodia's independence. It was an independence that was to last barely six months, until October, when the French began to return to take control of the kingdom once again.

There were clear indications even during this brief period of qualified independence of the political problems that were to dog Cambodia for nearly a decade. Sihanouk's closest advisers were firmly conservative in outlook. They held no brief for parliamentary democracy, any more than he did. Nor were they pleased that Son Ngoc Thanh, who had returned to Phnom Penh from his exile in Japan, sought to gain popular support for a parliamentary system that would undermine the position of the king.

THE FRENCH RETURN

In the event, Cambodia's Japanese-sponsored independence came to abrupt end. Assisted by the British army, the French returned and Son Ngoc Thanh was arrested and ultimately tried and sent into exile. It was to take nearly two years before a shaky parliamentary system was introduced that satisfied neither Sihanouk and his advisers, nor the small band of enthusiasts for something approaching a democratic system of government in which the king would be a constitutional monarch, who reigned rather than ruled.

As for Phnom Penh, it had stagnated during the war, and little was to change in the appearance of the city's centre over the next few years. There are relatively few descriptions of Phnom Penh between 1945 and 1953. Cambodia was by no means completely detached from the war being led by the Viet Minh against the French, but it was a bit player when compared with the savage hostilities taking place in Vietnam. One direct result was that few journalists covered developments in the country. The historian John Tully, in his *France on the Mekong*, quotes two contrasting journalistic views of Phnom Penh in the early post-war years. The first is the description of the city in 1946 by Philippe Devillers, writing for the Parisian daily, *Le Monde*. For Devillers, Phnom Penh was "a modern Oriental town" with a "calm atmosphere", a view that probably reflected the extent to which the city's pervasive somnolence contrasted with the frenetic activity that he had just experienced in Saigon. Writing for *The Scotsman*, three years later, Patrick Donovan had a more sombre view. Phnom Penh, he observed, "once as clean and swept as a French housewife's kitchen is now sinking into dusty oriental squalor."

A similar impression emerges from one of the few extended descriptions of Phnom Penh in the period between the end of the Second World War and Cambodia's independence. This is the account provided by

Norman Lewis, the famed British travel writer in his book *A Dragon Apparent: Travels in Cambodia, Laos, and Vietnam*, which describes Phnom Penh as he saw it in 1952. Much admired for his writing about the Sicilian mafia and towards the end of his long life for his sharply critical commentary on the Indonesian treatment of the indigenous people of Papua, Lewis wrote of Phnom Penh and its inhabitants with a barely concealed degree of racial superiority. This is apparent in his description of Cambodians as a people "who quite clearly didn't care in the slightest how they lived or dressed." The same tone is evident in Lewis' description of the "cast, brazen clamour of Phnom Penh's centre", an area he describes as having been "taken over by the Chinese... a local breed of Chinese, cheerful vulgarians raised in the country, very much to be preferred to the arrogant immigrants from Hong Kong that lord it in Saigon."

As for the Royal Palace, where Lewis went to call on King Sihanouk, it was, he wrote, "pagoda architecture and one feels that if the pinchbeck glitter of the gilding could be subdued it would provide, perhaps, a charming and discreet lakeside ornament." Echoing other, French, visitors to the palace, he remarked that: "We have seen buildings of this kind so often in colonial exhibitions that we have come to associate them with impermanence, and even suspect that may be supplied in sections with simple instructions for erection."

In his short time in Phnom Penh Lewis duly interviewed Sihanouk, who made clear his determination to see an end to the French control of Cambodia. He also followed the well-trodden route of many visitors by visiting Mère Chhum's opium den, curiously written up in his book as "Madame Shum's", attended a Chinese-owned dance hall and witnessed a "procession of the twenty-five spirits". Taking place over two days in the middle of the first lunar month in the Chinese calendar, this last event was usually referred to in the 1950s and 1960s as the "Fête des Génies". The account he provides matches what still could be seen in those later years. It involved individuals from both the city's Chinese and Vietnamese communities parading through the streets of Phnom Penh in a tranced state, some with their faces pierced by lances, others slashing their tongues with swords, while still others sat on chairs of nails.

Throughout, Lewis leaves a world-weary impression that Phnom Penh is a backwater that is most likely to remain just that. He gives no indication that its atmosphere was likely to be transformed by the young king

A Chinese medium parading in the Fête des Génies in 1960

who though thirty years of age, appeared ten years younger as he lectured his visitor on France's many failings, a lecture delivered in perfect French. As Lewis received Sihanouk's lecture the king was steadily moving to neutralize his political enemies while, at the same time, a low intensity war was being fought in the countryside. Through all of the twists and turns of post-war politics in Phnom Penh one theme was abundantly clear. This was Sihanouk's determination to match political ascendancy to his royal status. As he pursued this aim, aided by a loyal group of conservative advisers and associates, governments came and went in Cambodia's embryonic parliamentary system and a few well-known opponents, such as Son Ngoc Thanh, were briefly important. Many others who played a part at this time have been forgotten, not least by Cambodians. The essential fact was that by 1952 Sihanouk had achieved a political ascendancy and for the moment had placed himself in a position from which he could devote all his energies to gaining independence from France. In doing so, he showed himself ready to sanction the use of force against opponents, a harbinger of the ruthless politics that were seldom written about while he was in power, and a certain factor in the savage response that eventually came from his extreme left-wing opponents.

But as he did so, this new war, the war of the French against the various groups fighting for independence throughout Indochina, brought an influx of internal refugees from the countryside to the outskirts of the capital where they established themselves in squalid shanty towns. They were a foretaste of what was to come when, twenty-five years later, Cambodia's own civil war led to a flight of people in their tens of thousands to seek dubious safety in Phnom Penh. Simply stated, there were two groups fighting against the French in Cambodia. There were a small number of men who had linked their fortunes to the much more powerful Vietnamese communists fighting the French in Vietnam, and there were the Khmer Issaraks (Free Khmers), non-communist Cambodians of various political persuasions.

Linked in various ways to the communist cause was a small group of young Cambodians who had studied in France and returned to Phnom Penh. Among them were Saloth Sar, the future Pol Pot, Ieng Sary and Khieu Samphan. Sihanouk's security services were aware of them, as was the king himself, and they were seen as a potential threat to the kingdom. Yet for a variety of reasons these leftists (mostly but not exclusively men) and their associates, who came to power in 1975, survived in succeeding years. Some, such as Pol Pot, did so by going into clandestine exile in the countryside, others, such as Khieu Samphan, by appearing to "play the rules of the game" in Cambodia's parliament, before finally realizing in 1967 that the game had run its course, and that to remain carried the risk of execution. It is important to know that these men existed, and that they were plotting revolution in Phnom Penh more than twenty years before they finally seized power. The history of this group is charted in the pioneering work of Ben Kiernan, *How Pol Pot Came to Power*, and more recently with the biographies of Pol Pot written by David Chandler and Philip Short, plus the work of other less well-known but still important scholars dealing with the Khmer Rouge. Today we are aware of a vital aspect of Cambodia's political life that was most imperfectly understood, if at all, in the 1950s and 1960s.

By the end of 1952, and with Sihanouk having pushed aside the squabbling politicians in Phnom Penh, he was able to claim that he had brought the guerrilla forces in the countryside to heel. Next, and with great panache, he outwitted the French, who were desperate to remove Cambodia as a problem as they struggled with impending defeat in Vietnam, and forced them to concede independence in November 1953. As Sihanouk achieved his goal he revelled in the description of him by the commander of the French forces in Cambodia as "a madman of genius".

With independence successfully achieved, Phnom Penh was poised to experience the most dramatic series of changes that had ever taken place in its existence as the country's modern capital. Cambodia's and Phnom Penh's political new dawn came on 9 November 1953, the day when the transfer of sovereignty took place. The event was marked by a march-past of the French forces during a torrential downpour, with Sihanouk joining the French High Commissioner and the commanding French general on the reviewing stand. It was almost exactly ninety years since France had established a position in Cambodia, and eighty-seven years since Sihanouk's great grandfather had moved his capital from Udong to Phnom Penh.

Chapter Eight

"Sihanouk Time", 1953-1970

In a city in which today seventy per cent of the population is under thirty years of age, and fifty per cent is less than twenty years old, awareness of what life was like in Phnom Penh when Sihanouk was in power is scanty at best, often notably distorted, and for the majority practically non-existent. Not surprisingly, for those city dwellers who are alive today and lived through the period from 1953 to 1970, there is a widespread inclination to think of that time as a "golden age", often referred to simply, when spoken of in English, as "Sihanouk time". There is no expectation that such an age can ever return, but its contrast with what came afterwards make the years before Sihanouk was overthrown a period to be treasured. Like many other imperfectly remembered golden ages, there was, in fact, as much dross as precious metal in the daily lives of Cambodians while Sihanouk dominated political life. Yet despite all these necessary qualifications this was a time, indeed the time, when for a period Cambodia's present and its future prospects seemed bright under a charismatic ruler. Retrospect makes clear that it was also a time when stirrings of opposition to Sihanouk, deep below the apparent surface calm of life, were slowly building to form part of the tragedy that began with Pol Pot's Khmer Rouge forces marching into Phnom Penh in April 1975.

Sihanouk's Formula for Success

Central to this sense of well-being was Sihanouk's success in eliminating the ebb and flow of parliamentary politics. Buoyed by his achievement of independence in 1953, he capitalized on his essentially unassailable position by two masterstrokes. The first was his decision to abdicate the throne in March 1955, so as to engage directly in politics without any limitations that might be imposed upon him as a monarch. Ensuring that his father succeeded him meant that he now entered the domestic political fray with all the prestige of a king while insisting that he was a simple citizen. His second notable decision, taken immediately after his abdication, was to announce the formation of the *Sangkum Reastr Niyum* (People's Socialist Community). It was a mass movement—never a political "party" as Sihanouk repeatedly insisted—designed to incorporate all Cambodians,

supposedly regardless of political sympathies, with the essential requirement that membership involved loyalty to the Cambodian throne and to
Sihanouk's policies. Membership of the Sangkum was reinforced by the
formation of the curiously named Royal Cambodian Socialist Youth (Je-
unesse Socialiste Royale Khmère, JSRK), a body that was a fixture at all
major national functions, its members dressed in a scout-like uniform and
occasionally convoked to do "good works". Membership of the civil service
was pretty well synonymous with membership of the JSRK. Age was no
barrier to membership of this "youth" corps, so that many of its members
were in their forties and even fifties.

The *Sangkum* mass movement did not initially put an end to
factionalism. In the world of open politics there were still men, both on
the right and the left, who were ready to challenge Sihanouk's
determination to rule without constraint. But by 1960, and after
Sihanouk was successful in 1959 in putting down an attempted rebellion
backed by the South Vietnamese government and with peripheral United
States involvement, there appeared to be no remaining challenge to his
rule. What neither he nor any other observers knew was that a small
group of leftists, men and women who had studied in France, had chosen
to go underground rather than risk openly defying the prince and his
powerful security services. Among them was Saloth Sar, the man whom
the world came to know as Pol Pot. Determined to have their own,
Cambodian identity rather than to be linked to the Vietnamese
Communist Party, they met in the railway workshop area behind Phnom
Penh's station in September 1960 to form the Cambodian Communist
Party (the Communist Party of Kampuchea, often cited simply as the
CPK).

Knowledge of the underground left was not to emerge for years, particularly for foreign observers of Cambodia. As for the small number of
Cambodians, whether of the left or the right, who remained in the world
of open politics and chose to make their opposition to Sihanouk known,
life could be dangerous indeed. Largely unknown, or at least disregarded,
by foreigners living in Phnom Penh, was a dark underside to life in the
capital as Sihanouk's security apparatus operated ruthlessly to neutralize the
regime's opponents. On occasion this involved secret assassinations, at
other times imprisonment without trial or beatings carried out with impunity. There can be no doubt that Sihanouk both knew about and sanc-

tioned this activity, however much he sought to give the appearance to the contrary. Only rarely did he become publicly involved in the brutality which was part of his rule. Such was the case in 1963, when at a mass meeting of the Sangkum in Phnom Penh he ordered the death of a right-wing opponent and had the execution filmed to be shown in cinemas throughout the kingdom. Only later, as rebellion spread through the state after 1967, did he abandon any pretence of being divorced from the harsh measures which had long been part of his rule, to the point where he boasted publicly of giving orders for the summary execution of two hundred rebels in 1968.

But until the mid-1960s, and in Phnom Penh no less than in the countryside, Sihanouk appeared to bestride Cambodia as its political colossus. He had seen off challenges from the left and the right. Even the un-expected death of his father in April 1960 only appeared to strengthen his position as a little later he assumed the new position of chief of state. He seemed to have triumphed over threats of all kinds, even those from his hostile neighbours to the west and east, Thailand and Vietnam. Cambodia was at peace and Phnom Penh was a testimony to his success as it experi-enced a building boom such as it had not known since the years before the Second World War.

What is more, with a foreign policy that succeeded for a period in keeping Cambodia at peace while neighbouring Vietnam sank deeper into conflict, Sihanouk was able to claim that his policy of neutrality was both the right and only policy to be followed while at various times his nearest neighbours were his country's bitter enemies. With an ap-parent assurance from China that it would protect Cambodia from the communist Vietnamese and following a series of difficult encounters with American politicians and officials, Sihanouk seemed to have the best of all worlds. He criticized the Americans, but they aided his economy and his army. He said that he did not trust the Soviet Union, but it, too, gave aid to his country. It seemed that only China was free from his acerbic tongue. Often spoken of by outside observers as "mer-curial" and with a foreign policy that was compared to a high wire act, the truth was that Sihanouk's policies could only work so long as a con-stellation of external factors were aligned in his favour. When by the mid-1960s those external factors began to shift sharply he and his country came under threat.

Phnom Penh in its "Golden Age"

What was life like in Phnom Penh during this "golden age" for Cambodians and foreigners, whether Chinese, Vietnamese or Europeans? The question has to be asked in respect of these separate groups, since however much the inhabitants of Phnom Penh intermingled they lived essentially different lives. And it is important to remember that the Chinese and Vietnamese each represented about a third of the city's population in the 1960s.

Cambodians in Phnom Penh found their lives dominated by Sihanouk. The elite, and in particular those who served in his revolving door cabinets and in the upper levels of the administration, lived at Sihanouk's beck and call. They could be summoned to his residence at any hour, required to accompany him both within the country and abroad, and in the last years of the 1960s prevailed upon to take part in his self-proclaimed "feature-length films". Membership of the elite provided a passport to the many and often complex opportunities for corruption. It was not just that the elite owned the buildings that could be rented out to foreign residents at prices that often matched or surpassed those to be found in the western world. To be an elite figure was to be able to skim a percentage off government contracts, and to receive sweeteners from less elevated figures, particularly from Chinese businessmen who provided the capital and skills to keep the Cambodian economy turning over.

Membership of the Cambodian elite meant, almost axiomatically, to have had some French education, whether in Cambodia itself or in France. If there were rare exceptions among adults in this group, there were almost none among their children. Overall, they lived well, at a level even their middle-class compatriots could not imagine aspiring to, let alone Phnom Penh's poor. Their families often had villas at Kep, on the sea coast, and they would journey there in their chauffeur-driven cars. Few had much interest in Cambodia's history, with a princely member of this group once observing to me that he had been to see the great temple ruins at Angkor once and felt no pressing need to visit them again. The young men of the elite patronized the *dancings*, ate and drank at the wide range of restaurants and bars available in Phnom Penh, and seldom thought of a future that was other than linked to living in the city. The exceptions to this rule were those who had joined the military or the upper ranks of the civil service, which meant they would have to serve away from Phnom Penh during parts of their career. Their female counterparts had fewer choices. Many saw their life as destined to involve being married and raising children. Only occasionally did they make choices that led to careers.

Within Phnom Penh's elite, while Sihanouk was still a dominant figure, the royal family was a large, sprawling element, and one that Sihanouk never quite trusted. Even though Cambodia had a system, similar to that in Thailand, whereby the titles and status of royalty diminished in importance with the passage of generations, there were still dozens of princes and princesses living in Phnom Penh in the 1960s. And whatever their actual status, in theory all princes who were descended from King Ang Duang, who died in 1860, had a theoretical right to succeed to the throne. In reality only a small number would ever have been considered, and in any event Sihanouk's assumption of the position of chief of state put paid to the possibility of succession for anyone, though he did nominate one of his sons as his eventual successor. Some princes held important positions in government or were linked to commercial operations. Others had no employment but held honorary positions, such as was the case with one of Sihanouk's aunts who was head of the Cambodian Red Cross, an appointment which ensured that she never lacked for funds.

The Cambodian middle class, a loosely defined group that included mid-level members of the civil and military administrations, teachers, and a relatively small number of businessmen, had limited immediate contact with Sihanouk, but the effect he had on their lives was profound. They paraded when asked to do so, attended the national congresses of the Sangkum, which passed for a form of participatory democracy, and hoped that their position would give them some access to the pervasive web of minor corruption that was essential for a reasonable standard of living.

Then, below the roughly defined middle class, there were the city's poor. Just what proportion of Phnom Penh's population they represented is difficult to know. European foreigners had little awareness of them, except when they took a ride in a *cyclopousse*. Overall they were an almost invisible mass, living well away from the city centre in shanty towns, eking out a living in various forms of manual labour.

Cambodians of all economic and social groups flocked to observe or take part in the great public festivals that marked the Cambodian calendar: *Chaul Chnam* (New Year, falling in April) an occasion feverish gambling; *Chat Preah Nengkal* (the Ploughing of the Sacred Furrow, in May), *Bon*

Oum Tuk (the Water Festival that marks the end of the rainy season and the reversal of the Tonle Sap's flow from the Great Lake). All also observed the more private religious ceremonies of the Buddhist calendar, such as *Pchum Ben*, a festival falling in October when Cambodians honour their ancestors.

Among the foreigners resident in Phnom Penh the most visible and important group were Chinese. They were businessmen first and foremost, with links throughout Cambodia and to the Chinese diaspora beyond, particularly to the great Chinese trading centre in Cholon, Saigon's twin city in southern Vietnam. The rice trade was in their hands. They controlled the purchase and export of the high-grade pepper grown around Kampot on the Cambodian coast and monopolized the salt trade from the same region. The buses that travelled the length and breadth of Cambodia were owned by Chinese, as were the *cyclopousses* on Phnom Penh's streets. Poor Cambodians rode these distinctive vehicles, but they rented them from Chinese entrepreneurs. Chinese were restaurateurs, shopkeepers, traditional doctors, dentists and pharmacists, barbers and cinema owners. If there was a commercial opportunity they seized it. Not all were successful, and there were Chinese coolies working on the Phnom Penh docks alongside Cambodians. But with their commitment to education as a key to advancement and their embrace of an entrepreneurial work ethic seldom shared by Cambodians, the Chinese population of Phnom Penh provided the commercial drive for Cambodia's capital city. Important, too, was the fact that intermarriage between Chinese and Cambodians was quite common. Indeed, there were few leading Cambodian families that did not have some measure of Chinese ancestry. Only in a few and particular areas of commerce were the Chinese unable to make their mark. Banking was in the hands of French and British firms. Until 1963, when Sihanouk nationalized the import-export trade, European agency houses controlled key import commodities. The rubber plantations were still dominated by the French, a situation preserved by the technical expertise they were able to provide.

If Phnom Penh's Chinese community made its vibrant presence felt without apology, the same was not true for the resident Vietnamese. They were seen by Cambodians as foreigners of a different kind. Although marriage between Cambodians and Vietnamese was not unknown, it was uncommon. A substantial number of the Vietnamese living in Phnom Penh were Roman Catholics, in contrast to the small number of Cambodians who had embraced this western religion. During the untroubled years of Sihanouk's Cambodia, the Vietnamese occupied a minor place in the pecking order of Phnom Penh's commerce. They were tailors, shoemakers and bookshop owners, the latter selling material sympathetic to the Vietnamese communist cause. Vietnamese were clerks in banks and foreign businesses, maintaining relationships established before Cambodia's independence. A few found employment as clearance agents for imports and exports, but many more worked as domestic servants in the households of Europeans. They were an introverted community, apprehensive that Cambodians' ethnic hostility towards them might boil over into violence, as it finally did in 1970.

There were other identifiable minority communities. Indian cloth traders who doubled as moneylenders worked in the shops that ringed the main market, the Psar Thmei. But they were few in number. Then there were the Chams, followers of Islam, a sizeable group, most of whom lived on the northern outskirts, and who in the 1960s were little affected by Middle Eastern cultural movements—a situation that was to change markedly in the period after 1979. Many of this group were less than fully observant, mixing a basic commitment to Islam with rituals that paid as much attention to local traditions.

Most visible of all the foreigners were the French. At the beginning of the 1960s they may have numbered almost 6,000, though their participation in almost every facet of Cambodian life made their community seem larger. Acutely aware of Sihanouk's likes and dislikes, they drew on their previous experience as the colonial power to do all that they could to preserve their interests. In this they had the benefit of Sihanouk's genuine affection for much that was French—for aspects of French culture instilled during his education, for French food and wine, and most importantly for the independent foreign policies pursued by Charles de Gaulle, whom Sihanouk looked to as a father figure.

In Phnom Penh the French seemed to be everywhere, their presence symbolized by the fact that Sihanouk's doctor was a French army colonel, Colonel Riche. The French trained the Cambodian military and taught in the Lycée Descartes, where elite Cambodians sent their children. Some of the teachers at this school were on short-term contracts, but others had made Phnom Penh their home, as was the case with Mademoiselle Carrère who, always dressed in white with a mantilla and took her evening *apéritif* at the Hôtel le Royal. In the world of commerce Frenchmen presided over the Phnom Penh headquarters of the great rubber plantations. They occupied positions of great importance to Cambodia's cultural life, even if the true degree of interest in institutions such as the National Museum on the part of the Cambodian elite was limited indeed. No matter, the museum's director was a Frenchwoman, Madeleine Giteau, while the head of conservation at Angkor was Bernard-Philippe Groslier, son of George Groslier. Then there were the well-known "old hands" who were unprepared to sever their links with an *Indochine* that no longer existed, men such as Jean of the Bar Jean and Monsieur Mignon of La Taverne. By far the best known of these was Dr. Paul Grauwin, the famed "doctor of Dien Bien Phu", the soldier-surgeon who had gone on working in appalling conditions until the ill-fated French garrison was overwhelmed by the Vietminh forces in May 1954. Distrusting French governments of every stripe, he chose to end his working days in Phnom Penh, where he was much in demand for his expertise in treating venereal diseases. His dislike for metropolitan France and its politicians meant that when General de Gaulle visited Phnom Penh in 1966 Grauwin was required to exile himself from the capital.

There was yet another identifiable group of Frenchmen, those who worked for Sihanouk as speechwriters and journalists, positions that in a few cases carried with them the rather uncertain status of being an "adviser" to the prince. The most prominent was a somewhat sinister figure, Charles Meyer, whose past had included working for a ruthless group of gangsters in Saigon, the Binh Xuyen, in the early 1950s. After he moved to Phnom Penh following France's departure from Vietnam, he was almost certainly in the pay of two foreign intelligence services, the French and the Chinese. A skilled cartographer with a serious interest in Cambodia's history, Meyer had a justified claim to be an "intellectual". He worked for and with Sihanouk in the latter's various publishing ventures, but just how much influence he had on the prince remains a matter of debate. Other Frenchmen oversaw the publication of the weekly semi-official *Réalités Cambodgiennes* and the daily news bulletin of the Agence Khmère de Presse (AKP). The latter was the one publication that had the status as a document of official record. No matter what Sihanouk said in his endless round of lengthy speeches, if the approved text did not appear in the AKP it did not exist. The benefits of such an arrangement were obvious, permitting Sihanouk to denounce all and sundry, both foreign and domestic governments and individuals, but not to take responsibility for what he said. In a government world which in many ways resembled a royal court, it was Sihanouk's French journalists who not only ghost-wrote his letters but also penned remarkable panegyrics, such as the description of him as "the man whom heavenly wisdom has provided at the appropriate time so that Cambodia may travel forward in order and peace to the destiny reserved for it."

Then, until 1963, the year when Sihanouk stated that he would no longer accept aid from the United States, there was a large American community in Phnom Penh. Given the size of this community, they were a less than obvious foreign element. Cosseted by the existence of their own commissary and with personnel who were often monolingual, many tended to socialize with each other. This said, there were some among the Americans who were as well informed as any other foreigner and spoke Cambodian better than most. But apparent to Cambodians and others or not, the American presence in Phnom Penh drove much of the city's economy until the rejection of aid in 1963 and the break in diplomatic relations two years later. From 1965 to 1969 there was no official American presence in the city, a fact that contributed greatly to the economic decline that set in from 1965 onwards.

Where, out of office hours, were foreigners to be found in the "good" years? If they were inclined to sporting activities these could be accessed at the Cercle Sportif, located in the area now occupied by the American Embassy. Here there was a swimming pool and tennis courts as well a small club house. For sailing and boating there was the Société Nautique at the confluence of the Mekong and the Tonle Sap, with a club building that no longer exists. But the chief diversion for foreigners posted to Phnom Penh was eating at one of the many restaurants, with first-class European and Chinese cuisine available. At the lower end of the price range there were also good Vietnamese restaurants. The only cuisine that seemed to be lacking, at least to foreigners, was that of the country itself, unless one chose to eat at one of the ubiquitous food stalls that less prosperous Cambodians patronized.

BUILDING BOOM

During the years following independence and particularly before the mid-1960s, Phnom Penh witnessed a sudden surge in construction. This reflected both the long period of neglect that had persisted since the 1930s and the need to provide a range of buildings for an independent state where none had existed previously. Moreover, it was only with independence that a programme of building was undertaken to deal with the increase in the size of the urban population, which had been growing steadily since the end of the Second World War. All of these factors combined to mean that the area of Phnom Penh doubled between 1953 and the late 1960s.

In 1953 there were no qualified Cambodian architects working in Phnom Penh, but soon afterwards a small number returned from training in France. By far the best known of these was Vann Molyvann, but mention should also be made of Lu Ban Hap, Mam Sophan and Ung Krapum. In Van Molyvann's own words, what he and a number of his colleagues sought to achieve in their buildings was "the modern movement adapted to the Khmer context". In particular, this awareness of the "modern movement" paid homage to Le Corbusier. What this meant was exemplified in four major constructions designed by Vann Molyvann: the national sports stadium, the Preah Suramarit National Theatre, now existing only in a ruined form, the Chatomuk Conference Hall, and the Royal University buildings beside the Pochentong Road. Wherever possible the architect sought to incorporate the use of water that echoed the great reservoirs of the Angkor complex in his designs. He also designed roofs that alluded to traditional construction, as he did with the National Theatre and the conference hall. In the case of the university buildings, there was a reference to traditional Cambodian domestic architecture, with the buildings raised on stilts, while space was left to accommodate water so mimicking the moats of Angkor's temples while providing protection against flooding during the wet season.

Sadly, as a reflection of a lack of satisfactory urban planning plus the presence of commercial greed, none of these projects can be seen as they were designed, with the exception of the conference hall. The theatre burned down in 1996 and has never been reconstructed. The national stadium is increasingly boxed in by shoddy commercial developments, and the water features around the university buildings are being filled in. But nowhere is the sad fate of the innovative architecture of the post-independence period clearer than in relation to the apartment buildings constructed to the south of the centre of the city, beyond the Sihanouk

Boulevard, and along the Bassac river. These buildings, constructed as "machines for living", have now fallen into terrible disrepair and have become noisome squatter camps. Since this area is slated to be developed as a diplomatic quarter, it seems inconceivable that these dilapidated buildings will not be razed. The fact that they are occupied by large numbers of squatters is unlikely to inhibit the government from acting.

The Independence Monument, sited at the intersection of the Norodom and Sihanouk Boulevards, is another product of the post-independence period. In style it is a conscious evocation of the great temples at Angkor, and so yet another example of Sihanouk's efforts to suggest an unbroken link with the period of Angkorian grandeur. Nevertheless it was constructed, its architect Vann Molyvann, has said, with dimensions that drew on modulars established by Le Corbusier.

Many other buildings from this period can be seen in contemporary Phnom Penh. These include sections of the Pochentong airport, now considerably remodelled, the Russian Hospital and the Council of Government building. The large Cambodiana Hotel was begun in the final years of Sihanouk's rule but not completed until the beginning of the 1990s.

A "Fairy Tale" Kingdom

If there was some reality in the idea that Sihanouk's rule was a golden age, even the most generous commentator would have to acknowledge that Cambodia's image as an "oasis of peace" (Sihanouk's phrase) or a "fairy tale kingdom" (the words of his French publicists) was beginning to come under both domestic and external pressure by the mid-1960s. To some extent this was not Sihanouk's fault. Despite his sometimes erratic foreign policy, he had kept Cambodia out of the Vietnam War, but as the pace of that war began to accelerate, preventing Cambodia from becoming involved was becoming more and more difficult. Convinced that ultimately the Vietnamese communists were going to win—though he feared this possibility—Sihanouk slowly but significantly began to make gestures towards the communists that made his claims to neutrality much less believable. As he did so, his domestic situation was affected by economic decline following his renunciation of American aid in 1963, a decision taken in the belief that Washington was seeking to undermine the Cambodian state.

The end result of these decisions was a notable decline in the support, whether active or passive, that he received from the Phnom Penh elite and the city's middle class. For the truly wealthy there was no longer a pool of wealthy Americans ready to rent property. Nationalization of the economy following the cutting off of American aid did not eliminate corruption, but it did limit the opportunities to benefit from it. By 1966 there was a general sense that Cambodia and its capital were running down, and as part of that perception Phnom Penh's inhabitants were beginning to ask whether Sihanouk had lost his magic touch. A key reason leading them to pose this question was the prince's sudden decision to devote much of his time to making "feature length films" designed, he insisted, to present a true picture of Cambodia to the outside world. In doing so he was, in part, responding to critical comments about Cambodia made by the actor Peter O'Toole after the actor had spent time in the country when the Angkor temples were used as a location for a film version of Conrad's novel, *Lord Jim*.

Beginning in 1966, Sihanouk spent endless hours writing the scripts, composing music and on occasion acting in a series of films of an embarrassingly amateur quality. Designed as both entertainment and propaganda, Sihanouk's films used as actors some of his closest associates, as well as his wife. Far from presenting Cambodia in a realistic light they were works of fantasy. *Apsara*, which had its "world premiere" in 1966, was supposed to show both the readiness of Cambodian's military to repulse attacks by aggressive "imperialists" (read the United States and South Vietnamese allies) and at the same time to depict the beauty of Phnom Penh. In this latter aspect of the film, and although Sihanouk did not realize it, the emphasis on expensive cars and over-decorated mansions, not to mention the high jinks of the upper ranks of Cambodian society, proved to be a potent propaganda weapon in the hands of the slowly growing rural revolt led by Cambodia's communists. *The Enchanted Forest* was fantasy pure and simple, and featured Sihanouk as a forest spirit, dressed in a gold lamé jacket, dispensing beneficence in a fairy tale setting.

Phnom Penh's bourgeoisie were deeply embarrassed by Sihanouk's films and took them as yet another indication of the decline of his authority as he gave increasingly less time to the demands of government. At the same time it was becoming ever clearer that sections of Cambodia's eastern border were being used by Vietnamese communist forces, so calling into question Sihanouk's claim that Cambodia was neutral. Matters reached a point of high absurdity when the pretence that Sihanouk was a world-class filmmaker became institutionalized through the inauguration of a Phnom Penh International Film Festival. It was only held twice, in 1968 and 1969, and on both occasions Sihanouk was awarded the grand prize, a solid gold statue in the form of an apsara, a heavenly female deity. At the 1969 festival, where undiluted praise was heaped on the prince, Sihanouk's entry was entered and won in a special class in which he was the only competitor. The prize was handed to him by that staunch supporter of leftist causes, the novelist Han Suyin, who like so many of Sihanouk's other admirers on the left either knew little, or did not care, about the fact that he had waged a long-term and often brutal campaign against those who dared to embrace left-wing politics in his own society.

The last film Sihanouk made before he was deposed was *Joie de Vivre*, which he described as his "first film of passion". I saw it in Phnom Penh in February 1970, just weeks before the *coup d'état* that toppled him from power. It says something of both the quality of the film and the atmosphere of the period that when I went to the Cinéma d'Etat to watch it there were barely two dozen in the audience—a handful of Cambodians and the rest East European foreigners. Sihanouk may have thought of it as his first film of passion, but it was much the same in character as his initial effort with *Apsara*. There was a faithless woman who hopped in and out of bed with minor princes, who were in turn depicted as absorbed with lust and gambling. Everyone lived in villas furnished at great expense and in bad taste, and drove about Phnom Penh in Cadillacs.

Phnom Penh at War

By early 1970 Phnom Penh was a city adrift. In terms of politics, Sihanouk had ceded much of his power to a right-wing government that by this stage was engaged in a deadly if largely unreported battle with a growing rural insurgency. There were reports that Sihanouk had sanctioned the payment of bounties for the heads of rebels to be brought to Phnom Penh as a sign that repression was being effective. Whether or not this was true did not matter, as the Phnom Penh elite believed it. Meanwhile the AKP carried accounts of Sihanouk's anger with the rebels, including his public declaration, already mentioned, that he had given the order for the summary execution of hundreds of those fighting against the Phnom Penh government. Corruption was rampant, not least among a powerful group close to Sihanouk's consort, Monique. Efforts to raise money through casinos, one in Phnom Penh and one on the coast at Sihanoukville, had little effect on the country's economic problems. But these were seen as a further example of moral decline as individual fortunes were won or lost on the turn of a card, with reports of a sudden rise in suicides among those who had squandered their funds. To add further weight to the sense of unease that was so apparent in Phnom Penh, there was now widespread recognition of how little control the government had over its eastern border regions which were occupied by increasing number of Vietnamese communist troops as the Vietnam War grew in intensity. It was in this atmosphere and with Sihanouk absent in France that some of the prince's closest, if not always his most trusted, colleagues, men of the right without exception, concluded it was time to throw him out of office.

Discussion of the coup that overturned Sihanouk's long-time hold on the direction of Cambodian affairs has been bedevilled by his own determination, and that of many foreign commentators, to depict it as an event planned and orchestrated by the American Central Intelligence Agency. This characterization of the complex events that took place in the early months of 1970 is wrong. It is true that there is incontrovertible evidence that some American agencies were aware of the plans considered by the principal plotters, General Lon Nol and Prince Sirik Matak, both at this stage leading members of the government that had been voted into office in 1966. But to describe the coup as "American" is to ignore the factors that led Lon Nol, Sirik Matak and their associates to take this momentous step. In his *The Tragedy of Cambodian History* David Chandler provides the most detailed account of the serpentine manoeuvrings and high drama that preceded their final decision, which ultimately involved Sirik Matak threatening to shoot Lon Nol if he did not agree to participate in the coup. What is so often disregarded by those commentators who continue to see the hand of the CIA behind the coup is the abundant evidence that by 1970 Sihanouk's policies had led to a dead end in so many fields of government action, a fact that it seems clear he had partially come to recognize himself. And in a striking fashion that underlined this situation, the coup, when it took place, did not provoke any major reaction in the capital. There was one significant provincial demonstration against the event, but for the most part Phnom Penh remained calm.

Phnom Penh was now to become the capital not of a kingdom but of the Khmer Republic and with General Lon Nol as its nominal leader. This fateful decision signalled the start of a terrible civil war, which was to last five years. Sihanouk, enraged by his deposition and determined to exact vengeance, willingly lent his name to the political and military front that now formed under the control of the Cambodian Communist Party, with the support of both the Chinese and Vietnamese communist leadership, to oppose the new government in Phnom Penh. In acting in this way Sihanouk recognized the supreme irony of his joining forces with those who had so recently been his bitter enemies. But his thirst for revenge was strong and he concluded that it was only in association with the Cambodian communists that the Lon Nol regime could be defeated. Moreover, his decision was approved by the Chinese leadership whose judgment he respected. Yet while he was under no illusion that the Khmer Rouge were not using him for their own purposes, he appears to have believed that he still would have a role to play in a future Cambodia dominated by the communists with whom he was now aligned.

At first, Phnom Penh seemed little affected by the war, other than by the fact that some key ministries were surrounded by barbed wire and protective sandbags and officials began to dress in khaki clothing. But the costs to some of Phnom Penh's population became sharply and tragically apparent. This was particularly so for the young men, many of them students, who flocked to join the army and then marched off to confront the enemy. Poorly trained and armed, they found they were fighting not just members of the communist-led Cambodian insurgents, but, more devastatingly, regiments of battle-hardened Vietnamese communist troops. Against these well-trained opponents, the young volunteers died in their thousands.

Close to the capital there was a tragedy of a different sort, the unprovoked massacre of upwards of a thousand of Vietnamese residents living in the Chruoy Changvar region, just across the Tonle Sap from central Phnom Penh, in May 1970. No truly satisfactory explanation has ever been proposed for this event, which at one level seems to have been a reflection of atavistic rage directed against an ethnic group seen as traditional enemies. Possibly, too, the police and soldiers who took part were venting their anger at the high casualties suffered by Phnom Penh's troops as they now found themselves fighting Vietnamese communist forces in the countryside. Whatever the explanation, the massacre led to a large number of Phnom Penh's Vietnamese residents fleeing across the border to what was still South Vietnam.

What occurred at Chruoy Changvar prefigured an increasing sense of moral decay within Phnom Penh as the war continued. The sense of this decay is vividly captured in a chapter with that title in William Shawcross' outstanding exposé, *Sideshow: Kissinger, Nixon and the Destruction of Cambodia*. As refugees steadily came out of the countryside seeking refuge from the war to be housed in growing shanty towns, and as shortages of medical supplies were an ever-growing problem, some of Lon Nol's military commanders saw nothing amiss in profiting corruptly at this time of crisis. They drew the pay cheques of non-existing soldiers to line their own pockets and even sold weapons to their enemies. Corruption was so pervasive and so often covered up by a handshake that it was known cynically in Phnom Penh as *bonjour*, the French daily greeting.

The war fought in the countryside was as vicious as any modern conflict. Both sides took part in atrocities, but it was not until 1973 that the full effects of the war struck home physically in Phnom Penh. In that year the insurgent forces steadily gained control over the countryside close to the capital. That the war was drawing ever closer was emphasized by two attacks on the Japanese Bridge across the Tonle Sap which severed the road link between Phnom Penh and Chruoy Changvar peninsula. Then as the year drew to a close the Khmer Rouge forces were close enough to launch rockets into the city. By the beginning of 1974 they could also use captured artillery to add to the random destruction wreaked by the rockets. Amazingly enough, remarkably little physical damage was done to central Phnom Penh, but the costs in lives lost was high and there was a terrible psychological burden since no one was ever certain where the rockets and shells were going to fall. As the war dragged on, refugees had flooded into the city. Just how many we will never really know, but it is probable that by the time of the Khmer Rouge victory in April 1975 Phnom Penh's population had at least doubled in size to more than two million inhabitants. They lived in squalid shanty towns and in half-built buildings, such as the Cambodian Hotel, whose construction had halted in this period of war.

By early 1975 Phnom Penh was under siege, effectively cut off from the rest of the country except for air links with a few provincial capitals and supplies brought up the river from South Vietnam. It was remarkable that

River ferries near the Japanese Bridge linking Phnom Penh and Chruoy Changvar peninsula

it had not fallen to the enemy earlier. In part this is explained by the relentless secret bombing campaign of Khmer Rouge base areas in eastern Cambodia that President Nixon had authorized and which continued until it was stopped by the American Congress in August 1973. (This is a subject dealt with by William Shawcross.) In part, too, the city did not fall earlier because of the extraordinary bravery and courage of some of the forces defending it. Though there were shocking examples of corrupt commanders selling weapons to their enemies, as they claimed the wages of non-existent troops under their command, there were equally remarkable examples of devoted service even as it became ever more certain that the Khmer Rouge forces would be victorious. But courage and devotion could not save Phnom Penh as the insurgents drew a noose ever more tightly around the city. With the Pochentong airfield under relentless fire, the delivery of supplies into the city became increasingly difficult. In January 1975 the last shipments up the Mekong to Phnom Penh ceased, since it was no longer possible for shipping to run the gauntlet of fire laid down by the Khmer Rouge batteries sited along the river. Many of those, both Cambodians and foreigners, who could afford to pay for flights out of the city had already left in the weeks preceding the final Khmer Rouge victory. Those departing included the ailing head of the government that had supplanted Sihanouk, Lon Nol, now self-promoted from general to marshal, who left on 1 April. Then, in a deeply symbolic departure, the American ambassador, John Gunther Dean, and his remaining staff left the city by helicopter on 12 April.

Remarkably, as it became apparent that Phnom Penh could no longer be defended, many senior Cambodians, both civil and military, remained in the city. Some did so from a sense of duty, as was the case with the Khmer Republic's last prime minister, Long Boret, his deputy, Prince Sirik Matak, and my firmly apolitical friend, Colonel Kim Kosal. They held this view despite the fact that their enemies had repeatedly announced their intention of executing the leaders of the regime in Phnom Penh. Others, particularly among the city's educated class, stayed in the belief that since the war had been between Cambodians an end to it would not involve the winners exacting vengeance from the defeated. Surely, their thinking went, the fact that Sihanouk was associated with the Khmer Rouge forces provided a guarantee that there would be reconciliation between the victors and the defeated. The hollowness of their expectations was to be demonstrated almost immediately after the guns fell silent. And, of course, the overwhelming majority of those who remained in Phnom Penh had no other choice.

Finally, on 16 April, with the Khmer Rouge forces at the gates of the city, the need for surrender became apparent, and by the early hours of the following morning a ceasefire was effectively in place. It was arranged as much as the result of individual commanders from the opposing sides talking to each other as by an organized procedure involving the leadership of the victors and the defeated regime.

Then, around midday on 17 April 1975, the victorious Khmer Rouge forces marched into Phnom Penh. They came, as their leaders said, "not to negotiate. We are entering the capital through force of arms." The tragedies of war were now to be followed by the tragedies of peace, tragedies that some would argue were more terrible that all that had happened in the preceding five years. Cambodia was now to be under the control of *angkar*, the shadowy "organization" in whose name the Khmer Rouge forces had fought and which was, in fact, a pseudonym for the secret Cambodian Communist Party, or the Communist Party of Kampuchea to cite its official name.

Chapter Nine

THREE YEARS, EIGHT MONTHS AND TWENTY DAYS: PHNOM PENH UNDER POL POT

Since the overthrow of the Khmer Rouge regime in January 1979 there has been a steady flow of memoirs from Cambodians who survived the period when Pol Pot and his associates imposed their tyrannical regime on their largely helpless compatriots. For the most part, these memoirs deal with life away from the capital in the vast agricultural forced-work camps to which most of the population was sent. Accounts of life in Phnom Penh are much more limited in number, and for reasons discussed later in this chapter some of the most detailed material on the Pol Pot period in Phnom Penh relates to the regime's most horrific institution, the Tuol Sleng extermination centre—or, as it was known by members of the Khmer Rouge ruling group, S-21. This was an acronym derived from the Cambodian compound term *santebal*, which combined the words for "security" and "police" with 21, a code number assigned to the institution. There were other similar extermination centres in the provinces that have received less attention, but which are now being investigated. Among those carrying out this research is a French scholar, Henri Locard, whose preliminary findings suggest that these provincial establishments had a terrible record of torture and executions to match that of S-21. Overall, academic research has tended to focus on the Khmer Rouge regime as a whole, rather than on the more restricted subject of Cambodia's capital. Among the books covering this period, Ben Kiernan's study, *The Pol Pot Regime*, discusses much of the inner workings of the regime, but gives relatively little attention to the capital. This makes the work currently being undertaken by Paul Reeve, which promises to provide the most detailed look at how Phnom Penh functioned between 1953 and 1982, all the more welcome. While we now have a relatively clear picture of some aspects of life in Phnom Penh between April 1975 and January 1979, there are many gaps in our knowledge. Yet we do know enough to be sure that Phnom Penh, for a period just short of three years and nine months, was at the heart of a political enterprise that may surely be described by that much overused word as "evil".

ENTER THE KHMER ROUGE

The dramatic events that occurred when the Khmer Rouge troops entered Phnom Penh have been described many times, both by Cambodians and by foreigners. Almost all reports of the events during these tense first few days in the capital are marked by a sense of the surreal, for scarcely anyone had envisaged what was about to happen. And if what occurred proved to be beyond most inhabitants' worst expectations, some events, however shocking, were not unexpected among those who had held a pessimistic view of the likely aftermath of the Khmer Rouge victory. In this category were the immediate executions of leaders of the defeated Phnom Penh government who had remained in the city, including Long Boret and Kim Kosal. They and others were taken to the grounds of the Cercle Sportif near the *phnom* and killed immediately, so fulfilling the repeated threats from the Khmer Rouge that they would act in this way. Senior military commanders were also executed almost at once. There is some disagreement as to how many senior figures from the defeated regime were killed over the next few days, but most accounts settle for a figure of around a thousand. At the same time, perhaps another one hundred individuals were shot as they failed to obey the orders of the city's new masters.

Then, in the early afternoon of the first day of peace, came the order that no one had expected. Phnom Penh, the inhabitants of the conquered city were told, had to be evacuated. This was to be done immediately, and no one was exempt from the order. In fact, it is clear that the evacuation took place over a period of four or five days as different Khmer Rouge groups enforced the command in different ways. While many of the deported inhabitants were pushed out of the city on 17 April, some like another of my pre-war friends, Ping Ling, left on 18 April, while others even managed to stay until 20 April. By then the Khmer Rouge's evacuation plan had been successfully completed.

Two aspects of what was happening shocked the urban population, and most particularly those with some education. The first was the character of the Khmer Rouge soldiers who now controlled the city. It has to be remembered that some of their leaders were well known to Phnom Penh's educated class. They were men and women who had shared educational experiences both in Cambodia and overseas, particularly in France, with those living in the defeated city. Even at a less elevated level, many in Phnom Penh were aware that people they had known for many years had gone over to the fight in the ranks of the Khmer Rouge, disgusted by the failings of the Lon Nol regime and believing that Sihanouk had a future role to play once the Khmer Rouge forces were victorious. But these former members of Phnom Penh's middle class were not the men and women who had provided the bulk of the troops that defeated Lon Nol's forces and had marched into the city on 17 April. Instead, Phnom Penh's citizens were confronted by an army that seemed to be made up of a disproportionately large number of very young soldiers, some indeed barely into their teens. Through their actions these young soldiers showed themselves to be drawn overwhelmingly from Cambodia's poorest regions, parts of the kingdom that were foreign to city dwellers.

Unsmiling and quick to take offence if their orders were not followed, they were clearly from a segment of society which had almost no acquaintance with the modern aspects of a city. They must have seen motor vehicles before, but they did not know how to drive them. They were totally without understanding of modern plumbing, so that they drank from toilet bowls and defecated in bidets in the houses they ransacked. They seized watches from the wrists of city dwellers but showed little understanding of their purpose. In every way their behaviour validated the arguments of those who had already suggested that the Khmer Rouge had drawn its forces from the most marginal of Cambodia's population. These were men and women, and perhaps above all children, who had dwelt on the outskirts of society, for whom the cities and those who lived in them were centres of corrupt behaviour inhabited by their oppressors. They were the people who had been shown Sihanouk's films as a way of teaching that Phnom Penh was a noxious den of self-indulgent individuals who had never cared for those who struggled for their existence on a daily basis. If they had had any contact with representatives of the governments who had ruled in Phnom Penh in the past, it was as victims of pervasively corrupt and often brutal officials.

THE EXODUS

There are many descriptions of the exodus from the city that now took place. It occurred at a time of the year when the weather was at its most uncomfortable, with soaring temperatures and the humidity hanging heavily in the air. The climatic cycle was steadily building towards the relief of the south-western monsoon, but this was still weeks away. Father François Ponchaud, a French missionary priest who had lived in Cambodia since 1965, has left one of the most vivid pictures of this mass movement of people in his book, *Cambodge année zéro*:

> ... a hallucinatory spectacle: thousands of the wounded and sick were leaving the city, the less seriously ill painfully dragging themselves along, others were carried by friends, while still others were being pushed along on their hospital beds by their families with their plasma and IV drips bumping alongside. I shall never forget one cripple who had neither hands nor feet writhing along the ground like a cut worm. Or a weeping father carrying his ten-year-old daughter in a sheet tied around his neck like a sling. Or the man with his foot dangling at the end of a leg to which it was attached by nothing more than skin.

No distinction was made between young and old, and those who tried to preserve their belongings or even to use a car as they left the city, soon found that these were not permitted aspects of the new Cambodia the conquerors were establishing. Memoirs from those who survived the exodus make it clear that some of the victors treated their charges better than others. But the overall picture is one of bewildered and fearful incomprehension among the deportees as the vast human columns moved slowly out of the city.

Estimates of how many died in this mass departure vary greatly, but a figure of around 20,000 seems believable and includes the deliberate killing of people as they left, particularly officers from the defeated regime. There was also an uncertain proportion of men, women and children who simply could not sustain the rigours imposed on them. Old people died from exhaustion, as seems to have happened with a kindly older prince and princess who had helped me with my research in Phnom Penh in 1966. They were sent south out of the city towards Ta Khmau and simply disappeared after having fallen by the roadside. Pregnant women gave birth as the mass of deportees moved slowly on; some survived, many did not. Some thousands of men identified as possessing technical skills were plucked from the columns and returned to Phnom Penh to ensure that basic services in the city were maintained. At the time many of their relatives feared that these men were being taken off to be executed, and it would be years in many cases before they learned that some had survived.

As the reality of what was happening sank in, the fear of being identified as part of Phnom Penh's privileged sector became pervasive among the men and women pushed out of the city. Individuals did not have to witness the executions that took place to learn of them, and in the bizarre world that now existed without newspapers and radios reports of what was happening travelled rapidly by word of mouth. My friend, Ping Ling, an engineer by profession, was part of the exodus, and he survived the Pol Pot period, to recount his experiences to me later when I met him in a refugee camp in Thailand in 1981. It rapidly became clear, he said, that to be identified with the educated class was to be at risk. In this extraordinary situation it was dangerous to be wearing spectacles, since they too suggested education. So, along with thousand of others, and with his spectacles hidden, my friend was driven north and east and set to work labouring in the fields planting rice. Then, by some form of luck that he cannot explain, and after several months of working as a field hand, he was suddenly taken from the fields to return to Phnom Penh where, with his engineering skills, he joined the technicians that even the Khmer Rouge needed to keep basic services in the city functioning.

To be an unassimilated Chinese was also a cause for suspicion, for such people were regarded as part of the exploiting class. Yet in one of the many ironies associated with this period, the new regime's distaste for ethnic Chinese living in Cambodia went hand in hand with the fact that the Chinese government in Beijing was to be Democratic Kampuchea's most important supporter, sending hundreds of advisers to Cambodia. China maintained its support for the Khmer Rouge both throughout the entire period of the Pol Pot regime, and afterwards through the 1980s as its remnants fought a guerrilla war against the new Vietnamese-supported regime in Phnom Penh.

Why did this mass movement of people take place? And what lay behind the decision taken by the Khmer Rouge leadership? At the time it was taking place and shortly after, western apologists for the Khmer Rouge were swift to offer explanations that flew in the face of later, incontrovertible evidence. In doing so they backed the propaganda statements of the regime itself, including justifications offered by Pol Pot. The city was emptied, they argued, because there was no food to feed the swollen population that had crowded into Phnom Penh in the final phases of the civil war. Furthermore, as Pol Pot himself was also to say, the decision to order the forced exodus was necessary to prevent "lackeys" of the United States mounting a counterattack against the new regime. As Pol Pot's biographer Philip Short has pointed out, both these explanations are misleading. The apologists were wrong in suggesting there was not enough food to feed the city's population. And while it is true that forcing almost all of the population out of the city certainly did disrupt whatever remnant CIA networks were still in existence, there is no basis for thinking that there was an American plan to try and reverse the Khmer Rouge victory. Equally, the suggestion that the city had to be abandoned against the possibility of an American bombing raid is not borne out by any available evidence that there was planning for such a raid to take place.

Instead, and after reviewing all the evidence, Philip Short has concluded that the decision had been taken some six months previously, and for a complex range of deeply ideological reasons which made sense to the *über*-revolutionaries who dominated Khmer Rouge policy-making. Stripped to its essentials, the decision reflected the fact that the Khmer Rouge planned to remake Cambodian society totally, for in Pol Pot's eyes Cambodia's revolution had no place for half measures. To ensure the revolution succeeded it was essential to transform the urban dwellers into tightly controlled agricultural labourers by "extricating them from the filth of imperialist and colonialist culture." In a fashion that it is difficult for anyone who did not embrace the political philosophy of the Khmer Rouge leadership to understand, this adherence to a total transformation of society was soon to be reflected in the tragic irrationality of S-21, the Tuol Sleng Extermination Centre. Emptying Phnom Penh of its population was not just a case of the ends justifying the means. The ends were the means. As Henri Locard has shown in his carefully collated examples of the slogans used by the Khmer Rouge leadership, the forced exodus accorded with the exhortation, "Let us transform the countryside so that it becomes the city."

THE FOREIGNERS DEPART

Placed against the terrible drama undergone by Phnom Penh's population, what happened to the foreigners who had remained in the city pales by comparison. Yet this was the experience that has been most accessible to a foreign audience, both through some gripping memoirs and because of the impact of the Roland Joffé-David Puttnam film, *The Killing Fields*. Herded together into the French Embassy compound, the city's foreigners found that their political beliefs and the positions they had taken in relation to the war that had just ended meant nothing to the victors. The personnel from the Soviet Union were expected to share the humiliation of being controlled by the Khmer Rouge in the same manner as the American journalists who had stayed in the city. As for the French, the readiness their governments had shown from the time of Charles de Gaulle onwards to try and find a *modus vivendi* with the communist forces throughout Indochina availed them nothing.

No one has told the story of the tensions and agonies of what happened within the embassy compound better than François Bizot in his outstanding book, *The Gate* (originally published in French as *Le Portail*). The dramatic immediacy of Bizot's book reflects the fact that he had had a long personal association with Cambodia as a member of the Ecole Française d'Extrême-Orient and was fluent in the Khmer language. He documents in excruciating detail the ultimately unsuccessful efforts made by westerners held in the embassy compound to save Cambodians who had taken refuge there. It is a story that was also told with equal passion and empathy by Sidney Schanberg, the *New York Times* correspondent, who had remained in Phnom Penh and who sought unsuccessfully to find a way to prevent his cameraman, Dith Pran, from being taken away by the Khmer Rouge. These events are recounted in Schanberg's book, *The Death and Life of Dith Pran*. From Bizot, Schanberg, Jon Swain and others, there are heart-rending accounts of those, among them the wife of Long Boret and Prince Sirik Matak, one of the leaders of the defeated regime, being handed over to the Khmer Rouge. There is also the equally moving story of the refusal that had to be given to the sixty-six-year-old Prince Sisowath Monireth, Sihanouk's uncle, as he sought to enter the compound, wearing his Legion of Honour decoration. Passed over by the colonial authorities for succession to the throne in 1941, he had nevertheless been decorated by the French government. But now, under the rules enforced by the Khmer Rouge victors, he was ineligible for sanctuary in the compound since he was not a French citizen.

In the end, all who were foreign and had taken refuge in the compound were able to leave, on 30 April. This meant that only a limited number of people remained in Phnom Penh and then survived to give an account of what life was like in a city whose inhabitants now totalled some tens of thousands, not the millions who had lived there only days before. Of particular interest is the fact that one of those who came to live in Phnom Penh some months after the Khmer Rouge victory and who later wrote a detailed account of his period under house arrest was the former king and chief of state, Norodom Sihanouk.

AN EMPTY CITY

In the immediate aftermath of the Khmer Rouge arrival in Phnom Penh there appears to have been only one instance of the destruction of an iconic building that could have been seen as offensive to the primitive communist concepts held by the new regime's foot soldiers. On 18 April, victory day plus one for the Khmer Rouge, a massive explosion wrecked one wing of the National Bank on Norodom Boulevard. The best explanation for this event seems to be that it was not sanctioned by the Khmer Rouge leadership but was rather the work of a small, rogue element in the victorious forces for whom the traditional lure of gold was enough to overcome a general order against the destruction of buildings. Bank notes from the Lon Nol regime were scattered in the blast and were still lying in the gutters of streets near the bank building in 1981. If there was a general prohibition at this stage against damaging the built environment—the destruction of Catholic churches and some markets came later—there was no such ban on a disorganized orgy of vandalism. The sacking and destruction of houses and offices can only be regarded as some kind of atavistic act of violence against objects and possessions that were seen as contaminated by their association with the corrupt lifestyle of the city dwellers.

Houses were ransacked with their contents destroyed, as, tragically, were the records held within the Phnom Penh headquarters of the Ecole Française. This institution, which had been at the forefront of research on Cambodian history, archaeology and general cultural studies, housed records of the greatest importance going back many decades. But this meant nothing to the illiterate youths who destroyed them. One of the losses involved the stone-by-stone catalogue of the great collapsed Baphuon temple at Angkor, which had been assembled as a basis for its eventual reconstruction. The books that formed the library of the Catholic cathedral were burnt, as were some at least of those which lined the shelves of the national library. (What was not destroyed from the library at this time did not survive the period shortly after the Pol Pot regime was defeated in 1979. Then, the new authorities pulped the remaining books when there was a desperate need for paper.) Eye witnesses speak of other libraries being destroyed in an orgy of book burning as the Khmer Rouge consolidated their hold over Phnom Penh. Other symbols of urban modernity were smashed or destroyed in these first few tense days—cars, shops and their contents, and medical laboratories. But within a week control was established over the troops as the Khmer Rouge leadership came together in the city.

Governing Cambodia from Phnom Penh

The first important meeting of Khmer Rouge leaders (including Pol Pot, who reached the city on 20 April from his headquarters in the countryside) took place in Phnom Penh's railway station. Yet in one of the great ironies of these early days, the first full leadership meeting was held shortly after in the Silver Pagoda at the southern edge of the Royal Palace compound. It is hard not to see this choice of venue as an act of great symbolic moment, given Pol Pot's condemnation of all that was associated with the Cambodian monarchy, which he had once described as a "running sore". But it may have been a decision based on mere convenience; situated within the palace compound, surrounded by high walls, the pagoda was a clean, empty space that was available and could readily be protected.

Overall, the degree of destruction within the centre of the city that had preceded the Khmer Rouge victory was limited. It was in the swollen squatter villages where refugees from the countryside had taken up residence that the bulk of the damage had taken place under the rain of shells and rockets. In the period immediately after April 1975 there was little destruction of buildings on ideological grounds; as we have seen, the Catholic cathedral and smaller Catholic churches such as that in the grounds of the former Ecole Miche, where Norton University now stands, were not destroyed until the following year. The actual destruction of the cathedral took enormous effort, as is described by Ong Thong Hoeung, in his *J'ai cru aux Khmers rouges* [I Believed in the Khmer Rouge] discussed later in this chapter. All that survives from this massive effort to rid Phnom Penh of its prime Christian symbol are a couple of bells sitting on a terrace of the National Museum. Lacking any identification, they stand in mute

One of the bells from the demolished Catholic Cathedral

testament both to the determination of the Khmer Rouge regime to rid the city of its western religious association and as a reminder of how unsuccessful the efforts of western missionaries have been since the time of the Iberian visitors in the sixteenth century. At a later, uncertain date during Pol Pot's reign the buildings of the French Embassy were demolished.

Neither were Buddhist pagodas in the city destroyed or desecrated, in contrast to what happened in many provincial centres. The inscriptions on some stupas in the grounds of Buddhist pagodas were defaced, as was the case at the Wat Botum Vaddei near the Royal Palace—the pagoda in which Pol Pot had once studied as a young novice in the 1930s. Yet if the capital's pagodas were largely untouched, this was not the case with the Buddhist religion itself, for under Pol Pot Buddhism was outlawed. The deeply ingrained tradition in which most male Cambodians become monks, if only for a short period during their lives, came to a sudden end.

During the immediate post-conflict period a major market not far from the Royal Palace was badly damaged but, surprisingly, Phnom Penh's most symbolic buildings were not targeted by this supremely ideological regime: not the palace, nor the National Museum. Neither did the new regime damage the superstructure of the Grand Market. The National Library was simply left alone, despite the destruction of some of its books, while the National Archives building directly behind the library appears to have been used at different periods as a piggery on its ground floor and for accommodation. Although newspapers held on the ground floor were destroyed, there was no systematic effort to attack the thousands of archival dossiers held on the upper floors.

What explains the fact that no effort was made to damage the palace buildings, given Pol Pot's visceral dislike of royalty? No one has been able to offer a certain answer to this question or as to why the museum, too, remained essentially untouched. One possible explanation is that, while Pol Pot and his associates never intended that Sihanouk should play a role in the government of Democratic Kampuchea, they wanted to keep him as a bargaining chip for the future. They may also have taken into account the fact that the Chinese government retained an interest in the former ruler's well-being. In these terms, preserving the palace might have been a decision linked to the man who had once been its former occupant and who, in the latter part of 1975, became its occupant again.

The Cambodian communists now had a whole country to govern and, in a sense, Phnom Penh was not the most of important of their concerns. Ever fearful of the possibility of a counter-revolution, they believed that it was unlikely to come from the cowed elements of the population who were now held in the city under the control of the heavily armed military. What was more important was for the deported population in the countryside to work to build the grand, autarchic vision of an independent Cambodia that depended on its own resources for its existence. In the eyes of Pol Pot and his close associates, this reformed country would be capable of recapturing the greatness of the Angkorian empire. It was not for nothing that Democratic Kampuchea, as the country now called itself, adopted a flag which, like its predecessors, featured a silhouette of the Angkor Wat temple with its distinctive towers. But before the regime's planned greatness could be achieved it was essential that Cambodia should boost its agricultural production. More advanced forms of economic activity could come later. And while the country was being transformed, assistance would be acceptable from China, a country that Pol Pot and others in the leadership admired, not least for the totalitarian aspects that had been an essential element in the Great Proletarian Cultural Revolution. At this early stage relations with Vietnam were correct, but nothing more, for Pol Pot had long ago concluded that the Vietnamese Communist Party could not be trusted and hoped, eventually, to dominate Cambodia.

More mundanely, Phnom Penh had to be cleaned up, since in the words of the regime's foreign minister, Ieng Sary, when he later spoke to the American journalist Elizabeth Becker, the city smelt. The crowded living conditions of the final months of the war and the damage done by shells and rockets in the suburbs had left a city far removed from its prewar reputation as one of the most attractive in Asia. Soldiers were duly put to work to clear the streets of garbage and to store possessions in warehouses. Some of this clearance work gave a sharp reflection of the dislike the regime's leaders harboured against the lifestyle of those they had defeated. While they themselves were ready to travel in chauffeured vehicles, the cars that had been abandoned by the deported population were cleared away to be heaped on pavements, where they still remained when I visited Phnom Penh in 1981.

Remarkably little of what was happening in Phnom Penh during the first year the Khmer Rouge were in power was known to the world outside

Cars wrecked by the Khmer Rouge still lying beside the street in 1981

Cambodia. By the middle of 1975 upwards of 6,000 Cambodians had fled across the border into Thailand, and they recounted experiences that seemed too awful to be given credibility. As it was, the passage of time and the final defeat of Pol Pot made clear that they were simply telling the truth. The regime's fraternal allies, whether Chinese and, at this early stage, still Vietnamese, gave no account of what they saw and knew to be occurring. Indeed, with diplomatic representation limited to a few friendly "socialist" countries, foreigners in the city were also reluctant to report on the new dystopia—that is even if they knew much about what was taking place, since they were prevented from travelling or moving about Phnom Penh unescorted.

By early 1976, the much-reduced population of Phnom Penh had settled into a steady, if far from natural, routine. The leadership had by then moved into the houses that were now their homes, where they lived at a level of comfort conspicuously greater than the rest of the city dwellers. The latter were the men and women who worked in the new government's ministries, laboured to keep the city functioning and maintained production in a limited number of factories. These servants of the regime all lived in barrack-like quarters, and all, it seems, were regarded with constant suspicion. Among the most revealing records of this time is the memoir of

Laurence Picq, *Beyond the Horizon: Five Years with the Khmer Rouge*. Picq, a French woman who had married a Cambodian, was allowed to return with him to Phnom Penh as a supporter of the new regime. Her memoir offers a detailed and disturbing picture, as she describes how her commitment to an extreme left-wing cause enabled her to rationalize abnormality into acceptability. Everything was done to rob individuals such as Picq of their identity, including the requirement to wear uniformly drab clothing. As a sympathizer she found this liberating, at least for a time, though her Cambodian husband treated her with contempt for being insufficiently revolutionary, in his eyes. She had behaved in the same manner, she reflected years later, as those who become members of religious sects and submerge their individuality as they surrender all to a single, dominant idea. Working at the foreign ministry, she accepted the drudgery and the restrictions as the necessary costs of building a new state. But her experiences there led her later to denounce Ieng Sary and all that he stood for as a leading member of the Khmer Rouge.

This was hardly the outlook for Ping Ling, my engineer friend, who lived and worked in fear after he was brought back to Phnom Penh. Charged with keeping a range of equipment working, he was able to do so because he was familiar with the workings of machines of American or European origin and found Soviet and Chinese models relatively easy to understand. But the uncertainty of existence was such that, in his own words, life in Phnom Penh under Pol Pot was an endless nightmare. Accommodated in barrack-like buildings with dozens of others, he never knew if he would survive from one day to another, as fellow technicians would be taken away without warning, never to return. They were said to be going to attend "seminars", but there was little reason to believe that they were destined for anything else but execution. Indeed, even before the end of 1975 the regime had embarked on a bizarre and terrifying programme of arrests, torture and killing that was designed to root out and dispose of traitors to the state. This involved the establishment of S-21, the former high school that was transformed into the extermination centre better known as Tuol Sleng.

EXTERMINATION CENTRE

At first glance, and in an effort to understand Tuol Sleng and those who worked there, it is tempting to look at other examples of state-sponsored terror and extermination. Are we perhaps helped by looking at the Nazi extermination camps, at what took place during the military dictatorship in Argentina in the "dirty war" period, or at the functioning of the Soviet gulags under Stalin? David Chandler, who in his book *Voices from S-21* has written the most detailed and thoughtful analysis of the institution, rightly observes that ghastly behaviour involving the shedding of humane norms has not been unique to Cambodia. But he warns against too easily seeking understanding through analogy. Yet if analogies will not provide the answer, what might explain this remarkable and terrible instrument of state power?

Some explanations have looked to Cambodian history as an explanation for the existence of S-21, since the simplistic image sometimes promoted of Cambodia as "a gentle land" represents a patronizingly misleading view of the past. It disregards the well-documented existence of past violence in favour of an idealized view of a people locked in the embrace of Theravada Buddhism's peaceful doctrines. Other explanations have suggested that it is wrong to analyse the actions of the Pol Pot regime in terms of a commitment to a particularly brutal, but nonetheless recognizable version of Marxism and Leninism. Instead, this view suggests, what occurred in Cambodia between 1975 and 1979 was the outcome of inchoate peasant rage at the nature of Cambodian society translated into unconstrained vengeance. The problem here is that, whatever was the case for the bulk of the population, men like Pol Pot, Ieng Sary and Khieu Sampan were not peasants, but educated men. The same was true for the two men most closely associated with the functioning of S-21, Son Sen and Kang Keck Ieu (better known by his pseudonym of Duch, sometimes transliterated as Deuch). This is a difficult issue for which the present writer has no clear answer. Rather, it becomes necessary to balance what are now a range of explanations against the simple if puzzling facts of what we know took place. What follows is a brief summary of the workings of S-21 (Tuol Sleng) between late 1975 and the end of 1978, during which time at least 14,000—possibly 17,000—people were taken to the centre, tortured until they made confessions of their "crimes" and then were killed. Of those who entered S-21 as prisoners, barely a dozen survived, among them Vann Nath, part of whose story appears briefly below.

Because of the records that were left behind at S-21 when the Vietnamese captured Phnom Penh in January 1979, we know much about its workings and the personnel employed there. Central to its existence was the presumption of the Khmer Rouge leadership that its control of Democratic Kampuchea was constantly under threat from spies in the pay of its enemies and from domestic counter-revolutionaries. Inherent in this view was a deep element of paranoia, much of it directed towards Vietnam. That Vietnam had evil intentions towards Cambodia was a deeply held conviction on the part of Pol Pot and his colleagues. The Vietnamese may have been the allies of the Khmer Rouge between 1970 and 1975, but the leadership of the new Democratic Kampuchea did not believe that this reflected Vietnam's true intentions. Indeed, it did not only require paranoia to be concerned about Vietnam's future intentions towards Cambodia. After all, the Vietnamese had dominated Cambodia for a period in the nineteenth century, and the Vietnamese communist leadership had long envisaged that a future relationship with Cambodia would be on their terms. Moreover, fear, dislike, and hatred of Vietnam and its people were not confined to those who embraced the ideas of the Khmer Rouge, as the 1970 Chruoy Changvar massacre showed. Neither has this deeply held ethnic antipathy vanished today.

Fearful that their grip on power might be sabotaged, Pol Pot and his circle showed no hesitation in arresting, incarcerating and, after torture, killing those whom they regarded as their enemies. To be taken to S-21 was to be presumed guilty, and as time passed after the victory of April 1975 the top leadership became ever more convinced that there were traitors at high levels within the country. In a manner that parallels the later stages of the Terror in the French Revolution, an increasing number of the men and women who were sent to S-21 had once appeared to enjoy the confidence of the top leadership. There they, too, finally "confessed" to being agents of the CIA, the Russians or the Vietnamese, desperately seeking to absolve themselves by incriminating others. One of the men regarded in the 1960s as a key member of Cambodia's revolutionary vanguard, Hu Nim, met his fate in this way after confessing to having served as an agent of the CIA.

What was remarkable about Tuol Sleng was not the killing of presumed enemies, however abhorrent such actions were, but rather the regime's insistence that before they were killed the prisoners had to confess to their alleged crimes. In this regard at least, any effort to find analogies with Nazi extermination camps during the Second World War is unsatisfactory. Yet it is difficult not to think that the misleading words at the gates of Nazi death camps, *Arbeit macht frei* ("work will make you free") had a similar echo in the slogan at the entrance to S-21, "Fortify the Spirit of the Revolution".

The conditions in S-21 were horrendous, a fact that remains vividly apparent to visitors today. In converting an anonymous set of four school buildings into a torture prison the regime installed a range of restraints, chains, shackles and bars, with bare iron bedsteads used to hold down prisoners while they were tortured. Some prisoners were held in groups, others in cells constructed within the existing rooms. With the requirement that confessions were extracted from the prisoners, S-21's staff routinely beat, burned and electrocuted the men and women in their control. Failure to give what was regarded as a "correct" response led to further torture, occasionally ending in death but more often in the physically and psychologically broken individual's final confession. The torture sessions could continue for as long as three months, and failure to provide the right answer prolonged the agony. Even before prisoners were tortured they were kept in terrible conditions. As Vann Nath, one of the few to survive imprisonment in S-21 records in his *A Cambodian Prison Portrait*:

> …my body began to deteriorate. My ribs were poking out and my body was like an old man of 70. My hair was overgrown like bamboo roots, and had become a nest for lice. I had scabies all over my body… I lived that way for more than 30 days. I was never released from the shackles…

For the first year or so confession was followed by execution and burial near S-21. But as the space available for burials became exhausted a new site was chosen outside the city, at what had been a Chinese graveyard near the village of Choeung Ek. This is what is known today as the "Killing Fields". There, at night, in the secrecy that surrounded the whole S-21 operation, thousands were executed by being smashed across the back of the skull with an ox cart axle. In 1981, when I made my first visit to S-21 and then to Choeung Ek, what I saw differed substantially from what greets visitors today. Then, the walls and floors of S-21 still bore the marks of bloodstains, while skeletons were still being excavated from the mass graves of Choeung Ek and the stench of corruption hung heavily in the air. S-21 still has the capacity to shock, but Choeung Ek today has more the air of

Exhumed skulls and bones at Choeung Ek "Killing Fields" in 1981

a tourist site, even with its tower filled with skulls, than the mass execution ground it once was.

Why was it regarded as so important to extract and record the confessions of the men and women taken to S-21, and why did the regime feel it necessary to preserve the confessions in a voluminous archive? These are among the many questions to which there are no certain answers, only suppositions. Perhaps, in the end, there is no better explanation than that offered by David Chandler when he suggests that the institution provided reassurance for a deeply paranoid group who could never quite believe that they were other than at risk. Possibly, too, the Khmer Rouge leadership required the "confessions" because they feared subconsciously that they had departed from expected human norms, for whatever their many deeply unattractive aspects, these were men who had experienced a substantial degree of education. Yet to think they really believed that the assorted and combined intelligence agencies conjured up in the confessions really were at work to topple them strains belief. No less horrific than the confessions extracted from Cambodians were those forced out of the dozen or so westerners who had the bad luck to fall into the hands of the Khmer Rouge. Most of these were yachtsmen, American, Australian, British and New Zealanders, who had strayed into Cambodian waters and who, following the terrible logic of S-21, ended by making pain-crazed admissions to being agents of the CIA.

If the Khmer Rouge's leadership's need for constant reassurance explains the existence of S-21, the same rationale would seem to apply to the wish to preserve the institution's records in an archive. The records provided material assurance that traitors had been found and eliminated. Nowhere do the contents of the archive evoke horror and compassion more forcefully than through the hundreds of "mug shot" photographs of the victims brought to S-21, some taken as they were brought in, others after they had been executed. Numbering six thousand in all, a selection of these photographs mounted on the walls of the Tuol Sleng building are perhaps the most confronting aspect of this supremely confronting institution.

"A CITY LEFT TO ROT"
Among the few detailed accounts of life in the capital under Pol Pot written by Cambodians is that of the city's former ruler, Norodom Sihanouk: *Prisonnier des Khmers Rouges* [Prisoner of the Khmer Rouge]. When Phnom Penh fell, Sihanouk was still in exile in Beijing where he had been since the coup of March 1970, apart from a brief visit to Khmer Rouge-controlled sections of Cambodia in 1973. Nominally head of the forces victorious in the civil war, he was torn between a desire to return in triumph, so he thought, over his usurpers and the concern he had begun to feel following reports of the grim developments taking place in the capital. In the end, he decided that he should return. At first the Khmer Rouge leadership showed little interest in his doing so, but in September 1975, more than four months after Phnom Penh had fallen, he was allowed to return. He left Beijing with a firm admonition from Chairman Mao Zedong that he should not undermine the new government.

When he and his wife, Monique, reached Phnom Penh they were "bowled over" by the sight of the deserted city. Whisked from the airport to the Royal Palace, they stayed within its grounds for the entire three weeks of their visit, except for one boat trip taken on the Mekong and Tonle Sap, during which they saw not a single soul. Whether genuinely felt or uttered as a way to placate his communist minders, Sihanouk later professed to believe the Khmer Rouge leaders who told him that the city's population had gone into the countryside voluntarily.

After acceding to the new regime's wish that he should speak at the United Nations on its behalf and tour those few nations that had recognized the new government in Phnom Penh, he returned to Beijing. Then, in December 1975, Sihanouk again flew back to the city to what he later described as a "humiliating return". After being greeted at the airport by a crowd of black-clad workers who shouted slogans extolling the peerless virtues of *angkar*, Sihanouk and his small group of family members and domestic staff were taken once again to the palace. This was to be what he called their "gilded prison" for most of the next three years.

The self-centred account Sihanouk provides of his house arrest is of interest to historians for the way in which it charts the rapid decline in his relations with the Khmer Rouge leadership, resulting in an effective break between them in April 1976 that left him without even a titular role in the new regime. But his book is remarkably lacking in detail regarding events in Phnom Penh outside the palace walls. Within those walls he was, for most of the time, effectively under house arrest in relatively comfortable circumstances. There is no doubt he had reason to be fearful that at any moment the Khmer Rouge leadership might choose to kill him, a fear heightened by the unexplained disappearance of one of his closest aides. Yet he was allowed to listen to international radio broadcasts and he lived in quarters that were air-conditioned. What his memoir does provide is an account of the slow decay of the Royal Palace's buildings through lack of maintenance and of its grounds, as buffalos, sheep and goats were driven into the palace to feed in the gardens.

Throughout his enforced stay in the palace, and then in the latter part of 1978 when he was moved to a secluded villa behind the Botum Vaddei pagoda, Sihanouk was taken on a series of short excursions to the countryside. While he describes these visits in some detail, expressing concern for his people but rather more for the destruction of his provincial villas, Phnom Penh as a city does not become a subject in his book.

We do have insights and some detailed information from another Cambodian writer who was treated very differently from Sihanouk. This was Ong Thong Hoeung, who had studied political economy in Paris and who returned to Cambodia as an enthusiast for the new regime in July

1976. Like a number of other returning Cambodian expatriates, many of whom were later killed at S-21, he had campaigned in France against the Lon Nol regime while the civil war still raged. Now he hoped to work for the new regime in his homeland. He wrote of his experiences in his book, *J'ai cru aux Khmers Rouges* [I Believed in the Khmer Rouge]. In it he charts his shocked disillusionment at what he observed and as he and his wife were sent to re-education camps. Through his account we learn a little of what was happening in Phnom Penh—of trees being cut down along the city's wide boulevards and replaced with coconut palms, of vegetables being grown on vacant land around the national stadium, and of the general sense of decay and emptiness that permeated the once bustling city. He tells of how, not long after he returned to Phnom Penh from Paris, he was ordered to form part of the work team that was set to work destroying the Catholic cathedral, a massive task as he and others reduced reinforced concrete to rubble with hand tools. But even with accounts such as Ong Thong Houeng's, it is from a foreign visitor, Elizabeth Becker, as detailed later in this chapter, that we gain perhaps the most rounded picture of the city's appearance during the Khmer Rouge period.

By early 1977 relations between Cambodia and Vietnam were becoming more and more strained. By this stage Pol Pot and the Khmer Rouge leadership were translating their deep antipathy towards the Vietnamese into action. They were now speaking, irrationally, of Cambodia's capacity to retake the areas of southern Vietnam that had once been ruled by the Cambodian court centuries before. The area involved, from Saigon south to the Gulf of Thailand and west to the Mekong, was and still is known to Cambodians as *Kampuchea Krom* (Lower Cambodia). Now, to underline his views and as a counter to what was believed to be Vietnam's intention to invade and control Cambodia, during March 1977 Pol Pot ordered savage attacks on Vietnamese frontier villages. These attacks, with men women and children massacred and property put to the torch, continued intermittently throughout the year. As the Khmer Rouge followed this aggressive foreign policy, an important number of mid-level officials started to take stock of their place within the regime, a course of action that was spurred by their realization that more and more of their fellows were being purged, seized from their positions and disappearing into the regime's jails. In 1977 the purges were particularly savage in the eastern region of the country, and it was from here that men such as future prime minister, Hun Sen, chose to flee to Vietnam. There, eventually, they were to form the nucleus of the National Salvation Front, whose members accompanied the Vietnamese into Cambodia during the invasion that began in late 1978.

Against this background and by early 1978 the central leadership of Democratic Kampuchea began to acknowledge that it was desirable to reinforce links with sympathetic foreign countries. This was undoubtedly given urgent emphasis by the Vietnamese attack into Cambodia that took place over the period from late 1977 to early 1978. The attack was clearly designed by Hanoi as a warning of what the Vietnamese army was capable of doing if the Cambodian regime did not cease its border attacks. Yet the intended lesson did not change Cambodian policy towards its eastern neighbour, as when the Vietnamese withdrew Phnom Penh argued that they could not defeat Cambodia's forces.

As the regime in Phnom Penh sought to bolster its image with those abroad whom it considered its friends, there is some reason to believe that it was responding to advice from China. Throughout the whole time that Pol Pot ruled Cambodia Chinese advisers—perhaps numbering around a thousand—played an important role within the country. During 1978 a wide range of visiting delegations were invited to come to Cambodia. With one important exception, discussed below, these groups were decidedly of the left, members of "fraternal" parties, or from countries in which such parties ruled. Whether American, Australian, Danish, Swedish, French, Belgian, Yugoslav or Japanese, almost all came *parti pris* to one extent or another and returned to their homes with scarcely a word of criticism of what they had seen. Some, indeed, were lavish in their praise. One of the first to arrive was a Yugoslav television team, which visited in March 1978, but some of its members, at least, displayed a degree of scepticism lacking among others.

From the Yugoslav reports we gain a picture of Phnom Penh's population being no more than 20,000, a figure that is rather lower than most other estimates, and a sense of the unease of its members as they saw young children labouring in state factories. As for the rest of the friends of the regime of whatever nationality, they allowed their political sympathies to override any capacity for critical thought, so that as witnesses to what Phnom Penh was like at this critical stage in Democratic Kampuchea's short history they offer us little that is enlightening. In this they contrast sharply with the reporting that emerged from the visit by two American journalists, Elizabeth Becker and Richard Dudman and a Scot, Malcolm Caldwell, in December 1978. Caldwell, a well-known and dedicated supporter of left-wing causes, had visited Cambodia once before, briefly in the 1960s. From his university base in London, where he had a small but enthusiastic group of supporters among his students, he had been an outspoken supporter of the Pol Pot regime. Dudman's experience was particular in character and essentially limited to a period dating back to the early stages of the civil war in 1970 when, as a reporter for the *St. Louis Post Dispatch*, he had been held for forty days as a prisoner of Vietnamese communist forces fighting within Cambodia. In contrast to her travelling companions, Becker had spent nearly two years in Cambodia in the early 1970s reporting for the *Washington Post*. Her account of Phnom Penh was thus informed by clear memories of what the city had been like before the Khmer Rouge victory. An account of that earlier period and of her experiences in December 1978 appears in her book, *When the War was over*.

Becker's first impressions were of a largely empty city in which, along the route she, Dudman and Caldwell travelled from the airport, buildings were freshly painted and gardens maintained. Housed in what had been a private home on Monivong Boulevard, once she was able to explore the streets away from this main thoroughfare she found a different city. Disregarding her escorts' warnings that members of the party should not leave their accommodation on their own, she set off early one morning and walked through sections of the city she had once known well. Leaving Monivong Boulevard she turned down side streets and found, as she puts it, that "the city had been left to rot." The yards of houses were overgrown and filled with rubbish. Close to the Psar Thmei market banana trees had been planted in intersections of roads. When she reached the Hôtel le Royal it was to find that it, too, had been treated like the buildings along the road in from Pochentong airport. Its façade had been painted, but the reality was revealed once she went through the hotel's doors to find it in a decrepit state. At this point in her travel through the streets of the city she realized that the Catholic cathedral, near the hotel, had simply disappeared.

Becker's enterprising exploration was soon brought to a halt and for the rest of this group's visit their movements were closely supervised. They were taken to the Royal Palace, Silver Pagoda and the National Museum, and then later to what they were told was the Institute for Scientific Training and Information. Here they saw child factory workers labouring to repair broken mechanical parts. Next came travel away from Phnom Penh into a countryside where Becker felt that what she and her companions saw was staged for their benefit, while the true state of the country and its inhabitants was hidden from their view.

Written with the knowledge of hindsight, Becker was able to analyse the falsity of what she saw and later to place it in the context of the savage purges that the Khmer Rouge leadership had organized, particularly in the east of the country. But in reporting on her experiences back in Phnom Penh she and Dudman achieved what no American journalist had previously been able to do. They were accorded an interview with Pol Pot, as was Caldwell, separately in view of his status as a "friend" of the regime.

MEETING POL POT

After the Khmer Rouge regime was defeated in early 1979, Pol Pot was the subject of a number of interviews with journalists, including one that has received much attention, which he gave to the American journalist Nate Thayer in 1997 shortly before he died. But the interviews he gave in the closing weeks of Democratic Kampuchea's existence—with Becker and Dudman, and later with Sihanouk—have a particular fascination for the insight they give into the extraordinary, some would say insane, view Pol Pot had of his country in the weeks immediately before the Vietnamese seized Phnom Penh.

When Becker and Dudman were summoned to meet Pol Pot on 22 December they were taken to the former residence of the head of the French administration, the building that was known as the Hôtel du Gouvernement during the years when Sihanouk ruled. Becker's first impressions were of a man who was "actually elegant", whose gestures were "polished, not crude". In short, he was someone who appeared a great deal less the tyrant she feared he was, even without having a clear knowledge of the full depths of his responsibility for the staggering death toll that had occurred while he was in power.

But within moments of his starting to speak, she knew she was listening to a man whose grasp on reality was tenuous. As he built his case to show Vietnam's hostile intentions towards Cambodia, he began to conjure up the fanciful prospect that there would be a war in Cambodia in which Democratic Kampuchea would be fighting with the forces of NATO against the forces of the Warsaw Pact aiding Vietnam. Both Becker and Dudman were staggered by Pol Pot's performance, which at no stage dwelt on the state of the country's population.

Their interview was followed by Malcolm Caldwell's solitary visit to Pol Pot. Other than Caldwell's recounting that he and Pol Pot had discussed revolutionary theory, we know little more than the fact that the Scottish leftist was delighted with the occasion and was told by Pol Pot that he would be welcome to return. We know no more since, in a dramatic and still unexplained incident—and with the party of three visitors due to depart for China by air the next day—Caldwell was assassinated in the guest house in which they were staying. Various theories have sought to explain his murder, but none can be accepted with absolute certainty. Pol Pot's most recent biographer, Philip Short, argues that the most likely explanation—one that has been largely ignored or discounted—was that the killing was carried out by a Vietnamese commando team, a reflection of the fact that by December 1978 Cambodia had become a highly insecure country. Just how insecure became clear on Christmas Eve, when during the night of 24-25 December the Vietnamese army began its full-scale invasion of Cambodia.

It was against this background that Sihanouk was called to see Pol Pot, a man he had last seen during a clandestine visit to Cambodia in 1973. If the interview Pol Pot had granted to Becker and Dudman was touched by a sense of the surreal, this was even more the case when Sihanouk met him in the evening of 5 January 1979. As with Becker and Dudman, Sihanouk was ushered into Pol Pot's presence in the former Hôtel du Gouvernement. By this time the invading Vietnamese forces were moving steadily towards Phnom Penh and the sound of artillery barrages could be clearly heard in the capital. Sihanouk was aware of this in general terms, partly because he was able to listen to international short-wave broadcasts, and partly because he and his small entourage had, just four days before, set off by road from Phnom Penh to take refuge in Thailand. Before they reached the border they had been returned to Phnom Penh by their Khmer Rouge minders without explanation.

Pol Pot greeted Sihanouk courteously, addressing him by his royal titles and using the prescribed forms of the Cambodian language for conversation with royalty. Their meeting lasted four hours, with Sihanouk saying little as he nervously sipped orange juice while Pol Pot painted an entirely optimistic picture of the battles taking place close to the capital. Within a matter of months, he assured Sihanouk the Vietnamese would be driven from Cambodia. In spite of himself, Sihanouk found that Pol Pot possessed a seductive charisma, even if it was clear that he was talking complete nonsense. The next day Sihanouk was flown out to Beijing in a Chinese aircraft.

THE KHMER ROUGE DEPART

Even as Pol Pot and Sihanouk talked, senior Khmer Rouge figures had already begun to flee Phnom Penh. So, too, had the Chinese diplomats and advisers, still numbering more than six hundred, who had played an important part supporting the regime during its three-year-plus existence. With much of the city surrounded by five Vietnamese divisions, the railway line running to the north-west and the Thai border became the means of escaping the advancing Vietnamese and two heavily loaded trains pulled out from Phnom Penh's station on 7 January as Vietnamese troops entered the city's southern suburbs. Ben Kiernan adds a bizarre and chilling footnote to this hurried flight of important Khmer Rouge figures. One of the last to leave Phnom Penh, he notes, was the director of S-21, Duch. He was still at his post at noon on 7 January, by which time Vietnamese tanks were rolling through the centre of the city. Before he left he supervised the killing of the prisoners, including some still chained to the iron bedsteads used to restrain them while they were being tortured.

With Vietnamese troops taking over Phnom Penh, the city was rid of the Khmer Rouge. But those who now controlled it were foreigners. It was to be fourteen more years before what became known as "the Cambodia problem" was finally resolved and Phnom Penh began to move slowly towards something approaching normality.

Chapter Ten

WRITING OBITUARIES FOR "OLD PHNOM PENH"

It is perhaps not surprising that Phnom Penh in particular and Cambodia more generally have not generated the same amount of literary material, or even serious reportage, as Vietnam. Before Sihanouk was bundled out of office in 1970, setting in train the period of civil war and then the Pol Pot tyranny, Cambodia was little known in the world at large. In some ways it was less well known after the Second World War than in the 1930s, at least to that group of writers whose personal circumstances allowed them opportunities to travel. The country that had attracted the interest of travellers and writers such as Somerset Maugham and Osbert Sitwell as well as many less well-known *littérateurs* seemed much less attractive a destination during the period of the First Indochina War (the Franco-Viet Minh War) that began in 1946. In this regard, Norman Lewis' *A Dragon Apparent*, discussed earlier, is decidedly an exception to the general rule. Even when a kind of peace came to the Indochinese region in 1954, following the Geneva Conference that ended the war, Cambodia remained a little-known, if exotic destination, visited by those who wanted to see the Angkor temples. As for Phnom Penh, it was off the tourist track and seen as a backwater, if it registered on people's minds at all.

Those of us who lived in Phnom Penh during the 1950s and 1960s had, of course, a different view. We found its capital fascinating. But there have been few books published from those years that echo the interest of the city's "old hands", with the 1950s particularly neglected. An interesting exception is the memoir of an English writer, Christopher Pym, who visited Cambodia in the 1950s. After offering an account of travelling to Angkor from the coast of Vietnam in his *The Road to Angkor* (1959), he went on to record his impressions of daily life in Phnom Penh in a sympathetic fashion in *Mistapim in Cambodia* (1960). The book is a lively account of what can be achieved by an enterprising visitor in a foreign city, which in Pym's case included interviewing King Suramarit, Sihanouk's father, and Sihanouk himself. Long out of print, it rewards a search to locate the book in libraries.

The paucity of novels from earlier decades was matched by the post-Second World War period. The contrast with Vietnam is unmistakable. If Graham Greene's *The Quiet American* heads the list of any fictional writing about Vietnam, the war that followed the period he wrote about—the "American" war in Vietnam—produced other writers of fiction of a high quality. Philip Caputo's *A Rumour of War* and Tim O'Brien's *Going after Cacciato* immediately come to mind.

In contrast, there are only two novels of substantial literary quality that have Cambodia, and Phnom Penh, as central to their plots, and these are discussed below. Otherwise there were only a small number of books about Cambodia published in the 1960s, and an even smaller number that had Phnom Penh as their principal focus. One novel with a Cambodian setting by the prolific author Han Suyin dating from 1963 is *The Four Faces*. But this satirical book has Siem Reap, the provincial capital close to the Angkor temples, as its setting rather than Phnom Penh. And when brief reference is made to the capital she locates it twice as far away from the temples of Angkor than is actually the case. Han Suyin is at her sharp-penned best, or worst, in this book as she skewers the pretensions of a series of recognizable types who are serial participants in international conferences devoted to high-minded issues. It is probable that some of her characters are based on real-life figures, and that the book is a *roman à clef*, but read from the distance of over forty years it is difficult to know just who is being mocked. Only Sihanouk, who plays a small part in the book, escapes unscathed, for Han Suyin was one of his most uncritical admirers. In this she typified a number of western writers who supported leftist causes. Ignoring Sihanouk's readiness to deal harshly with his own domestic left, they offered him unqualified praise and received in return a warm welcome when they visited Phnom Penh.

FACT AND FICTION

The onset of the civil war in 1970 led to some outstanding reportage as the world press found that events in Cambodia could no longer be ignored. In the face of the tragedy associated with the war and its terrible aftermath, a few writers who had known the country before the war wrote their memoirs of a different time. Common to all the writing discussed in this chapter is the contrast between what Phnom Penh was and what it became.

As such, it may be regarded as either the forebodings of tragedy or as obituaries for a vanished Phnom Penh.

Just as Anthony Burgess was writing about Brunei in his novel, *Devil of a State* (1961) but set his story in a mythical African country, so Andrew Graham, a former military attaché at the British Embassy in Phnom Penh in the 1950s, chose to set his light-hearted satire on diplomatic life, *A Foreign Affair* (1958), in the mythical "Kingdom of Parasang" rather than in Cambodia. For anyone familiar with diplomatic life, there are cameos in this novel that are close to the bone. As for the novel's locale, it is not hard to see traces of the Cambodian royal family and its associates in the characters, but Phnom Penh is barely recognizable in the picture the author provides. In striking contrast, British diplomat Leslie Fielding's recent, real-life memoir, *Before the Killing Fields: Witness to Cambodia and the Vietnam War*, offers a warts and all account of diplomatic life in Phnom Penh in the 1960s that is genuinely absorbing. It depicts a time when there still seemed to be hope that Cambodia would escape the war that was already engulfing Vietnam.

Phnom Penh appears as a "backdrop" in a limited number of novels, few of which possess much real literary merit. One such is Loup Durand's *The Angkor Massacre* (1983). The author covered Cambodia as a journalist for seven years. This first-hand experience shows in his references to Phnom Penh street names of the pre-Pol Pot period, and to such landmarks as the Hôtel le Royal, La Taverne restaurant and Thai-San hotel, the last an establishment patronized by Cambodians and expatriates alike for its excellent Chinese restaurant, which still exists today. Well-known expatriate figures appear, either under their own names, as with the *conservateur* at Angkor, Bernard-Philippe Groslier, or as recognizable figures such as Walter Blackett, a character clearly modelled on the Australian communist journalist, Wilfred Burchett, who lived in Phnom Penh in the 1960s. Regrettably, Durand misses an opportunity to develop Blackett/Burchett's character in his book. This controversial figure, whom I saw from time to time in 1966 in Phnom Penh, played something more than a bit part in the drama of the Second Indochina War period. An admirer of the Vietnamese communists and of the Chinese until he began to have grave doubts about the meaning of the Cultural Revolution, he also spoke in favour of Cambodian "neutrality" for a period. In many ways he was a stereotype of a certain kind of foreign correspondent—hard drinking, hard working and in his particular case, deprived as he was of an Australian passport, close to maudlin on occasion as he remembered his childhood home in Gippsland.

Apart from one descriptive passage describing the Grand Market, the city barely intrudes on the Durand's complicated story of the adventures of a French plantation owner in the period leading up to the Khmer Rouge victory in 1975, whose family's long association with the region had led him to think of himself as Cambodian.

The best-selling author of "airport" novels suffused with sex and violence, Eric Van Lustbader, sets much of his 1987 novel *Black Heart* in Phnom Penh. As with Durand's novel, the rise to power of the Khmer Rouge is an element in the story. But even more than in *The Angkor Massacre*, *Black Heart*'s characters are paper thin and in some cases clearly appropriated, along with various of the episodes described in the novel, from other writers. I am listed as one such.

Against this discouraging background are two clear exceptions: the novels of John Le Carré and Christopher Koch. These are, respectively, *The Honourable Schoolboy* (1977) and *Highways to a War* (1995). The second volume in Le Carré's "Karla Trilogy", *The Honourable Schoolboy* at times reads like an extended satire, as it moves from the London haunts of the Secret Intelligence Service, the "Circus", to the hotels and clubs of Hong Kong, with an inimitable re-creation of the legendary Australian journalist, Richard Hughes, as "Craw". But throughout the novel, and certainly the sixty pages that deal with Cambodia and Phnom Penh, Le Carré's writing reflects his research on the ground before he wrote the book. This is clear in the realistic depiction he offers of life in Phnom Penh in the closing stages of the Khmer Rouge's march towards victory. He captures the indulgent seediness of that time, as foreign journalists, the "warries", booze in the garden of the Hôtel Phnom, the former Hôtel le Royal—its name had been changed to assuage the sentiments of the republican regime that had ousted Sihanouk. In the same garden are still young women remaining in the capital who have found time to sunbathe in their bikinis beside the hotel's pool.

Le Carré's protagonist, the Honourable Gerald Westerby, who gives the book its title, is a Circus agent operating under deep cover. He knows he is visiting Phnom Penh as time is running out for the city. With an unerring eye for atmosphere, Le Carré has Westerby reading Conrad as he

A Chinese merchant's mansion, now UNESCO headquarters

flies into the capital, for it is "the last of the true Conrad river ports". It is also a city "like nowhere else Jerry had ever been," as the "war took place in an atmosphere of peace"—a comment on the way in which journalists journeyed out each day to see the fighting and then returned to the relative safety of Phnom Penh to file their stories. For sixty pages, Le Carré writes of Phnom Penh at war with a sharp immediacy as the sun shines and a rocket falls in the city to kill yet another eight or nine children.

The scenes of fighting just outside the capital are realistic, as the Khmer Rouge forces press ever closer to the city and most Cambodian provincial towns, with the exception of Battambang, fall to the communists. Then there are the passages in which Le Carré takes his literary scalpel to the life still being led by foreign diplomats in the doomed city. The British Embassy counsellor's wife is "tall and Harrods and amused by the idea of a *journalist*, as she was amused by anyone who was not a diplomat, and of counsellor rank at that." Later, in an observation that summons up what was so often to be found in the houses of diplomats in Phnom Penh, she is referred to as the owner of "an indifferent collection of pilfered Buddhas". Satire though much of this novel may be, it accurately captures the despair that lay just below the surface of life as April 1975 drew ever closer. This was now a city with two burgeoning refugee camps where aid workers "struggled with the impossible, the only water filthy, a rice handout twice a week…"

If much of what John Le Carré wrote in *The Honourable Schoolboy* is in a satirical mode with touches of black comedy, Christopher Koch's *Highways to a War* is more sombre in tone. Its story is told against backgrounds ranging from Tasmania to Vietnam, and from Thailand to Cambodia. Most of all, it contains descriptive passages that are lyrical in character and which capture the emotional hold Phnom Penh and Cambodia have had on so many who have spent time there. The central character in the book is Mike Langford, a combat cameraman who, as Koch tells his readers, is "only partly" based on the real-life Neil Davis, a renowned Australian cameraman who covered the wars in Vietnam and Cambodia for a decade. He survived endless exposure to danger only to be killed in a failed coup in Thailand in 1985. Newsmen like the fictional Langford knew Phnom Penh before full-scale war came to Cambodia in 1970. This was when it was a "river city. Hot silence; and Phnom Penh's noises were the muted, magic sounds that come to you in a doze: an afternoon siesta when you're having good dreams." But all this changed after the coup that overthrew Sihanouk; after that, if you drove your car out of Phnom Penh "all highways led to the war."

There are many descriptions of Phnom Penh in the novel, none more evocative than that of the Psar Chaa, the "scruffy" Old Market. But Langford's friend, Harvey Drummond, describes it as something different, even as the war rages in the Cambodian countryside. It sold everything, "from flowers and fruit to notebooks, pencils and clothing". (I could also add that it was something of a thieves' market when I first went to Phnom Penh in 1959. Books ordered from abroad seemed to move effortlessly from the post office to the market, where the intended recipient was permitted to buy back the stolen items for a modest premium over the original cost.) Thieves' den or not, it was a welcoming place where "the combined scents made you tipsy; the coloured mountains of produce hurt your eyes. Rambutans, durians, mangoes, oranges, bunches of lotus buds; Cambodia's horn of plenty, not yet run dry."

Whatever aspects of the past the novel conjures up, the reader is never able to forget that Cambodia's capital lives a fragile peace, as its inhabitants look across the Mekong to see the passage of tracer bullets in the night. It is a city that also trembles to the sound of B-52s dropping their bombs.

The war in the countryside can never be forgotten by the correspondents as they tour the bars, eat dishes laced with hashish and visit opium dens. There is a barely controlled frenzy to their activity that fails to blot out the war's stark reality however much they try.

Highways to a War matches Christopher Koch's previously highly acclaimed book with an Asian setting, *The Year of Living Dangerously* (1978), set in Indonesia. Both are the products of detailed research transformed into gripping stories of high literary quality. It is no surprise that *Highways* should have been awarded one of Australia's highest literary awards as well as receiving the plaudits of fellow authors such as Larry MacMurty and Anthony Burgess.

Acknowledging, as Koch does, the importance of Tim Bowden's 1987 biography of Neil Davis, *One Crowded Hour*, it is worth turning to that book for Davis' own grim words about the final days in Phnom Penh as the Khmer Rouge drew ever nearer. What for Le Carré were words in a novel about a rocket attack on a school were for Davis a sight he witnessed, filmed and recorded in his audio diary in February 1975. A 107 millimetre rocket had hit a school, and:

> I got there less than a minute later. The rocket had gone straight into a classroom with children aged six to nine. There were fourteen or fifteen dead, thirty or forty seriously wounded, and it was like a scene from Dante's *Inferno*. Bloodied children wounded and screaming in terror were trying to get out of the school… It was the most horrifying sight I remember from the Cambodian War.

If the number of novels dealing with life in Phnom Penh is limited, the same is true of detailed personal accounts by Cambodian writers of life in the capital before and after the Khmer Rouge victory. Most of the books dealing with the period from 1975 to 1979 focus on experiences after their authors were driven out of Phnom Penh, and many of these are difficult to find. In addition to those already mentioned in the previous chapter, one of the few readily accessible books to deal with Phnom Penh before 1975 is the memoir of Someth May, *Cambodian Witness* (1986). A member of Phnom Penh's middle class—his father was a doctor—Someth May's book is particularly valuable for the manner in which it covers his school and university days, the latter coinciding with the period of the highly corrupt Lon Nol regime. Ong Thong Hoeung's *J'ai cru aux Khmers Rouges* has already been mentioned for its account of life in Phnom Penh in the Pol Pot period. But in other available Cambodian memoirs such as Pin Yathay and John Man's *Stay Alive, My Son* (1987), Molyda Szymusiak's *The Stones Cry Out* (1987) and Joan D. Criddle and Teeda Butt Mam's *To Destroy You is No Loss* (1987) the emphasis is not on Phnom Penh. Rather, these provide accounts of what happened to the authors once the city fell to the Khmer Rouge and they were driven into the country.

Spanning the categories of reportage, travelogues and memoirs is Maslyn Williams' *The Land in Between: the Cambodian Dilemma* (1982). Written after an extended visit to Cambodian in the late 1960s, it recalls the kind of travel writing that was popular in the 1930s, with its evocation of place and people in a deliberately mannered fashion. We join the author in his modest hotel by the post office square and take coffee with him in the restaurant, which he does not name but is clearly my much-regretted La Taverne. He has a journalist's eye for major celebrations in Phnom Penh, such as the Water Festival, and is not afraid to be accurate in his descriptions, whether of the bustling markets or the shabbiness of the Buddhist pagoda sited on top of the *phnom*. But for all the echoes of earlier travel writing, Williams has a shrewd eye for the reality of power, and the Phnom Penh he describes is marked by political contradictions and the failings and errors of Sihanouk. Frequently forgotten when a list is made of books to read about Cambodia in the closing stages of Sihanouk's rule, Williams offers perceptive descriptive passages along with a gentle debunking of the readiness of some commentators of that period to describe both Cambodia and its ruler in idealized terms.

Much less successful is Williams' novel *The Temple*, which like Andrew Graham's book, is set in an exotic Asian kingdom, "Punan", clearly Cambodia. Its central figure is unmistakably based, in part at least, on Sihanouk, hence the observation that: "it was not difficult to see why the less reputable sections of the western media called him 'The Royal Chorus Boy' or 'The Pin-up Prince'."

Although not strictly memoirs, several books by journalists reflect their personal experience in Cambodia or association with the subjects of their books. The Pulitzer Prize-winning *New York Times* journalist Henry Kamm's *Cambodia: Report from a Stricken Land* (1998) draws on his experience in covering Cambodia both before and after the Lon Nol coup in 1970, as well as carrying the story of the country forward into the late 1990s. He is particularly successful in capturing the dangerously naive and enthusiastic spirit of Phnom Penh's youth as they marched off to war in 1970, totally unprepared for the practised enemy they would encounter. He also provides sympathetic portraits of individuals who never understood why and how they would be abandoned by their American patrons. More than incidentally, Kamm deserves the highest praise for being one of the first western journalists to draw international attention to the horrors of the Pol Pot regime once it gained power in 1975.

Tim Bowden's biography of Neil Davis, *One Crowded Hour*, making extensive use of Davis' own journals, has much that is characteristic of a memoir. Phnom Penh and Davis' life in the city feature only briefly in the biography, which is most rewarding reading for the non-nonsense account of what war in the Cambodian countryside was really like. A legendary figure among Australian newsmen, Davis was an affable and informative figure to all who knew him and I, like many others, remember the interest and pleasure to be had in talking to him.

More strictly a memoir, and at the same time an example of high-quality reportage dealing with both Vietnam and Cambodia, Jon Swain's *River of Time* (1995) provides some notable descriptions of the life led by journalists using Phnom Penh as their base before the city fell, and of what happened when the Khmer Rouge achieved their victory. Unfairly described as "mawkish" by one critic, on account of Swain's love affair with a French-Vietnamese woman, one chapter alone makes the book worth reading. This is the description Swain gives of his travel by ship from Saigon to Phnom Penh shortly before the Khmer Rouge succeeded in closing the river to all traffic. The chapter entitled "River Ambush" is an outstanding and exciting piece of reporting as the vessel on which Swain travelled came under Khmer Rouge attack. It brings home to the reader the reality of the increasingly desperate circumstances in Phnom Penh in the closing stages of the civil war when all access to the capital by road had been cut off and when the only way of transporting heavy equipment into the city was by ships that risked being targeted by artillery and heavy machinegun fire.

Although not written in the style of a memoir, two books by French authors deserve mention for the positions their authors held in Phnom

Penh during the time when Sihanouk still ruled. These are Charles Meyer's *Derrière le sourire khmer* and Bernard Hamel's *Sihanouk et le drame cambodgien*. As we have seen, Meyer held an unusual position in Sihanouk's Cambodia. Although never as influential as he presented himself to be, he was nonetheless probably the foreigner who was most frequently in contact with Cambodia's ruler during the 1950s and 1960s, though this proximity ultimately led to the bitter tone that marks this book. He was a highly intelligent man with a wide, if somewhat uneven, knowledge of Cambodia and its people. For this reason his book, when it deals with the nature of Cambodia society and its politics, is well worth reading. Hamel's book is less rewarding, but it does provide another insight into political life in Phnom Penh in the closing stages of Sihanouk's rule.

Among other memoirs mention has already been made of Leslie Fielding's account of diplomatic life in the mid-1960s, when he was *chargé d'affaires* of the British Embassy. My own contribution to the small number of readily accessible memoirs by foreigners that deal with the Sihanouk years is *Before Kampuchea: Preludes to Tragedy*. Distilled into a few paragraphs in the opening chapter of this book, it recounts the period I spent as a Cornell graduate student in Phnom Penh in 1966 and is based on a detailed journal I kept over that period. As much concerned with people as places, the book seeks to give a sense of what life was like in Phnom Penh as Sihanouk's rule was observably becoming less sure than it had previously been. Hindsight allows us to know that 1966 was Sihanouk's and Cambodia's last "good year".

After the fall of the Pol Pot regime there is little that can be described as literature that covers the period from 1975 to 1991, when the United Nations assumed its role of custodian of Cambodia. One further novel deserves mention for completeness, though its inclusion owes more to the standing of its author than to the manner in which it treats Cambodia. This is Margaret Drabble's *The Gates of Ivory*, which has a brief section drawing on reports the author had read about Phnom Penh. Set in the post-Pol Pot period, it has Liz, a figure from the comfortable middle-class world of literary London, setting out to find what has happened to a friend who has disappeared in Cambodia. A sequel to Drabble's earlier two novels, *The Radiant Way* and *A Natural Curiosity*, it is more concerned with the inner lives of its London-based characters than with the exotic world of Thailand, Vietnam and Cambodia where they briefly find themselves.

Chapter Eleven

AMBIGUOUS CITY IN AN AMBIGUOUS COUNTRY, 1979-1993

Accounts of life in Phnom Penh from the time the Vietnamese marched into the city on 7 January 1979 to the period of United Nations administration of the country under UNTAC (the United Nations Transitional Administration in Cambodia) in 1992-93 are limited in number. What is more, among those that are available there is a set of still-unresolved divergent judgments about the motives and actions of the chief actors involved: the Vietnamese who invaded; their Cambodian protégés whom they installed as the new government in Phnom Penh; and those members of the international community who supported efforts to force the Vietnamese from Cambodia, even though this meant giving aid to the defeated Khmer Rouge as well as to non-communist groups. With Cambodia forced into the position of a pawn in the hostile rivalry between China and Vietnam and more broadly caught up in the last decade of the Cold War, few of the state actors emerge with credit. If one searches to find figures to admire during the 1980s they are surely to be found among the personnel of the NGOs who placed the interests of the Cambodian people above political considerations.

As for accounts of Phnom Penh between 1979 and 1991, put bluntly, an observer's political sympathies were often reflected in any interpretation of the city, its population and how it was governed. In particular, these sympathies—or lack of them—were most apparent in the view individuals took of the role of the Vietnamese. They tended to be seen either as saviours or as quasi-colonizers who were determined to shape a Cambodia responsive to their interests. I declare my own position in judging that the Vietnamese invasion should surely be regarded as having liberated the Cambodian population from Pol Pot's tyranny. But I am unprepared to see it and the subsequent role Vietnam played throughout the 1980s as essentially an exercise in altruism. There can be no doubt that the immediate motivation behind the Vietnamese invasion was to put an end to the cross-border attacks that Pol Pot's regime had undertaken. That this meant freeing the population from Democratic Kampuchea's control was to be applauded. But once this was achieved, I believe Vietnam sought to support a new government in Phnom Penh that paid close attention to its interests, with the hope that it would achieve its long-term goal of being the dominant partner in an Indochinese "federation" (whether or not it was described overtly in such a fashion) composed of itself, Cambodia and Laos.

Moreover, I believe that Vietnam ultimately withdrew from Cambodia and abandoned direct involvement in its affairs essentially as the result of international opposition and the collapse of the Soviet Union, which was its foreign patron. It was not a choice it would otherwise have made. All this said, the picture that emerges of Phnom Penh in the 1980s is of a city that slowly became, once again, a city of Cambodians, ruled by Cambodians. A necessary qualification is that this did not always mean the lives of the bulk of the city's population were free from petty irritation, at best; what was on occasion rigid political control with a Marxist bent; and the endemic Cambodian problem of corruption and the impunity enjoyed by those who held the levers of power, at worst.

The new Cambodian rulers of the post-Pol Pot period and the Vietnamese who mentored them, assisted them, and for much of the time simply directed them what to do, faced a task that was staggering in size and character. Some of the leaders who played an important part in the early days of what became known as the People's Republic of Kampuchea (PRK), such as Chan Si and Pen Sovann, are names that were scarcely known to most outsiders, while others, such as Heng Samrin, Chea Sim, and most notably of all, Hun Sen, steadily became recognized as figures of importance through the 1980s into the years after the UNTAC period, or at least they did to those who studied Cambodia.

We now know that upwards of two million people had died while the Khmer Rouge ruled Cambodia. The country was shattered physically and the number of those who remained alive and who possessed the skills required to make the country work had been drastically reduced. Only a tenth of the doctors who had been in the country in 1975 were still alive in 1979. There were even fewer teachers, proportionately, who had survived. Malnutrition was endemic among children, and within six months of the Vietnamese invasion the whole country was on the brink of famine.

THE VIETNAMESE ARRIVE

Just how many people remained in Phnom Penh as the Vietnamese troops streamed into the city on 7 January is uncertain, but a figure of around 30,000 is believable. These were the men and women who had provided the services required by the Khmer Rouge administration and who worked in the few factories the regime had maintained to produce basic goods such as textiles. As the Vietnamese forces arrived these Cambodians were sequestered in their barrack-like accommodation, uncertain of what was happening and how it would affect them. This meant that the Vietnamese and the Cambodian members of the National Salvation Front who accompanied them found an empty city, with deserted streets, buildings that had been important to the departed regime ringed with barbed wire, and the debris of wrecked cars and items such as washing machines and refrigerators still piled on pavements.

It was not until the next day that the extermination centre at Tuol Sleng was found, stumbled upon by chance by two Vietnamese photographers who were alerted to its existence by the stench of decaying bodies coming from a compound enclosed behind an iron fence. Inside the compound they found the corpses of prisoners still chained to the iron bedsteads, their throats cut and the blood that had poured onto the floor still not fully dry. Over the next few months the Vietnamese, assisted by Cambodians, went about making what they had found into a genocide museum. At the same time and of great importance for the knowledge we now have of what took place at S-21, Vietnamese and Cambodians took charge of the vast archive of records that had been preserved during the extermination centre's operation. As David Chandler has pointed out, these did not directly link the top leadership of Democratic Kampuchea—men such as Pol Pot or Ieng Sary—with the functioning of S-21. Nevertheless, that it was an agency of the central committee of the Communist Party is beyond dispute. Equally beyond dispute is the falsity of the claims repeatedly made by the surviving top Khmer Rouge leadership that they did not know of S-21's operations.

A NEW REGIME

The day after Phnom Penh was liberated from Pol Pot's control a new Cambodian government was installed in the form of the Kampuchea People's Revolutionary Council. Later in the year it mutated into the government of the People's Republic of Kampuchea. It was avowedly social-ist (Marxist) in character and deeply indebted for its existence to the Vietnamese. As the Vietnamese and the Cambodians tried to come to grips with controlling Phnom Penh, they faced a situation in which the defeated Khmer Rouge still had armed forces in excess of 30,000—some estimates place their size at twice that figure—who continued to herd an unwilling section of the rural population towards the Thai border. As they did so they fought rearguard actions against the Vietnamese. At the same time, those hundreds of thousands of people who had been released from the control of the Khmer Rouge in the countryside began to return to the towns and villages in which they had previously lived. People were on the move all over Cambodia and were travelling in the worst possible condi-tions. The retreating Khmer Rouge had burned granaries, and at the same time those who had been released from their bondage tended to consume whatever they found along the way, whether rice or draft animals. The conditions that ultimately led to the near famine conditions in the latter part of 1979 were being set in train.

In those first few months of 1979 a steady stream of returnees reached the outskirts of Phnom Penh. They were the surviving remnants of its middle classes: civil servants, technically qualified people and members of the pre-Pol Pot commercial class. But the best estimate of how many trained Cambodians remained among them suggests that it was no more than 15 per cent of those alive before 1970. Concerned at any possibility of an undermining of the new regime, both the Cambodians who were now struggling to form an administration and their Vietnamese mentors moved slowly to select those allowed to return into the city. For a period of some months Phnom Penh was ringed by holding centres while the ac-ceptability of those looking for employment was established. When they were selected they had to undergo "re-education" before they took up places in an administration in which Vietnamese "advisers" had the last word over every important action. The Vietnamese ambassador to Cambodia throughout the 1980s, Ngo Dien, was in effect a proconsul who had found, he told Henry Kamm, the *New York Times* journalist, that the abilities of the protégé government were "below the level required by their task". This comment, which Kamm recorded in his *Cambodia: Report from a Stricken Land*, was made more than a year after the 1979 Vietnamese invasion.

Seen from one point of view, it is unsurprising that the Vietnamese should have assumed a directing role as they did. On the one hand, they had every reason to be concerned about the continuing capacity of the Khmer Rouge to fight against them, and on the other they could not abandon their Cambodian protégés to flounder in a ravaged country. As Nayan Chanda of the *Far Eastern Economic Review* recounts in his *Brother Enemy*, the Vietnamese government sent thousands of its citizens into Cambodia to bring Phnom Penh back to life, to restore its electricity and water supply and to furnish basic health service, which had otherwise totally collapsed. At the same time a smaller number of Cambodians were rapidly taken to Vietnam to be trained in the basic elements of running a modern state. But hand in hand with this rescue exercise was another side to the Vietnamese presence, described again by Chanda, writing of developments in the early months of 1979, as the Vietnamese looted the city:

> Convoys of trucks carrying refrigerators, air conditioners, electrical gadgets, furniture, machinery and precious sculptures headed towards Ho Chi Minh City. All these had been left behind by a population brutally evicted from the city in 1975.

A Phnom Penh street shortly after the defeat of the Khmer Rouge in 1979

As one of the first journalists to visit Phnom Penh, in July 1979, Chanda found it "a ghost town... The once busy Chinese business section of Phnom Penh looked like a scene after a cataclysmic storm. Every house and shop had been ransacked."

Chanda's picture is echoed by almost all foreign observers whom the Vietnamese allowed in to see the city. John Pilger, the Australian journalist known for his sympathy for progressive causes and in this instance for the Vietnamese communists, wrote of his visit in August 1979 and of "entering a city the size of Manchester or Brussels in the wake of a nuclear cataclysm which had spared only the buildings." He detailed the dreadful conditions that existed in the functioning hospitals within the capital—lack of trained staff, lack of drugs, insanitary conditions. Two months later Henry Kamm made his first visit for six years to Phnom Penh, a city he knew well. Accompanying a group of American and Australian politicians who were seeking ways to improve the supply of food into Cambodia, he spent a day in the city. Writing of this first, brief visit, he records how those he spoke to were preoccupied with hunger and of how there was still no monetary economy in place. Instead of money, prices were calculated in terms of the amount of rice required to fill an empty condensed-milk tin. As I was two years later, he was surprised to find the Catholic cathedral had been demolished. But this reaction was totally overshadowed by the horror of seeing the extermination centre at Tuol Sleng.

Visiting the following year, Kamm again found a preoccupation with hunger and, in his eyes, the unquestionably dominant role of the Vietnamese, but it is clear that by the end of 1980 a degree of fragile stability had begun to return to Phnom Penh as the use of currency was reintroduced and a combination of large-scale smuggling and international assistance had overcome the near famine conditions that had existed shortly before. William Shawcross reported a similar picture of 1980 Phnom Penh in his *The Quality of Mercy*. A market economy had begun to function, but it did so against a background of continuing fears of famine, periods of obstruction from the new government in the distribution of aid, and an uneven capacity on the part of key government ministries.

By this stage the new government had, in August 1979, held a five-day trial of Pol Pot and Ieng Sary before a Popular Revolutionary Tribunal in Phnom Penh. The trial took place without the presence of a proper defence for the accused, with invited observers from friendly (socialist) countries. It is recognized to have been a "show trial" in nature, even by writers sympathetic to the new regime such as Margaret Slocomb, the author of *The Peoples Republic of Cambodia 1979-1989*. After four days of proceedings lacking any suggestion of balanced legal procedure it condemned both men to death in absentia for "genocide".

RETURN TO PHNOM PENH

One of the important decisions taken by the PRK in its first year of existence was to permit the return to a central part in Cambodian life of the Buddhist *sangha*, the Buddhist "establishment" with its monks and its organizational identity. While its readiness to see the Buddhist church functioning again reflected an awareness of the importance of religion to the population at large, the government clearly intended it to be under strict state control. Evan Gottesman, who has written with great insight on the evolution of Cambodian politics in the 1980s in his *Cambodia After the Khmer Rouge*, details the manner in which, in September 1979, the PRK arranged for ethnic Cambodian monks from southern Vietnam to come to Phnom Penh to officiate at the consecration of former monks at Wat Unnalom. Even so, the PRK was not prepared to see the revival of the Thommayut sect, presumably because of its royal connections (described in Chapter Four). Only when Sihanouk was welcomed back to Cambodia in 1991 was this minority Buddhist sect allowed to function again. More generally, and while the number of monks in Cambodia today has returned to the level of the 1960s, the religion revived slowly, partly because away from Phnom Penh many pagodas had been damaged in the Khmer Rouge period.

It was against this background that I was able to visit Phnom Penh in late August-early September 1981. Tellingly, it was a visit facilitated by the Vietnamese. My first impression after reaching the centre of the city was of its pervasive and extraordinary decrepitude. Buildings had been left unpainted and un-maintained for years, large piles of garbage littered the streets and there was a curious contrast between areas such as Monivong Boulevard, where people swarmed, and other areas that were sealed off and were totally empty. Efforts to find out why some areas were not accessible were turned aside by my escorts without explanation other than that this was a "government decision". When darkness fell in the evenings there was a limited amount of electricity, so that whole districts of the city relied on lamps and candles. In the occupied sections there was a surprising amount of motor traffic, much more than I had seen in both Hanoi and Saigon in the days immediately before reaching Phnom Penh. And, in great contrast to the Phnom Penh of the 1960s, there were many horse drawn carts used for the transport of people and goods. Some streets were free of debris, as opposed to garbage, while others still had wrecked cars piled up at the side of the road.

It became rapidly clear that no one knew exactly how many people were living in the city. The official estimate, I was told, was 300,000. But the consensus among foreign NGOs in the city settled on an approximation of around 400,000. The uncertainty reflected the fact that a large proportion of the city's population at this time were squatters. Visiting the building that had housed the Australian Embassy when I worked there in the early 1960s, I found it occupied by four families of squatters, with a pig tethered in the driveway. A major problem was the fact, admitted readily to me by Mat Ly, the Deputy Minister for Agriculture, whom I interviewed at length, that many of the squatters were peasants without jobs, representing an unproductive drain on urban services.

By this time, more than two years after the defeat of Pol Pot, there was a clearly mapped-out circuit of visits available to visitors, and one of my first was to Tuol Sleng and then to Choeung Ek—described earlier in this book. Following these shocking experiences the rest of my itinerary included a textile factory and a distillery, both revealing a severe lack of trained personnel, and a visit to the 17 April Hospital, once a private Chinese hospital and curiously named after the date of Pol Pot's victory in 1975. It now functioned with the help of a Cuban medical team. I noted in my journal that "it probably fits into the 'appropriate technology' category, but for a western visitor it is pretty grim, with a lack of cleanliness, crowded wards, relatives living with patients." Indeed, the whole health issue at this stage was "pretty grim". On a later, unescorted visit to a World Vision-supported paediatric hospital, I was told that malnutrition among the city's children was serious, exacerbated by the absence of a balanced diet. This contrasted, I was told, with the situation in rural areas, where there were often inadequate quantities of food but what was available was essentially balanced between protein and non-protein intake. Children in the capital, on the other hand, were subsisting on a diet of rice alone. As

I absorbed this information I saw the tell-tale signs of kwashiorkor in the children in the hospital with their swollen bellies and hair turning orange in colour.

Visits to the Royal Palace, including the Silver Pagoda, and to the national museum were reassuring to a degree, for it was clear that they had not been looted as had been claimed. A visit of a particularly personal character to the Archives building, where I had spent so many hours in 1966, revealed less damage than I had feared. Nearby the old Hôtel le Royal was once again functioning after the years of neglect. It was now renamed the Samaki (Solidarity) Hotel and was occupied by long-term residents from the NGOs in the city. Both in Phnom Penh and in my travels to the provincial centres of Battambang and Takeo—and despite the decisions taken in relation to religion in 1979 and 1980—I saw no more than twenty Buddhist monks. At this time, Takeo was little more than a collection of ruined shophouses. Battambang, by contrast, appeared to have recovered much better from the years of war than Phnom Penh, probably because of its relative proximity to the Thai border and opportunities for smuggling goods into the city.

Within Phnom Penh the Vietnamese presence was discreetly low-key. The official Cambodian position was that whether military or civilian, the Vietnamese were in the country at Cambodia's request. Outside the city the situation was very different, with key infrastructure such as bridges guarded by clearly visible units of Vietnamese troops. The Vietnamese military presence, amounting to some 50,000 troops, was essential as the forces opposed to the new regime grew in strength, a fact that led to a development that severely dented the reputation of the new Phnom Penh government and its mentors. Beginning in the 1982-83 dry season, then accelerating in 1984-85, the Vietnamese-backed regime embarked on a massive work programme to build a physical barrier consisting of ditches and earth ramparts against a possible invasion from the west, a strategy which almost certainly originated within the Vietnamese high command in Cambodia. But it was the PRK government which conscripted upwards of 100,000 labourers to work in difficult conditions. They were poorly fed, often harshly treated and exposed to areas plagued by rampant malaria without adequate medicine. Known as the K5 plan, this exercise in forced labour brought a high cost in lives—no one really knows how many were lost—and did much to diminish the new regime's support among the population in general, not least because it was apparent that there was widespread corruption in the disbursement of funds earmarked for the K5 barrier's construction.

LIMITED NORMALITY

Despite all of the point scoring and manoeuvring that had bedevilled the provision of aid to Cambodia in the first four years following the Vietnamese invasion, from 1984 onwards a fragile kind of normality began to take hold in Phnom Penh, if not in the countryside, where the unlikely coalition of forces opposed to the government and its Vietnamese supporters launched attacks. The ideologues, both Cambodian and Vietnamese, who initially hoped for an almost textbook application of Marxist economic planning principles, came to the realization by 1984 that it was impossible to prevent the private sector from operating. From that date on, to use Gottesman's well-chosen term, Phnom Penh, as it had been in both colonial and Sihanouk's time, was once again caught up in "Mekongisation". This meant that the PRK leadership "gradually permitted the Chinese dominated merchant class to recreate the traditional economic relationship between Saigon and Phnom Penh." Nevertheless, a slow return to this qualified sort of normality did not disguise the fundamentally authoritarian nature of the regime. John Tully is correct in calling it "Stalinist", with its reliance on secret police—initially Vietnamese, but then the Cambodian successors they had trained—detention without trial, torture and the rhetoric of denouncing dissidents as "traitors to the regime".

Based on his long acquaintance with the city, Henry Kamm's account of returning to Phnom Penh in 1987 is particularly valuable for its detail. He found it "shocking". When he had visited in 1980 he thought he had seen the signs of a rebirth; now he found it "an overgrown rural settlement":

> The pigs, poultry, and occasional cattle that had been driven to the popular quarters were now comfortably roaming the city... The litter of years lay ungathered everywhere, breeding rats, flies, and sickness... Medical relief workers told me that no more than one per cent of the people had access to safe drinking water. The deputy minister [of health] said few people were heeding advice to boil the water. She seemed to

give no thought to the evident proposition that a population that had barely enough money to ward off starvation had none to spend on firewood.

Eight years after the defeat of the Pol Pot regime, life in Phnom Penh for all other than the most senior officials and the re-emerging merchant classes still revolved around survival. While those who worked for the government were granted rations to supplement their meagre pay, the common pattern was for one partner in a marriage, usually the wife, to conduct some form of petty commerce. Supplies of all kinds were limited, with aid from the socialist bloc, and in particular the Soviet Union, insufficient to overcome the constant shortages that hindered a full economic recovery. Rubber plantations were only slowly being brought back into production, and in Phnom Penh those factories that were operating had to contend with frequent power interruptions. The most important factory in the city, a textile factory at Tuol Kork, was lucky to operate three days a week, beset as it was with both electricity blackouts and shortages of yarn.

Yet change was close to hand, indeed closer than Henry Kamm's unhappy experiences in 1987 could have led anyone to believe. It was change, moreover, that would dramatically transform Phnom Penh both in political and in physical terms in the course of four years. As has been the case so often in Cambodia's history, the fate of the country and of its capital city was to be determined by other powers.

A Changing World

By 1987 the leadership in both Moscow and Beijing had changed, and the two giants of the communist world, the Soviet Union and China, now led by Mikhail Gorbachev and Deng Xiaoping, had begun a shared retreat from the doctrinaire policies of the past. The possibility of a Sino-Soviet rapprochement opened the way for a resolution of the festering Cambodian problem. So long as it remained unresolved it left Phnom Penh in the state Henry Kamm described. This state of affairs was an ever-growing drain on Vietnam's military and its meagre finances. There was no hope that the coalition forces ranged against the Hanoi and Phnom Penh governments could defeat them, but there was equally no way that these enemies of the PRK, backed as they were principally by China, the United

States, Thailand and Singapore, could be prevented from acting as a debilitating pressure on the Cambodian state.

Yet despite the continuing low-level hostilities that existed between Phnom Penh and the coalition forces ranged against it, trade with Thailand was becoming an integral part of the city's day-to-day existence. In all of these changed circumstances it slowly became apparent that a deal could be struck that would free Cambodia from its isolated state as a Vietnamese dependency. The essential requirement for Phnom Penh's opponents—the ASEAN countries, with Thailand and Singapore in the lead, China and the US, all of whom were supporting a coalition of Cambodian forces dominated by the Khmer Rouge—was that Vietnamese forces should withdraw completely from Cambodia. In March 1987 the Vietnamese Prime Minister, Pham Van Dong, stated that all Vietnamese troops would be out of Cambodia by 1990 (by the time he made this statement, a large number had in fact already left). As negotiations moved at what seemed at times a glacial pace, the outlines of a settlement slowly became clear. As part of this process the Vietnamese finally withdrew all of their troops from Cambodia in September 1989.

Now, in a gesture that was designed to indicate its changed character, the Cambodian government renamed itself the State of Cambodia (SOC), so dropping the reference to a "people's" republic in its official title and, by implication, its claim to be a socialist revolutionary state. At one level this change of title was more than cosmetic, for it coincided with a visible change in Phnom Penh's character and appearance. But if the government was relaxing its control over everyday life, it was certainly not ceding any power to others where politics were concerned. Nevertheless, the capital began to rediscover its life. New shops and restaurants began to open and consumer goods flooded in from abroad. As Evan Gottesman points out, there was an accompanying rise in social vices, of prostitution, gambling and drug taking. In this area the regime found itself unable to control society, or indeed members of its own administration. The new reality of this period is wonderfully captured in a quotation Gottesman records in which the Deputy Minister of the Interior observed, "If madams [of Phnom Penh's brothels] are our staff or cadres, we have a hard time [making arrests] and there might be protest."

Finally, and as the Berlin Wall came down in November 1989, the path leading to a settlement of what was now routinely called "the

Cambodia problem" began to become clearer. After tortuous negotiations, all of the powers with interests in the country signed the "Accords on a Comprehensive Settlement of the Cambodia Conflict" in Paris on 23 October 1991. These accords contained the essential provision that a United Nations Transitional Authority for Cambodia (UNTAC) would assume responsibility for a national election to take place in 1993, in conditions of peace. A key feature of these accords was their provision for the Khmer Rouge's participation in the process leading up to the election.

"BOOMTOWN"

As the advance guard for UNTAC began its task in November 1991, Phnom Penh was being further transformed. The American journalist Stan Sesser reached Phnom Penh a month later. In his book *The Lands of Charm and Cruelty* he describes how he found a "boomtown" that had embraced capitalism with a vengeance, from the "Welcome to Cambodia— Heineken Beer" sign at Pochentong airport to the abundance of Mercedes-Benz and BMW cars travelling the streets. Foreign NGOs had begun to pour into the city, fuelling the demand for new restaurants and pushing up property prices as there was a growing demand for rental accommodation. The Hôtel le Royal had reverted to its original name, been repainted and ran a popular, noisy disco, while the long-neglected Cambodiana had finally been completed and was operating as the best hotel in town. Vice and corruption were part of this boomtown atmosphere, from the members of the government who were ready to sell off state property to the highest bidder to the Vietnamese prostitutes who had flocked into the city. Sihanouk himself had returned, with a retinue of chefs from China. He had played an important part in the final conclusion of the settlement, but certainly did not recognize at this stage that, despite his undoubted hopes to the contrary, he would never again be able to play the dominant role in Cambodian politics.

As Sesser accurately observed, whatever ritual bows the SOC made towards suggestions that Cambodia should emerge as a democratic state once UNTAC had overseen elections, the political leadership now headed by Hun Sen was determined not to give away the dominance it had enjoyed throughout the 1980s. Hun Sen's political party, now calling itself the Cambodian People's Party (CPP), kept a tight grip on power and did not hesitate to use that power to arrest those who challenged it.

This provoked student riots in December, which were largely inspired by resentment of the corruption associated with the regime's leadership, including Hun Sen and his wife, Bun Rany. The riots were brutally suppressed—a forewarning of what the government has been prepared to do since.

THE UNITED NATIONS

With its headquarters in Phnom Penh but branches spread throughout the country, UNTAC was a hydra-like body covering everything from the planned elections to peacekeeping, and from civil administration to humanitarian relief. Ultimately troop contingents came to Cambodia from nearly a dozen countries, some as peacekeepers, some as engineers and some as communications specialists. Sad to tell, among the military personnel who served during the UNTAC period were a number of men who were already HIV-positive. In circumstances of widespread prostitution, their legacy lives on in Cambodia's serious HIV-AIDS problems.

Some sense of the high ideals of many who worked for UNTAC—and the less than admirable qualities of others—is vividly captured in a memoir of the period by an American volunteer, Tom Riddle, who worked in the electoral headquarters as preparations were made for the 1993 elections. His *Cambodian Interlude* is marked by good humour, frankness and a healthy appreciation of the ridiculous. At the same time and with obvious sympathy for the Cambodian population, he evokes a city that was still trying to come to terms with the terrible two decades that that had preceded the 1991 Paris Agreements. It was still a city where fear of the Khmer Rouge, of bandits and other assorted thugs linked to political parties could make the thought of going out at night dangerous.

> … For Cambodians the night was frightening, dangerous and foreboding—time to lock the door, stay inside and sleep. The night, everyone knew, was the time for drunks, robbers and prostitutes. After eight o'clock at night most of Phnom Penh's streets were deserted.

An enthusiast in every way, Riddle delighted in the bustle of the Psar Thmei, ruefully dissected the rules of riding motor cycle taxis and found a way to live with the army of amputees who begged in the streets from any foreigner they could find.

The *Psar Thmei* or Grand Market completed in 1937

A counter-point to Riddle's book is Christopher G. Moore's 2004 thriller, set in the UNTAC period, *Zero Hour in Phnom Penh*. Consciously modelled on the hard-boiled novels of the Dashiell Hammet genre, Moore's Sam Spade is an American private eye resident in Bangkok, Vincent Calvino, who is sent on a mysterious mission to Phnom Penh where he encounters troubles of many kinds. Moore covered the final UNTAC period as a journalist and his novel offers a credible description of the places where foreigners gathered at that time. Warmly received in translation in Germany, it has at least the rare distinction of being a fictional account of life in 1990s Phnom Penh.

At one fundamental level UNTAC was a notable success. In July 1993 it presided over what was the first free and fair election ever conducted in Cambodia. (It may well have been the last, since intimidation has played a major part in each election that has followed.) But it was marred in two important ways. Before the vote took place the Khmer Rouge had withdrawn from the electoral process and made clear it was ready to fight on against the Phnom Penh government. Given the vicious background of this group, it will sound odd to argue that this was ultimately less important than the other shortcoming of the UNTAC process: the fact that the United Nations abrogated responsibility when Hun Sen and his CPP refused to accept the verdict of the voters and cede government to the party that won the most votes and seats in the National Assembly. This party was the clumsily named Front Uni Pour un Cambodge Indépendant, Neutre, Pacifique et Coopératif (FUNCINPEC), which had been formed in the 1980s in support of Norodom Sihanouk and which was led at the time of the elections by his son, Prince Norodom Ranariddh. Quite simply, and with power firmly in the hands of the CPP through their control of the forces of order and the key ministries, Hun Sen and his associates refused to give up power. The compromise arrangement that saw both Hun Sen and Ranariddh being designated as prime ministers did not disguise this fact and set the scene for the bitter rivalries of the following years that ended with Hun Sen's bloody putsch of July 1997.

As the United Nations effectively washed its hands of Cambodia's internal politics, the Phnom Penh they left behind had much of the appearance to be found more than ten years later. The Hôtel le Royal was still to be renovated, but the well-known Foreign Correspondents' Club was already functioning, having been opened in 1993. In the inner city the former Chinese Quarter swarmed with people, but the streets of this district had deteriorated to be little more than rough dirt tracks. Then, as now, building seemed to be taking place everywhere, and the main thoroughfares were filled with traffic including *cyclos* in streets such as the Boulevard Norodom, from which they are now banned. There were no taxis, nor the Phnom Penh version of *tuk-tuks* that began to appear in 2006, and so motorcycles, known as *motodop*, were the preferred means of local transport for foreigners. Norodom Sihanouk had returned to sit once more on the throne of Cambodia, but as a constitutional monarch—even if he showed little sign of recognizing this concept. In all of this, and despite the multiple problems Phnom Penh faced following the end of the UNTAC period, one point was beyond dispute. The city was fully alive again.

Chapter Twelve

TODAY'S CITY: SOMEHOW HOPE SURVIVES

It would be easy to present a picture of life in contemporary Phnom Penh that gives full rein to pessimism. And, without doubt, pessimism should be part of any assessment of the city, for there is much that that is deeply disturbing about the way it is ruled and the manner in which the majority of its people must live. But such a view is unlikely to be the impression gained by short-term visitors. Little of the corruption and impunity that dominate life for the Cambodian population of the city is apparent to the growing number of tourists. Most of these, like so many before them, spend only a day or two in the city, staying in what is now a wide range of comfortable and even luxurious accommodation, before or after a visit to the temples of Angkor. Visitors encounter smiling people who appear to have triumphed over a recent past and to have achieved a phoenix-like rebirth from the figurative ashes of the period when Pol Pot ruled. So the majority of visitors are unaware that the elections of 1993 did not spell an end to Cambodia's and Phnom Penh's political problems and were, instead, a departure point for a struggle for control of the country's destiny which was only fully resolved more than a decade later.

With the primacy of Hun Sen and the CPP now clearly established, no major steps have been taken to suggest that the government is prepared to address the running sores that corruption and impunity represent. This is well understood, of course, by Cambodians, and by those foreigners who work in Phnom Penh and are committed to improving the lives of the population in general. But faced with the alternative of trying to engineer change by cutting aid to the government, which would ultimately have an impact on the long-suffering population at large, or hoping that at some future date change of a positive kind might occur, the international community has chosen the latter course.

Whether or not the political and social ailments of Phnom Penh are apparent to another and very different group of expatriates, who stay longer than most tourists and are often ignored in accounts of the city, is a different question. Numbering in the few hundreds, the group in question is almost exclusively male, mostly blue-collar in occupational background, and committed to plumbing to its full depths the opportunities Phnom Penh provides for cheap alcohol, sex and drugs. They are a group distinct from the ubiquitous backpackers, who are equally likely to take advantage of cheap accommodation and drugs, but tend to move on fairly quickly to what they see as the more exciting cities of Saigon (Ho Chi Minh City) and Bangkok, or the even cheaper locales found in Laos. As Michael Hayes, the perceptive long-time publisher and editor of the *Phnom Penh Post* remarks, the group in question is seldom seen before six in the evening, when they emerge from their cheap lodgings to congregate in the less salubrious bars of the capital. They do not frequent the Foreign Correspondents' Club on Sisowath Quay, or the Deauville near Wat Phnom, but they can be found in the Heart of Darkness, or nowadays more likely at Sharky's, where beer is cheap and working girls are readily available. Whether most of them know it or not, they have their own laureate, Amit Gilboa, whose book *Off the Rails in Phnom Penh* (1998) charts the author's experiences in 1996 and 1997, from the drug culture of his associates and their use of heroin—he stopped at marijuana—to his readiness to visit the infamous brothels known by their location on the road leading to the north out of town as Kilometre 11.

There is, sadly, another sub-group of foreign visitors whose presence must be listed in any brief survey of contemporary Phnom Penh. These are the foreigners who come to the city in search of under-age sex. There is no possibility of quantifying the numbers of this cohort of paedophiles. Occasional arrests are a pointer to their existence, which ultimately reflects the pervasive presence of dire poverty that still leads to parents selling their young children to brothel keepers.

POWER POLITICS

As outlined in the previous chapter, the political architecture of contemporary Cambodia was determined, if not absolutely set in place, by events following the United Nations sponsored elections of 1993, when Hun Sen and the Cambodian People's Party refused to cede power to Prince Norodom Ranariddh and FUNCINPEC, despite receiving a smaller proportion of the vote and of the parliamentary seats contested in the election. Following those elections, the essential outlines of Cambodia's political contest became clear. Whatever prestige accrued to Ranariddh as a result of his royal birth and his party's association with his father, the now-reinstated King Norodom Sihanouk, Hun Sen's hands were on the levers of power that mattered. Because it had ruled during the 1980s, the CPP controlled the important ministries in the administration and the key elements within the forces of order, the army and the police.

Most observers have recognized this fact and taken it as the main reason that Hun Sen and his party have been able to dominate politics after UNTAC. But many of these commentators have given too little credit to Hun Sen's skill in building on this advantage, even if that skill has been accompanied by a readiness to sanction brutality when it seemed opportune. Too often, not least in the light of events in 1997 discussed briefly below, critics of Hun Sen have been reluctant to acknowledge his energy and political skills, not least his capability as a natural orator, and too ready to overlook Ranariddh's lack of these skills. As this political drama has played out since 1993, Ranariddh's father, Sihanouk, slowly came to the realization that there was little role for him to play in Cambodian politics, a decision that ultimately led to his abdication in favour of another of his sons, Norodom Sihamoni, in 2004.

To write in these terms is not to justify the methods that Hun Sen and the CPP have used to entrench their control over the country. Above all, Hun Sen's putsch of July 1997, when his forces mounted a full-scale assault against Ranariddh and those much weaker elements in the army that were supporters of FUNCINPEC, illustrated the lengths to which he was prepared to go. Not only did the CPP's forces comprehensively defeat their opponents in the battles that raged for two days in the streets of Phnom Penh, but they followed this victory with a brutal series of extra-judicial killings and torture of those they had defeated. Amit Gilboa gives an eyewitness account of this affair in his *Off the Rails in Phnom Penh*.

Since 1997, and admittedly simplifying to some extent what has been a sometimes complex set of circumstances, including clear evidence of tensions within the leadership of the CPP, Hun Sen has steadily imposed his personal control over the country, and consequently over Phnom Penh. Ranariddh, by contrast, has proven to be no equal to Hun Sen, with an inclination to spend long periods of time away from Cambodia and to pay too much attention to the interests of other members of the royal family. As the years have passed, more and more of those who once had been Ranariddh's supporters have decided that their best interests are served by working with the CPP, or defecting to join it. The endgame for Ranariddh came when, in late 2006, members of his own party dismissed him from the leadership of FUNCINPEC, effectively removing him from the possibility of playing a role in Cambodian politics.

In all of this another politician, Sam Rainsy, has played a courageous gadfly role, founding his own party and without question putting himself at personal risk by his open criticism of Hun Sen and the political system. But courageous though he certainly has been, Sam Rainsy has never appeared likely to assume a controlling role in Cambodian politics. Moreover, he has some personal characteristics which his western admirers frequently ignore or seek to minimize. He is, no less than other politicians, authoritarian in personal nature and bitterly anti-Vietnamese in outlook. The latter trait is one that does not always emerge in his speeches and statements made in English or French, but is a frequent theme when he speaks in Cambodian.

THE SHADOW OF THE KHMER ROUGE

By the beginning of 2007 twenty-eight years had passed since the Khmer Rouge were driven from Phnom Penh and eight years since Pol Pot had died, abandoned by most of his followers, who had turned against him and confined the sick old man to house arrest. Yet in all of the years that have passed none of the surviving leaders of the Pol Pot period has been brought to a proper trial—the Popular Revolutionary Tribunal, held in 1979, and mentioned in an earlier chapter, certainly did not meet the requirements of fairness and justice, however much the guilt of Pol Pot and Ieng Sary has been an accepted fact by the world at large. Finally, after years of procrastination by the Phnom Penh government, a tribunal was established in 2006 charged with trying surviving senior Khmer Rouge figures. With its official title as the Extraordinary Chambers of the Courts of Cambodia (ECCC), the judges for the tribunal are drawn from Cambodia and foreign judicial circles, with Cambodians in the majority. Given the clear evidence that a number of the Cambodian judges lack a record of independence from the government and its interests, as well as their dubious commitment to the best standards of jurisprudence, there are good reasons to hold a reserved view about the future functioning of the tribunal. For a time there was real doubt as to whether it would actually ever try cases. But in May 2007 disagreements over procedural issues between the Cambodian and international judges were resolved and it appears likely that the first cases before it will be heard in late 2007 or early 2008. Yet even now there are doubts as to whether the few most senior Khmer Rouge figures, men, such as Ieng Sary and Khieu Samphan, some of whom are in poor health, will survive to face prosecution.

Despite its protestations to the contrary, the government would have been happy if the trials had never been held, for far too many officials currently holding positions of power, from Hun Sen himself on down, were once members of the Khmer Rouge. In fairness, it should be noted that exhaustive investigations have not succeeded in linking Hun Sen with any specific crime against humanity in the period before he fled to Vietnam in 1977. There are many others who also served the Pol Pot regime and hold positions of power today. Although their names are seldom mentioned, their existence acts as a damper on public discussion. China, Pol Pot's closest international backer, would also have been pleased if the tribunal had foundered on legal disagreements. Its support for the Khmer Rouge has now become an embarrassment, even for a regime that is largely impervious to external criticism.

It is difficult to know what Phnom Penh's citizens think about this issue. The overwhelming majority of them were born after the Khmer Rouge regime was overthrown. Many have only the vaguest notions of what happened during the Pol Pot years, for despite the existence of Tuol Sleng, of the "Killing Fields" at Choeung Ek and the abundant foreign literature that recounts what happened during that awful time, history as it has been taught in Cambodian schools and tertiary institutions up till now has barely touched on developments after 1970. A text book that did give brief attention to the Pol Pot period was introduced in 2002, only to be withdrawn shortly afterwards. Craig Etcheson, who as the principal founder of the Documentation Centre of Cambodia has been at the forefront of those seeking a legal accounting for what happened between 1975 and 1979, underlines the problem in his book, *After the Killing Fields: Lessons from the Cambodian Genocide.* He cites the case of the eleven-year-old son of a journalist who has had the evidence of what happened made clear to him, but who simply does not believe that killing could have taken place on such a scale.

It now seems that efforts to change this situation are achieving some success. The Documentation Centre of Cambodia has now published *A*

History of Democratic Kampuchea by a young Cambodian researcher, Khamboly Dy, which reviews the period in detail. Yet it has failed to gain government approval for its use in high schools, with some members of the body that reviewed it finding it "inaccurate" and questioning the very desirability of students being exposed to the details of recent history. These details, of course, reveal the fact that many in the current government and administration were once actively associated with the Khmer Rouge. Instead, the government has said that teachers may use Khamboly's book as a supplementary reference only, until its own text book appears in 2009. Although it says this official text book will draw on the material provided by Khamboly, there seem grounds for wondering how far this will take place. As for those who did survive the years when the Khmer Rouge ruled, many have tried simply, and understandably, to put the period behind them. That many try to do this but do not succeed is apparent in the high rate of mental illness among those who were adults when Pol Pot was in power.

Moreover—and hard though it is to believe—there are Cambodians, particularly among those now living overseas, who forcefully seek to deny that large-scale slaughter took place during the Khmer Rouge years. This revisionist point of view sits well with the claims of those senior Khmer Rouge figures alive today that they did not know about the Tuol Sleng extermination centre. When Nuon Chea, the most senior surviving Khmer Rouge figure, at eighty-two, and the second most powerful man in the Pol Pot regime, was asked in early 2007 about Tuol Sleng, he simply claimed he knew nothing about it until after the Vietnamese invaded in 1979.

THE DECLINE OF ROYALTY

It is impossible to over-emphasize the change to Phnom Penh's identity in the years that have followed Norodom Sihanouk's overthrow in 1970. Put at its simplest, it has meant that Phnom Penh has ceased to be, first and foremost, a royal city. However much there was disenchantment with Sihanouk in the closing years of the 1960s—particularly among the urban population—he still retained his royal aura. This was particularly true for the country's peasantry, who certainly saw Phnom Penh as the home of their king. This did not change when Sihanouk abdicated the throne in favour of his father, King Suramarit, in 1955. Neither was the palace robbed of its importance after Suramarit's death in 1960. Sihanouk continued to be king in all but name, and his formidable mother, Queen Kossamak, living in the Royal Palace, reinforced all that was traditional, special, even quasi-divine about the concept of monarchy in Cambodia. But Sihanouk's deposition in 1970, the years of war and totalitarianism and the troubled period from 1979 to 1993, before Sihanouk was reinstated as king, all combined to strip the office of monarch of much, if not all, of its special mystique. In the period between 1993, when Sihanouk was once again crowned king, and his abdication in Sihanomi's favour in 2004, his efforts to play a role in the Cambodian political process only further weakened the sacral qualities associated with the monarchy.

The fact that Sihamoni was installed as Cambodia's king in a coronation replete with traditional pomp and ceremony does not detract from these judgments. He lives in a palace that is now as much a tourist attraction as the true, mystical centre of the kingdom. Men and women can be summoned to don traditional costumes for events such as Sihamoni's coronation, but there is no longer a true court, as once there was. In the same way, a group of dancers can be assembled to perform in traditional fashion on special occasions, but the court dancers who once lived permanently within the palace are no more. The Pol Pot period ended the lives of many of the teachers who once instructed the royal dancers. Those who survived or have trained since are associated with the Royal University of the Fine Arts, and today the classical dances are more likely to be seen in commercial settings. As a sad reflection on contemporary Cambodia, almost every time a traditional dance troupe travels to perform abroad one or more of its members defects to seek residence in a foreign country.

Other factors have contributed to reinforce the dilution of royalty's aura. While the government under Hun Sen has permitted the revival of what were previously *royal* ceremonies, that character has been undermined in a variety of ways. The Ploughing of the Sacred Furrow ceremony, held each May, was once the preserve of the king, and then after his father's death of Sihanouk as prince and chief of state. While the new king, Sihamoni, has taken the role of the "ploughman", this follows a period when the task has been performed by lesser royal figures or even government officials, and on one occasion by Hun Sen himself. While there are many in the Cambodian population who take the casting of the country's horoscope seriously, the ceremony has taken on the air of a tourist event.

A court brahmin blessing oxen at the Ploughing of the Sacred Furrow

Even more than with the Sacred Furrow ceremony, the festivities associated with the Water Festival are now marked more as a public holiday for Cambodians than as a ceremony with deep meaning. As a tourist attraction it brings foreign visitors to Phnom Penh in large numbers, but it is even more a time when Cambodians flock into the city from the countryside—one of the few occasions when this occurs through the year. As with the Sacred Furrow, the king presides over the Water Festival, but it has changed its character—made clear by the participation of teams of expatriates resident in Phnom Penh who regard it as another version of Hong Kong's dragon boat races.

In all of this, Hun Sen has been concerned to minimize the importance of royalty in Cambodia. Whether he really believes that members of the royal family, including former King Sihanouk, now known as the "King Father", and Ranariddh can undermine the changes that have reinforced his power, is difficult to judge. At first glance his concern seems misplaced. Sihanouk is an old man in indifferent health. Ranariddh has played himself out of the political game, and the many princes who are still keen to use their titles are essentially ineffective bit players in Cambodia's political drama. While Sihanouk still remained on the throne after 1993, though more often than not living outside Cambodia, he tried and failed to play an activist role and was blocked at every time that mattered by Hun Sen. It is interesting, nevertheless, that Hun Sen was happy to have had Sihanouk bestow on him the honorific title *Samdech* (perhaps best translated as "lord") as this was a title used frequently as a form of address to Sihanouk himself in other times. Now that Sihamoni is on the throne and playing a strictly non-interfering constitutional role there is no reason why the monarchy in Cambodia should not survive—for a period. Its long-term future is another matter.

Less easy for an outsider to assess is the extent to which Buddhism has remained central to contemporary Phnom Penh society, as was the case before 1970. At one level the judgment would appear to be positive, with a pervasive and genuine devotion to the religion among the population at large. Certainly this is the impression a visitor receives in visiting pagodas or observing the ubiquitous presence of Buddhist monks at ceremonies both public and private. But there is another aspect to contemporary Buddhism that cannot be disregarded. This is the extent to which the government has co-opted the Buddhist hierarchy, with the current Supreme Patriarch of the Mohanikay sect, Tep Vong, widely regarded as being closely aligned with Hun Sen and the ruling Cambodian People's Party. Critical voices, of which there are many, suggest that his knowledge of Buddhist texts and philosophy are much inferior to his understanding of Cambodia's power politics.

CONTEMPORARY SOCIETY
Of vital importance is the fact that Cambodia is a post-conflict society. This determines the character of the country's capital and the demographic profile of its population. The disruption of society between 1970 and 1993 (if this latter date does indeed represent a terminus) has made sure that attempts to introduce a political system complete with checks and balances have failed. Too many people died or fled the country during the troubled years, leaving a society deprived of talent and commitment, to make this an easy, or even a possible, task. It is against this background that uncontested power is what matters to those who rule, and the possession of power ensures access to wealth. As the population continues to recover from the years of war and loss, only a limited number of men and women

have profited from the aid money that has poured into the country and the opportunities to take a stake in commercial developments. And, axiomatically, those who have benefited enjoy the patronage of senior politicians, just as senior politicians benefit financially from those to whom they grant their favour. Many of the individuals who have worked in this symbiotic relationship with the government have also been rewarded with the honorary title of *oknha*, which confers a measure of nobility, very roughly equivalent to a British knighthood. It is not uncommon to hear them referred to in a generic fashion as a group of individuals who are, in all ways that matter, outside the normal legal constraints that apply to less well-connected people; as individuals and as a group prone to flaunt their wealth in large and expensive cars and SUVs; and as the fathers of sons who are often ready, with the assistance of their bodyguards, to throw their weight about in the bars and restaurants of Phnom Penh.

The fact that so much emphasis is placed on impunity and corruption in summary commentary on contemporary Cambodia is entirely justified. Yet, as David Chandler has pointed out, the existence of the sort of "connections", to use his word, that operate at the highest levels of Phnom Penh society are far from absent in less elevated circles. His point, in short, is that everyone, certainly in the capital, exists by being part of a series of connections. What is disturbing is the extent to which this mirrors that state of affairs in the late 1960s when there was a general revulsion against what was seen as the development of two kinds of corruption: corruption on a grand, even limitless, scale, and the corruption that existed at a functional fashion and which oiled the machinery of existence for all but the poorest in the city. In current circumstances, there has to be a concern that the apparently endless presence of grand corruption will ultimately lead to some form of social explosion.

Although it would be foolish to suggest such a development is inevitable, let alone likely, there are many other factors leading to the expectation that resentment against the present state of affairs will grow. An important factor is the inability of any Cambodian government, now and for the foreseeable present, to find employment for those leaving school and institutions of higher education. The World Bank estimates that there are 300,000 new entrants into the work force each year, with little capacity on the part of the economy to absorb more than a small percentage of this number. Job opportunities for young people who have completed tertiary education are not much brighter than for those who leave at the end of their schooling. With forty-seven institutions providing some form of tertiary education, and with the great majority of these located in Phnom Penh, the current estimate is that some 8,000 students graduate each year and begin looking for work. A frequently-quoted figure indicates that fewer than one in nine graduates are able to find a job after graduation.

The social implications of a large pool of unemployed youth are apparent in the high incidence of domestic violence, criminality involving youth gangs and drug usage, particularly of methamphetamines. While there is general agreement that the first steps towards halting the persistence of the country's many social problems, as well as continuing to contain the prevalence of HIV-AIDS, is increased access to education, it will be some years before Cambodia will be able to provide nine years of basic education for its young people. Politicians of all stripes proclaim their commitment to improving the education system, but it is only in the schools for the children of the elite in Phnom Penh—notably the Lycée Descartes and the Lycée Sisowath—that there is anything approaching the availability of adequate teaching materials and teachers who do not have to devote much of their time to low-level corruption in order to be able to pay for the necessities of life.

Amid the seemingly endless catalogue of social problems afflicting contemporary Phnom Penh, the success the government has had in containing the spread of HIV-AIDS deserves recognition. This has been a remarkable achievement given the multiple problems confronting those who have worked so hard to halt what, in the mid-1990s, seemed set to be the unstoppable acceleration of the infection rate. The combined response of government agencies, UNAIDS and a consortium of NGOs has succeeded in stabilizing the infection rate at 1.6 per cent for the whole of a population just short of 14 million—in 2003 the infection rate was estimated at 2.3 per cent. But there are still groups remaining at high risk, both the obvious, such as sex workers and those who combine other employment with occasional commercial sexual encounters. And there is a worrying group of older men who have decided that, after the lives they have lived over the past three decades, taking one more risk by resorting to unprotected commercial sex is an acceptable choice.

More positively, Phnom Penh functions as a city in which there is relative harmony between the overwhelmingly ethnic Cambodian and Buddhist element of the population and other ethnic groups. It is difficult to know just how many ethnic Chinese and Vietnamese now live in the city, except to be sure that in percentage terms they represent a much smaller proportion of the population than was the case before 1970 (generally accepted statistics estimate ethnic Chinese in the whole of Cambodia as five per cent of the population). That same figure is cited for ethnic Vietnamese, though there are suggestions that it is much too high. While those ethnic Vietnamese who live in Phnom Penh keep a low profile, the same is not true of the city's ethnic Chinese, particularly as political links between Cambodia and China have grown ever warmer in recent years. Chinese temples and schools are now much more prominent than was the case until recently, with one school thought to be the largest in all of Southeast Asia with no fewer than fifteen thousand students.

Seldom obvious in the centre of the city are Cambodia's Muslim citizens, the Khmer Islam. A group which suffered grievously under the rule of the Khmer Rouge, they probably number 500,000 throughout the whole of Cambodia today, with less than half of this number living either on the northern edges of Phnom Penh or in villages not too far distant, at Udong, for instance. While there are clear signs that an influx of Middle Eastern money has contributed to making the Khmer Islam community more observant than once was the case, the government under Hun Sen appears to have developed close and effective links with the country's Islamic leadership. Even so, there have been some indications of efforts to promote militant Islamism in Cambodia and it is clear that the government is alert to this as an issue.

Against this background of apparent social harmony, mention has to be made of the anti-Thai riots that suddenly erupted in January 2003. Supposedly sparked by a comment made by a Thai film star that the temples of Angkor really belonged to Thailand, the riots involved thousands of young Cambodians who looted and burned Thai properties in Phnom Penh and sacked the Thai Embassy, from which the Thai ambassador was lucky to escape uninjured. There has been little satisfactory analysis of the riots, and to some extent they should probably be seen as a reflection of deeper social problems. Although the Phnom Penh police keep a firm hand on petty crime, they have not been able to eliminate the presence in the city of gangs of young men who are engaged in standover tactics and assaults on their rivals in order to dominate protection rackets.

Spirit houses for sale in Phnom Penh, evidence of Thai influence

There seems little doubt that many of these gangs were engaged in the riots and that some, at least were encouraged by people linked to sections of the ruling CPP. In this regard, the riots could be seen as a warning from the pro-Vietnam factions within the CPP to Prime Minister Hun Sen that his government's links with Thailand were growing too close.

The riots also raised the question as to whether there was another division within Phnom Penh society, at least in historical terms. While he was in power in the 1950s and 1960s, Sihanouk lost few opportunities to criticize Thailand and its leaders, leaving the impression that the Thais were Cambodia's "traditional enemies" along with the Vietnamese. Yet the evidence is beyond dispute that the Cambodian court for centuries, up to and including Sihanouk's great-grandfather, Norodom I, regarded the Thai ruler as their suzerain. And well into the twentieth century Cambodian Buddhists seeking higher education in their religion went to study in Bangkok. So the question arises, and probably cannot be answered at this stage, as to whether the modern generation of Cambodians living in Phnom Penh have forgotten about the historical links between their royal family, and their Buddhist leaders, with Thailand. Or is what happened an example of unemployed urban youth being cynically manipulated by using Thailand as a whipping boy for particular political purposes?

THE ARTS AND LITERATURE TODAY

Writing about the arts in Phnom Penh is a difficult task and one made more difficult by the understandable tendency of many who write about the subject to place admiration for a recovering society above the actual level of achievement of the arts in question. Nowhere is this more apparent than in some of the writing that has been devoted to Cambodian cinema, which by any normal, external standards is mostly poor in plot and cinematographic quality. There may not be, as the saying goes, any room for argument about "art". But this does not mean that romanticizing achievement serves any good purpose.

Just as court culture has been greatly affected by Cambodia's grim recent past, so has traditional popular culture been damaged in a serious, but not yet fatal fashion. With support from foreign donors Cambodian musicians, dancers and shadow puppet masters have been able to renew their roles, including as teachers for members of a younger generation which for years had little access to traditional cultural expressions. Among the best known examples of this mentoring is the programme supported by the NGO, Cambodian Living Arts, which has backed the work of music masters such as Kung Nai, known as the "Ray Charles of Cambodia", who performs on the long-necked guitar known as the *chapei dong vang*. A foreigner finds difficulty in experiencing performances of these traditional arts, other than at the Royal University of the Fine Arts or at infrequent festivals or commercial shows. The last option preserves the art form being showcased but can scarcely be compared with performances in a "true" traditional setting. Harsh thought the judgment may appear, traditional entertainments are fighting what may be a losing battle against more modern forms of musical and theatrical expression. Pop music and karaoke are more to the taste of many young Cambodians, with members of the diaspora often greatly admired for their versions of popular music in their homeland. This is true for rap artists such as California-based Prach Ly, with the words delivered both in Cambodian and in English.

Despite the efforts of Cambodian Living Arts and other NGOs to preserve traditional popular culture, there is a question mark over its long-term survival. There is a real risk that music in the folk tradition and shadow puppetry, which never had the same hold in Cambodia as it had and has in Indonesia, will be preserved as quaint relics or the subject for foreign ethnomusicologists rather than being, as once was the case, an integral part of the community's life. As one Cambodian commentator expressed the problem to me, learning to perform the complex music known as *smot* that traditionally accompanied funerals requires a long apprenticeship. Why would a student devote the time and effort to doing this when it is possible to buy a tape or CD that will provide the music required?

Cambodian literature will remain largely inaccessible to foreign visitors to Phnom Penh, with few works available in translation. Surveys of Cambodian writing emphasize both the large volume of writing that took place before 1972—with the estimate of more than a thousand novels published between 1938 and that date—and the great difficulties that exist for any author seeking to live from writing in contemporary Cambodia. Those novels that are published have limited print runs of two or three thousand copies, while newspapers that previously provided opportunities for authors to publish novels in serial form are now reluctant to use space for this purpose. One of the few opportunities for foreigners to sample Cambodian creative writing is in the collection published as *In the Shadow of Angkor: Contemporary Writing from Cambodia*, edited by Frank Stewart and Sharon May. Significantly, several of the items produced in translation in this anthology were written before the Khmer Rouge seized power in 1975, or have been written since by Cambodian writers who live away from their homeland.

Far more than is the case in Vietnam, where there is a lively modern art movement, Cambodian visual art is struggling to establish a presence and an identity in contemporary Phnom Penh. Before 1975 there was an active art scene that benefited from the support of expatriates and foreign diplomatic missions. By far the best known artist of this period was Nhek Dim, whose landscapes were technically accomplished, perhaps reflecting the period he had spent working in the Disney studios. Like so many others who worked in the arts, Nhek Dim died during the period of Khmer Rouge rule. In almost any shop that hopes to attract tourists there will be paintings of all sizes with the Angkor temples, scenes from the *Ramayana* or idealized rural landscapes as their central themes. Few have any claim to artistic merit, but rather are exercises in repetitive composition.

Change is taking place in the visual arts, particularly with the return to Phnom Penh of members of Cambodia's diaspora who have trained overseas. The works of artists who have left behind the "temple and palm tree school" can now be seen in a limited number of the commercial galleries scattered along Street 178, which runs beside the National Museum, and Street 240. Perhaps the most promising development in the visual arts scene is the formation of a group under the title Visual Arts Open (VAO), which has united sixteen painters and three photographers, and which held the first group show in Phnom Penh since the 1960s. The driving forces behind the group are Sopheap Pich and Linda Saphan, both of whom have returned to live in Cambodia after living in the United States.

Although foreign coverage of the Cambodian cinema in the 1960s tended to focus on Sihanouk to the exclusion of the work of other filmmakers, there was a domestic film industry that survived despite the competition of imports, particularly from India and Thailand which, dubbed into Cambodian, appealed to a mass audience. Apart from a limited number of propaganda films made during the Khmer Rouge period, it was not until the early 1980s that a domestic film industry emerged once more that concentrated on low-budget productions, with plots concerned either with the miseries of the Pol Pot years or the retelling of Cambodian legends and stories of love and loss. By the late 1980s, however, the local industry had difficulty competing with the growing number of imported videos, and although films continued to be made during the 1990s, they were limited in number and quality.

Since the beginning of the present century there has been something of a renaissance in the local film industry, at least in terms of the number of films completed and shown in the dozen cinemas functioning in Phnom Penh. With rare exceptions Cambodian films do not attract an international audience, though the director Panh Rathy, who has made both features and documentaries, has had two of his films shown at the Cannes Film Festival, *Les Gens de la Risière* [People of the Ricefields, shown in 1994], and a film about Tuol Sleng, *S-21: The Khmer Rouge Killing Machine*, shown in 2003.

As for traditional handicrafts, particularly the crafting of silver and wood and stone carving, these can be found in abundance in contemporary Phnom Penh. Whether they should be seen as much more than attractive souvenirs is debatable, since for the most part they involve repetitive design. This is not a new phenomenon, for despite the efforts of George Groslier, whose association with the National Museum has been discussed earlier, efforts to bring a renaissance in these traditional handicrafts never succeeded in recapturing the verve of earlier artists and artisans. The recovery of the silk industry may be seen by some as a positive sign, but it is proper to note that silk weaving, an important aspect of artisanal activity in Cambodia, was largely associated with production in provincial centres, particularly in the Takeo region.

GROUNDS FOR OPTIMISM?

Some subjects have an obvious ending. Phnom Penh is not one of these. That the city itself and many of its people are better off in a material sense than in the 1980s and indeed the 1990s is arguably correct, but it would scarcely be the judgment of those who have just been evicted from their flimsy shanty towns or are waiting for this to happen to them. Neither would it be the outlook of those men and women who have fearlessly sought to establish trade unions to protect workers in the garment industry. For all who live in Phnom Penh, the promise inherent in the election of 1993, that something approaching democracy was in prospect for Cambodia, has well and truly failed to materialize.

Yet it is not the place of a foreigner, no matter how closely involved in the city, and no matter for how long, to deny the hope that is clearly held by many younger Cambodians that something better can be achieved than what currently exists in their capital and in their country. Given the real dangers associated with speaking out against the present governing regime, there is every reason to admire the courage of those in Phnom Penh, particularly the men and women associated with domestic NGOs, who bravely call for change and are ready to criticize the current political system. In a phrase that has entered the lexicon of any serious discussion of the country, David Chandler has written of "the tragedy of Cambodian history". Only a supremely unperceptive optimist would suggest that the tragedy is no longer part of drama played out each day in Phnom Penh. As the city and Cambodia as a whole stand poised on the threshold of sudden wealth flowing to the government from the oil deposits discovered in the Gulf of Thailand, might this mean that hope can finally triumph over tragedy? That there is no certain answer to that question is a sad but realistic reflection on life in contemporary Phnom Penh.

Appendices

APPENDIX A: THE ROYAL PALACE

At the time of writing, visits to the Royal Palace are restricted in access to the Napoleon Pavilion, the Silver Pagoda (official name the Wat Preah Keo Morokat or Temple of the Emerald Buddha) and to the adjoining small museum and gift shop in what were once the quarters for the Royal Guard and the Elephant Stables. Whether this situation will continue is impossible to predict, though with a monarch once more on the throne it may be that access to the Throne Hall, which was possible only a few years ago, will remain closed to visitors. As a collection of buildings, the palace evokes an immediate image of the much larger Grand Palace in Bangkok, underlining the extent to which at the level of the Cambodia royal family the Thai monarchy was in many ways a model. The architecture with the Phnom Penh palace is indistinguishable from that found in Bangkok.

The Royal Palace in Phnom Penh is poorly documented, with the one book devoted to it, Julio A. Jeldres and Somkid Chaijitvanit, *The Royal Palace of Phnom Penh and Cambodian Royal Life* (Bangkok, 1999), unreliable in some of the information it provides, particularly in relation to dates. A notable example is the photograph shown on pp. 22-23, which is

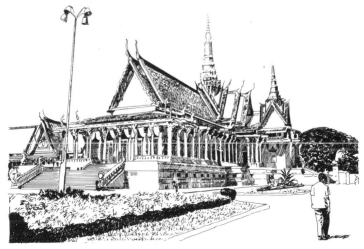

The Throne Hall in the Royal Palace

The Napoleon Pavilion in the Royal Palace

cited as being "in the early nineteenth century", when it clearly dates from the early twentieth century. The number "1806" which appears on this photograph is obviously a catalogue number and not a date. The book does, however, have the virtue of identifying the various buildings within the compound and providing pictures of these, and their interiors, which otherwise will not be seen by the public.

The Throne Hall, inaugurated in 1919 during the reign of King Sisowath, replaced a wooden building completed in 1869 after the court moved to Phnom Penh from Udong. The site for major ceremonies such as the coronation, the king's birthday and state receptions, it contains a magnificent throne and has highly decorated walls and ceilings.

The Napoleon Pavilion has already been discussed. Said by some French officials to be Norodom's favourite building within the compound, it now contains a range of memorabilia.

As noted earlier, the Silver Pagoda was completed shortly before Norodom I's death in 1902, and was renovated under the supervision of Sihanouk's mother, Queen Kossamak, in 1962. Its distinctive feature is its floor of 5,281 silver tiles. The cloisters surrounding the pagoda, known as the Ramayana Cloisters, contain murals originally painted between 1903 and 1904 and depicting the Hindu epic, the *Ramayana*, known by its

Buddhist monks walk past the Moonlight Pavilion of the Royal Palace

Cambodian name as the *Ream Ker*. The painting was done under the direction of the palace architect, Oknha Tep Nimit Tlak, the descendant of a famed sculptor who had studied mural painting at Wat Botum Vaddei where he took the robe between 1868 and 1874. Sadly, the murals have suffered from neglect over many years. In 1985 a Polish conservation team was brought in to stabilize them and they continued this work until 1992. Since then little has been done to repair the very evident ravages of time. Situated around the pagoda itself are a number of structures of varying importance, including memorials to King Norodom I and to King Suramarit, and probably of greatest importance to contemporary Cambodians the artificial mound known as Phnom Mondop, which contains a footprint of the Buddha and which is regarded as a primary site for leaving petitions seeking the Buddha's beneficence.

Nothing more sharply underlines the changes that have taken place in Cambodia, and in the Royal Palace in particular, than the extent to which the Chanchhaya Pavilion, the Moonlight Pavilion, has slipped from importance in Phnom Penh's life. Now only used occasionally, its prime purpose before 1970 was as the location of dance performances by the royal ballet. Completed shortly before the First World War, it contrasts sharply in size with the dancing pavilion Norodom I erected when he moved his capital in 1866 and which is depicted in part in an illustration prepared at the time of the French Mekong River Expedition in that year by the naval officer and artist, Louis Delaporte.

The National Museum

APPENDIX B: THE NATIONAL MUSEUM

Construction of the National Museum began in 1917, to a design by George Groslier, and it was opened to visitors for the first time in 1918. Initially inaugurated as the Musée du Cambodge in April 1919, it was then renamed the Musée Albert Sarraut, after the then Governor General of Indochina, in April 1920. It was renamed the National Museum in 1966; renamed again as the Archaeological Museum in 1979; and then reverted to the title of National Museum at the end of the 1980s. Until 1951 it was under the direction of the French administration, at which point it passed into Cambodian control, but France continued to provide technical support until 1966. In that year the first Cambodian director was appointed.

At the time of its inauguration the museum housed some 1,000 items in its collection. Today that collection has increased by several thousand and makes it the most important repository of Cambodian art in the world. Only the Musée Guimet in Paris has a collection of comparable quality. That the museum has survived the vicissitudes of Cambodia's modern history is remarkable. It was abandoned during the Pol Pot period when three of the museum staff who had been trained in France were killed. When the Vietnamese ended the Khmer Rouge regime in January 1979 the museum was in a parlous state as it had been totally neglected. But remarkably the collection was essentially intact, though some objects had been damaged by a lack of overall maintenance. Since then there have been extensive repairs to the building, but it continues to require attention and receives only limited funds from the government, so that it depends greatly on foreign assistance.

The collection is remarkable for its coverage of Cambodian art, from pre-Angkorian times, through the centuries of Angkorian greatness, to the post-Angkorian period. It is a rich collection, particularly of objects in bronze and stone, with two of the most notable examples of these categories being the giant Reclining Vishnu dating from the second half of the eleventh century and the presumed portrait statue of Jayavarman VII, dating from the end of the twelfth or the beginning of the thirteenth century. But impressive as the objects in bronze and stone are, a visitor should not neglect the museum's holdings of ceramics and objects in wood.

There is an up-to-date guide, *The New Guide to the National Museum* (Phnom Penh, 2nd edition, 2006), compiled by Khun Samen, available at the museum shop just inside the main entrance.

Further Reading

The following listing of bibliographic references, on a chapter by chapter basis, is confined to books, so that there are no references to what are frequently difficult-to-find journal articles. Where possible the references cited are in English, but given the link between Cambodia and France it would be derelict not to include some French references, though if an English-language edition is available this is cited. The most complete bibliography of publications on Cambodia is Helen Jarvis, *Cambodia*, vol 200 of the World Bibliographic Series, Oxford and Santa Barbara, California, 1997.

CHAPTER ONE

The period covered by my personal experiences in Phnom Penh is treated in the key published source for all Cambodian history, David Chandler's, *A History of Cambodia*, Boulder, Colorado, 4th edition, 2007. The same author's *The Tragedy of Cambodian History: Politics War and Revolution since 1945*, New Haven, Connecticut, 1991, provides the best overall coverage of Cambodia's modern history since the Second World War. My own memoir of Cambodia in 1966 is *Before Kampuchea: Preludes to Tragedy*, Sydney, 1979, new edition Bangkok, 2004.

CHAPTER TWO

David Chandler's *A History of Cambodia* is again important for the period covered in this chapter, as it is for the entire span of history covered in this book. Michel Igout, *Phnom Penh Then and Now*, Bangkok, 1993, is significant as the most detailed photographic record of Phnom Penh's development since 1866. The recently published survey of Cambodian cities by the distinguished Cambodian architect, Vann Molyvann, *Modern Khmer Cities*, Phnom Penh, 2003, should also be consulted for those with an interest in the evolution of Phnom Penh's urban character. Both Igout's and Vann Molyvann's books contain a copy of the sketch map of Phnom Penh in the fifteenth century prepared by George Coedès to which reference is made in this chapter. A very recent and important study of modern Cambodian architecture is Helen Grant Ross & Darryl Leon Collins, *Building Cambodia: "New Khmer Architecture"*, Bangkok, 2006.

CHAPTER THREE

The key source for the period covered in this chapter is by the long-term *conservateur* of the Angkor temples, Bernard-Philippe Groslier. This is his *Angkor and Cambodia in the Sixteenth Century, According to Portuguese and Spanish Sources*, Bangkok, 2006, now in this faithful and readable translation by Michael Smithies of the original French edition published in 1958. The original edition is long out of print. Although not listed on the title page as an author, the work is greatly indebted, and is acknowledged by Groslier as such, to the work of the notable English historian of Iberian overseas expansion, Charles Boxer. The early reference to Cambodia by Tomé Pires may be found in A. Cortesão, editor and translator, *The Suma Oriental of Tomé Pires*, London, 1944. Henri Mouhot, so often inaccurately described as the "discoverer" of Angkor, recorded his comments on Phnom Penh in 1859 in *Travels in Siam, Cambodia and Laos, 1858-1860*, originally published in London, 1861; more accessible modern editions were published in Kuala Lumpur in 1989 and 1992.

CHAPTER FOUR

In addition to David Chandler's *A History of Cambodia*, two general studies that cover the period of this chapter are John Tully, *France on the Mekong: A History of the Protectorate in Cambodia, 1863-1953*, Lanham, Maryland, 2002, and his *A Short History of Cambodia*, Sydney, 2005. My own *The French Presence in Cochinchina and Cambodia: Rule and Response, 1859-1905*, Ithaca, New York, 1969, new edition Bangkok, 1997, covers Norodom I's reign in the initial period of French "protection". Alain Forest carries the story of the French relations with Cambodia forward under Sisowath's reign in his *Le Cambodge et la colonisation française: histoire d'une colonisation sans heurts (1897-1929)*, Paris, 1980. For this and succeeding chapters, Penny Edwards' *Cambodge: The Cultivation of a Nation, 1860-1945*, Honolulu, 2006, breaks important new interpretive ground. Equally important for its new approach to the period is Gregor Muller, *Colonial Cambodia's "Bad Frenchmen": The Rise of French Rule and the Life of Thomas Caraman, 1840-87*, London, 2006. Of the authors contemporary to the period cited in this chapter many are not readily available, but those that can be found in reprinted editions include Mouhot, *Travels*, and Frank Vincent, *The Land of the White Elephant: Sights and Sounds in South-Eastern Asia, 1871-72*, London, 1873, new edition Boston, 2004. Charles

Meyer, *La Vie quotidienne des Français en Indochine, 1860-1910*, Paris, 1985, is a useful source for commentary on the French in the Indochinese region as a whole.

CHAPTER FIVE

There are relatively few analytic studies of the period from the accession of King Sisowath in 1904 to the death of King Monivong in 1941. One of the few writers to study the period in detail is John Tully, *Cambodia Under the Tricolour: King Sisowath and the "Mission Civilisatrice"*, Melbourne, 1996. Alain Forest's *Le Cambodge* ends its coverage in 1920, and Paul Collard, *Cambodge et Cambodgiens*, Paris, 1925 is a useful source up to the 1920s. As always, David Chandler's *History* may be profitably consulted, particularly for the killing of Bardez, which is considered in detail in his *Facing the Cambodian Past: Selected Essays*, Chiang Mai and Sydney, 1996. Penny Edwards' *Cambodge* is again important for this period. The "1916 Affair" is discussed in my *The Mekong: Turbulent Past, Uncertain Future*, revised edition, Sydney, 2004. Norodom Sihanouk's account of his surprise at being selected to fill the Cambodian throne may be found in his *L'Indochine vue de Pékin: entretiens avec Jean Lacouture*, Paris, 1972.

CHAPTER SIX

The following listing is of the books cited in this chapter in the order in which they appear and receive more than a passing mention. Pierre Loti, *Un Pélerin d'Angkor*, Paris, 1911; Roland Meyer, *Saramani, danseuse khmer*, Saigon, 1919, new edition Paris, 1997; George Groslier, *Le retour à l'argile*, Paris, 1931, new edition, Paris, 1996, and *La route du plus fort*, Paris 1925, new edition Paris 1997; Somerset Maugham, *The Gentleman in the Parlour*, London, 1930; Harry L. Foster, *A Beachcomber in the Orient*, London, 1923; Harry A. Franck, *East of Siam: Ramblings in the Five Divisions of French Indo-China*, New York, 1926; André Malraux, *La Voie royale*, Paris, 1930, English language edition, *The Royal Way*, New York, 1935; Walter Langlois, *André Malraux: The Indochinese Adventure*, New York, 1966; Sydney Greenbie, *The Romantic East*, New York, 1930; Pierre Billotey, *Indochine en zigzgs*, Paris, 1929; Guy de Pourtalès, *Nous, à qui rien n'appartient: voyage au pays khmer*, Paris, 1931; Robert J. Casey, *Four Faces of Siva: The Detective Story of a Vanished Race*, Indianapolis, 1929; Geoffrey Gorer, *Bali and Angkor: Or Looking at Life and Death*, Boston, 1936; Alan

Houghton Brodrick, *Little Vehicle: Cambodia and Laos*, London, 1949 (?); Vannary Inman, *When Elephants Fight: A Memoir*, Sydney, 2000.

CHAPTER SEVEN

David Chandler's *History* and *Tragedy* are fundamental sources for this period, with the latter particularly helpful for 1945-53. John Tully's *A Short History* is also useful, as is his *France on the Mekong*. A neglected but still useful study of the period's regional and international politics is Donald Lancaster, *The Emancipation of French Indochina*, Oxford, 1961. Sihanouk's *L'Indochine vue de Pékin* provides commentary on the period, as does his *Souvenirs doux et amers*, Paris, 1981. I have attempted a biography of Sihanouk in this period and beyond in *Sihanouk: Prince of Light, Prince of Darkness*, Sydney, 1994. Norman Lewis' *A Dragon Apparent, Travels in Cambodia, Laos, and Vietnam*, London, 1951, is valuable for the picture it presents of a period mostly neglected by travel writers.

CHAPTER EIGHT

Once again David Chandler's *History* and *Tragedy* are the first points of reference, with Chandler's account of the plot to overthrow Sihanouk dealt with in detail in *Tragedy*. John Tully's *A Short History* is also valuable for this period. Although remarkably little known at the time, the Cambodian communists, and in particular Pol Pot, were a growing clandestine force during this period. They are examined in the two important biographies of Pol Pot: David Chandler, *Brother Number One: a Political Biography of Pol Pot*, Boulder, Colorado, revised edition, 1999; and Philip Short, *Pol Pot: the History of a Nightmare*, London, 2004. The rise of the Khmer Rouge and their activities are charted by Ben Kiernan in *How Pol Pot Came to Power: a History of Communism in Kampuchea, 1930-1975*, London, 1985. Sihanouk's own reflections on his years in power are found in his *Indochine vue de Pékin* and *Souvenirs doux et amers*. Former adviser to Sihanouk, Charles Meyer, provides an insider's view of political life under Sihanouk in *Derrière le souirire khmer*, Paris, 1971. Among the limited number of books dealing with Phnom Penh politics in the years 1970 to 1975, Justin Corfield, *Khmers Stand Up! A History of the Cambodian Government 1970-1975*, Melbourne, 1994, is particularly useful. William Shawcross, *Sideshow: Nixon, Kissinger and the Destruction of Cambodia*, London, 1979, is an invaluable overview of the Second Indochina

War as it affected Cambodia. Jon Swain, *River of Time*, London, 1995, deals with the closing days of the Lon Nol regime. I cover the period treated in this chapter in my *Sihanouk*, and in a much earlier study, *Politics and Power in Cambodia: the Sihanouk Years*, Melbourne, 1973. My memoir, *Before Kampuchea*, offers an account of life in Phnom Penh in 1966.

CHAPTER NINE

In addition to the books by David Chandler already cited, his *Voices from S-21: Terror and History in Pol Pot's Secret Prison*, Sydney, 2000, is a thoughtful examination of the Tuol Sleng extermination centre. Philip Short's *Pol Pot* is important, as is Ben Kiernan's *The Pol Pot Regime: Race, Power, and Genocide in Cambodia under the Khmer Rouge, 1975-79*, New Haven, Connecticut, 1996. François Bizot gives a dramatic account of the first few days of Khmer Rouge rule in Phnom Penh in *The Gate*, London, 2003, as does Jon Swain in *River of Time* and Sydney Schanberg in *The Death and Life of Dith Pran*, New York, 1985. Another French author's account of the same period may be found in François Ponchaud, *Cambodge, année zéro*, Paris, 1977 (published in English as *Cambodia, Year Zero*, Harmondsworth, 1978). A less critical account of the Khmer Rouge period is found in Michael Vickery, *Cambodia: 1972-1982*, Sydney, 1984. Among the limited number of books written about Phnom Penh while the Khmer Rouge ruled are: Ong Thong Hoeung, *J'au cru aux Khmers Rouges: retour sur une illusion*, Paris, 2003; and Laurence Picq, *Beyond the Horizon: Five Years with the Khmer Rouge*, New York, 1989. Vann Nath, *A Cambodian Prison Portrait: One Year in the Khmer Rouge's S-21*, Bangkok, 1998, is a rare account by a survivor of Tuol Sleng. Elizabeth Becker, *When the War Was Over: Cambodia and the Khmer Rouge Revolution*, New York, 1986, is particularly interesting for the closing days of the Pol Pot regime. Sihanouk's *Prisonnier des Khmers Rouges*, Paris, 1986, is interesting in relation to his personal experience but tells a reader virtually nothing about life in Phnom Penh away from his prolonged period of house arrest. The interesting and revealing study of Khmer Rouge slogans by Henri Locard is *Le "Petit Livre Rouge" de Pol Pot, ou les paroles d'Angkar*, Paris, 1996. A thought-provoking examination of the Pol Pot years from an anthropologist's point of view is Alexander Laban Hinton: *Why Did They Kill?: Cambodia in the Shadow of Genocide*, Berkeley, California, 2005. Dealing with a later period than that covered in this chapter, Nic Dunlop' *The Lost Executioner: a Story of the Khmer Rouge*, London, 2006, covers the story of Duch, the former director of Tuol Sleng, through to the present day.

CHAPTER TEN

As with Chapter Six, the listing of books from this chapter follows the order in which they are cited, and books have received a previous listing are not listed again. Christopher Pym, *Mistapim in Cambodia*, London, 1960; Han Suyin, *The Four Faces*, London, 1963; Andrew Graham, *A Foreign Affair*, Garden City, New York, 1959; Leslie Fielding, *The Killing Fields, Witness to Cambodia and the Vietnam War*, London, 2007; Loup Durand, *The Angkor Massacre*, New York, 1983; Eric Van Lustbader, *Black Heart*, New York, 1987; John Le Carré, *The Honourable Schoolboy*, London, 1977; Christopher J. Koch, *Highways to a War*, London 1995; Tim Bowden, *One Crowded Hour: Neil Davis Combat Cameraman*, Sydney, 1987; Someth May, *Cambodian Witness: the Autobiography of Someth May*, London, 1986; Pin Yathay, *Stay Alive my Son*, New York, 1987; Molyda Szmusiak, *The Stones Cry Out: a Cambodian Childhood 1975-1980*, London, 1987; Joan D. Criddle and Teeda Butt Mam, *To Destroy You is No Loss: the Odyssey of a Cambodian family*, New York, 1987; Maslyn Williams, *The Land in Between: the Cambodian Dilemma*, Sydney, 1982; Henry Kamm, *Cambodia: Report from a Stricken Land*, New York, 1998; Jon Swain, *River of Time*, London, 1995; Charles Meyer, *Derrière le sourire khmer*, Paris, 1971; Bernard Hamel, *Sihanouk et le drame cambodgien*, Paris, 1993; Milton Osborne, *Before Kampuchea: Preludes to Tragedy*, Sydney, 1979, Bangkok, 2004; Margaret Drabble, *The Gates of Ivory*, London, 1991.

CHAPTER ELEVEN

The period between the defeat of the Pol Pot regime and the settlement of Cambodia's political problems is poorly covered by comparison with preceding years, particularly for the latter part of the 1980s. Once again, John Tully's *A Short History*, provides a useful overview. The atmosphere in Phnom Penh in the years immediately after the Vietnamese invasion is well described in the following: Nayan Chanda, *Brother Enemy: the War After the War*, New York, 1986; Henry Kamm, *Cambodia: Report from a Stricken Land*, New York, 1998; and William Shawcross, *The Quality of*

Mercy: Cambodia, Holocaust and Modern Conscience, London 1984. A generally sympathetic view of the PRK regime is contained in Margaret Slocomb's *The People's Republic of Kampuchea, 1979-1989: the Revolution after Pol Pot*, Chiang Mai, 2003. Of particular importance for the 1980s because of the access the author had to PRK documents is Evan Gottesman, *Cambodia After the Khmer Rouge: Inside the Politics of Nation Building*, New Haven Connecticut, 2003. Stan Sesser, *The Lands of Charm and Cruelty: Travels in Southeast Asia*, New York, 1993, provides a vivid picture of Phnom Penh in 1991 in the chapter "The Khmer Rouge have returned". Also dealing with the UNTAC period is Tom Riddle, *Cambodian Interlude: Inside the United Nations' 1993 Election*, Bangkok, 1997. Christopher G. Moore, *Zero Hour in Phnom Penh*, Bangkok, 2004, is a rare example of a thriller set in Cambodia in the recent past, while Amit Gilboa, *Off the Rails in Phnom Penh: Into the Dark Heart of Guns, Girls and Ganja*, Bangkok, 1998, offers an uninhibited account of the city in the mid-1990s. Also relevant, and of interest for the fact of its author being Cambodia, is Sorpong Peou' *Intervention and Change in Cambodia: Towards Democracy?* Chiang Mai, 2000.

CHAPTER TWELVE

The closer one comes to the present day the fewer are the number of books dealing with events in Cambodia, and even fewer that concentrate on Phnom Penh. A controversial survey of the period from 1991 to 1999 is David W. Roberts, *Political Transition in Cambodia 1991-1999, Power, Elitism and Democracy*, New York, 2001, which takes a very favourable attitude towards Hun Sen and the CPP. The long saga of developments associated with the Khmer Rouge Tribunal is discussed in Tom Fawthrop and Helen Jarvis, *Getting Away with Genocide: Elusive Justice and the Khmer Rouge Tribunal*, Sydney, 2004. On key personalities, see Harish C. Metha and Julie B.Metha, *Hun Sen: Strongman of Cambodia*, Singapore, 1999, and Harish C. Metha, *Warrior Prince: Norodom Ranariddh, Son of King Sihanouk of Cambodia*, Singapore, 2001. Recent developments in Cambodian Buddhism are covered in Ian Harris, *Cambodian Buddhism: History and Practice*, Chiang Mai, 2005. David M. Ayres, *Anatomy of a Crisis: Education, Development and the State in Cambodia, 1953-1998*, provides a helpful review of educational policies through the second half of the twentieth century. Frank Steward and Sharon May, editors, *In the Shadow of*

Angkor: Contemporary Writing from Cambodia, Chiang Mai, 2004, is an anthology of modern literature. An overview of Cambodian culture in the period since the victory and defeat of the Khmer Rouge, but now somewhat out-of-date is, May M. Ebihara, Carol A. Mortland and Judy Ledgerwood, editors, *Cambodian Culture Since 1975: Homeland and Exile,* Ithaca, New York, 1994. A more recent and very helpful commentary on contemporary Cambodian culture and politics is Leakthina Chau-Pech Ollier and Tim Winter, *Expressions of Cambodia: the Politics of Tradition, Identity and Change,* London, 2006.

Index of Literary & Historical Names

Index of Places & Landmarks